Crime, Punishment, and Policing in China

Asia/Pacific/Perspectives

Series Editor: Mark Selden

Crime, Punishment, and Policing in China

EDITED BY BØRGE BAKKEN

ROWMAN & LITTLEFIELD PUBLISHERS, INC.
Lanham • Boulder • New York • Toronto • Plymouth, UK

University of
Roehampton
London

Library Services

Barcode No. 0750 2516

ROWMAN & LITTLEFIELD PUBLISHERS, INC.

Published in the United States of America
by Rowman & Littlefield Publishers, Inc.
A wholly owned subsidary of The Rowman & Littlefield Publishing Group, Inc.
4501 Forbes Boulevard, Suite 200, Lanham, MD 20706
www.rowmanlittlefield.com

Estover Road, Plymouth PL6 7PY, UK

British Library Cataloguing in Publication Information Available

The hardback edition of this book was previously cataloged by the Library of Congress as
follows:

Crime, punishment, and policing in China / [edited by] Børge Bakken.
    p. cm. — (Asia/Pacific/Perspectives)
    Includes bibliographical references and index.
    1. Crime—China. 2. Punishment—China. 3. Prisons—China. 4. Police—China. I. Bakken,
Børge. II. Series.
    HV7118.5.C76 2005
    364.951—dc22
                                                                              2004025864
    ISBN-13: 978-0-7425-3574-9 (cloth : alk. paper)
    ISBN-10: 0-7425-3574-6 (cloth : alk. paper)
    ISBN-13: 978-0-7425-3575-6 (pbk : alk. paper)
    ISBN-10: 0-7425-3575-4 (pbk : alk. paper

Printed in the United States of America

♾™ The paper used in this publication meets the minimum requirements of American
National Standard for Information Sciences—Permanence of Paper for Printed Library
Materials, ANSI/NISO Z39.48-1992.

Contents

Figures and Tables

Preface

The present project began to take form at a workshop at the University of Oslo, Norway, as far back as 1999. The plan back then was to make papers from that workshop into a book comparing crime, policing, and punishment in Europe and China. That particular project was since scrapped (although not entirely forgotten), but some of the participants stayed in touch, and after a long and winding process of deliberation, the core group of China scholars at that workshop instead wrote entirely new papers for this anthology on crime, prison, and punishment in China. While China became the center of attention and the comparative aspirations were put aside in their original form, we still have comparison in mind, hoping to reach readers both inside and outside the "China field."

I moved from Scandinavia to Australia in the process, and the work of compiling this book took place at the Division of Pacific and Asian History, Research School of Pacific and Asian Studies, at the Australian National University (ANU) in Canberra.

I would like to thank each one of the participants for their contributions and their patience. Mark Selden deserves a special thank you for support and encouragement at a time when the project seemed to come to a halt. Three anonymous readers of the manuscript gave insightful and useful comments on the individual articles, and the staff here at the history division gave invaluable technical help. Lastly, I am indebted to the ANU Publications Committee who granted a much-welcome subsidy to assist in the final publication of this book.

Børge Bakken
Australian National University
Canberra, October 2004

Introduction: Crime, Control, and Modernity in China

BØRGE BAKKEN

Crime has been a silent partner in Chinese modernization. Law and order have been as central to the regime's priorities as economic growth and the promise of prosperity. This volume examines and theorizes the social, economic, political, legal, and practical parameters of crime and control, locating them within a broader milieu of development and transition. This is a novel approach in the case of China. The book analyzes historical and cultural contexts as well as offering broader comparative observations. Context is a key word, as crime and control are at the roots of modernity and its definitions. In many ways China is reliving the experiences of other industrializing countries in this respect. At the same time the practices of police and prisons are also painted with thick layers of historical memory. Comparative efforts must be balanced with the efforts to understand the unique quality of the Chinese situation. In the descriptions of campaign policing and contract policing we see approaches to control in a unique Chinese setting. While some chapters focus on the uniqueness in the Chinese approaches to crime and control, other chapters link the analysis to general criminological theory in order to demystify the developments in China. Cultural and historical context does not prevent a general comparative perspective. On the contrary, it strengthens our basis for comparison and deepens our understanding of the Chinese experiences.

China is thus seen in its own historical and cultural context as well as it is compared with other countries in their process of transition. Law, norms, and community are linked together in complex ways in China as they are in the history of Western societies. During the Industrial Revolution it became the fashion to look to Britain as a yardstick both in terms of economic management and organization of society. Policing was no exception. The London Metropolitan Police began developing into a relatively impersonal, bureaucratic, professional force only during the first half of the nineteenth century, and the London police force became the ideal of European thinking about the police. Established in 1829, the London Metropolitan Police was the world's first attempt to develop a relatively impersonal, bureaucratic, professional law enforcement agency. By contrast, developments in the United States at that time pointed in a somewhat different direction. The New York "cop" was a far more traditional type of policeman who enjoyed greater discretionary power.

The point is that old types of policing were practiced in step with the prevailing norms of society and that mere "law" had to step down when faced with the ruling "morality" of the day. In the case of China this has been the basic practice until quite recently. Of course, power defined the norms of the day, and police enforcement of morality and norms was part of that power. Policing was traditionally rooted in a community, and those in charge of representing the ruling order also participated in defining the ruling norm. One could say that this was a period when the social norm rather than the written law ruled. The police were a forceful part of their community more than they were law enforcement agents in the modern and professional meaning of the term. Those in charge of "policing" were expected to take care of the moral order rather than the impersonal black letter of the law. The Chinese police force of today was born in the political upheavals of anti-Japanese war, civil war, and revolution. Its task was to defend the revolution against political enemies. The beginning adaptation to modernity and professional policing came much later, and the rehabilitation of legal processes is part of that story. Until at least 1997 Chinese criminal law continued to "police the norm" rather than the law. It is an "analogous application" of the law to punish conduct that is viewed as harmful to society when such conduct is not criminalized by law. For instance, one could be sentenced by the statute that dealt with rape (*qiangjian*) when one had committed adultery (*tongjian*) only. Adultery was seen as an act of amorality not covered by the law. Such prosecution by analogy was specified in Article 79 in the 1979 Criminal Code:

> A crime that is not expressly stipulated in the Special Provisions of this Law may be determined and punished according to *the most closely analogous article (zui xiang leisi de tiaowen)* of the Special Provisions of this Law, but the matter shall be submitted to the Supreme People's Court for approval.[1]

This article was abolished in the 1997 Criminal Code. Such analogous application of law is now seen by Chinese legal authorities as unlawful and against the spirit of the law. This is undoubtedly an important achievement in Chinese law, but how does this look from the point of view of the policeman and policewoman on the beat? Policing the exemplary norms of society gave the police extensive discretionary power and elasticity in going about their job. Rome was not built in a day, and the same applies to Chinese practices of policing. The Chinese police with their culture and habits were definitely not changed in a day. For were they not the guarantor of the People's Democratic Dictatorship, and later the dictatorship of the proletariat, and was it not their duty as the People's Police to define the proletarian norms set by Mao and the inner circle of leaders? They were "policing the norm," the exemplary norm of the dictatorship of the proletariat. Their power emanated from that task, and not from the letter of the abstract law. We should bear this perspective in mind when we read the chapters in the present volume. These will not only look at how China copes with the rapid changes that occurred during the economic reforms, but will also gauge them in light of the experiences of an earlier period of modernization, that of the republican period.

A mistake one can make when talking about crime and control in China is to apply the seductive strategies of the press, Western as well as Chinese. There is a tendency to make alarmist assumptions about the crime of nearly any society in transition.[2] China might have its specific profile of crime, but the country has rarely been studied comparatively. To do so is to discover that there is no such thing as an oriental "mystique" to the developments we see in present-day China. We should approach China in the light of a more general pattern of modernity.

PRISONS AS CATHEDRALS OF MODERNITY

The prison, as Dikötter indicates in chapter 2, came to represent the very idea of modernity in republican China, and he proceeds to examine certain Chinese characteristics of that development. The educational aspect of prisons and punishment represented the idea of producing new citizens at the dawn of the new century, as these became symbols of order and producers of goodness. In the author's words, the prison became a "cathedral of modernity." This was the case across the industrializing and modernizing world at the start of the twentieth century, and China was a part of rather than an exception to that global trend. A new conception of the prison as a total institution in which the bad criminal was reformed into a good citizen was very much in line both with the thoughts of Enlightenment thinkers as well as it fitted into core values of human malleability and educability in Chinese thinking. The idea of the prison—producer of obedient citizens for a moral community based on the rule of law—paralleled the rise of the modern state and the extension of political rights. Prison reform became an indicator of a nation's "progress," and the prison became one of the most discussed indicators of a nation's capacity to survive in a context of struggle for survival.

Dikötter's discussion of developments in republican China sets the tone for a broader cultural and historical perspective on the durability and importance of administrative culture. Beginning with a discussion on penal reform in republican China highlights this perspective in contemporary debates of reforms in the People's Republic. One of the most fundamental ideas in penal philosophy in imperial China was that punishment should be designed to educate people in ethical norms; the law was an instrument of moral education.[3] Based on traditional notions of an inherently good human nature, the notion of *ganhua* (change by setting an example) sustained the belief that even criminals could achieve individual self-improvement through proper institutional guidance. Punishment in China, Dikötter explains, was meant to educate, and education was designed to consolidate the social bond between the individual and the collective. The *li*, or "rules of proper conduct," was a core concept of Confucian ethics. As much as in the imperial past, the administrative culture in republican China was preoccupied with the transformation of morality and the malleability of the prisoner. The principle of *ganhua* was transformed in twentieth-century China from a mere principle of penology to a more general political concept. Sun Yatsen hoped to develop the nation by virtue of propaganda and reformation, a process he styled *ganhua*. The present regime's current attempts at state building through "spiritual civilization" (*jingshen wenming*) is based on that same tradition. Even down to the details of rehabilitation, we can see the contours of a "statist" conception of law and social control. There are no direct assumptions of a liberal civic society in the Chinese law-and-order regime. Instead, the rules, methods, and practices of legal rationality are employed as managerial and regulatory instruments of state power. Law becomes a direct instrument to pursue the objectives of the state.[4]

Dikötter shows how the establishment of penology as a "science" was introduced in China during the republican period and gives us important glimpses into the scholarly debate. Early reformers believed, like most of their contemporaries, that criminal rates increased with the advance of civilization.[5] They also believed, however, that a nation could be improved through the engineering of its citizens, and Dikötter describes some of the sources of a disciplinary culture in which the promotion of strict rules of behavior is seen as part of an "exemplary society." *Ganhua* was one of the methods of human improvement. Some of this culture is indigenous, and some is imported from the West, both from the core area of Enlightenment ideas as well as from the Soviet system.

The prison was and still is part of an educative mission that places faith in the malleability of human beings while it is also a disciplinary project aimed to instill respect for and adherence to social norms. Modernizing elites in republican China viewed the reformation of criminals as a constitutive part of a project of national regeneration in which social harmony, economic development, and state power could only be obtained by molding obedient subjects. A penal philosophy emphasizing the moral reformation of the prisoner was proposed in Europe during the early nineteenth century. Faith in the capacity of prisons to effect moral reformation among prisoners was, however, undermined by the huge gap between articulated goals and observable realities, and the theories went out of fashion. Penologists in republican China nevertheless remained faithful to the principles of *ganhua* and upheld their belief in the perfectibility of human beings and the capacity of their penal institutions to reform the minds of men.

PRISONS AS WORK, EDUCATION, AND REHABILITATION

Xu Zhangrun and Michael Dutton's discussion on contemporary prison reforms in chapter 4 demonstrates that *ganhua* education still occupies an important part of Chinese thinking about prison reform. The emphasis on rehabilitation is taking place during a time when the rest of the world is struggling with the problem of resignation and a feeling that "nothing works" as far as rehabilitation of criminals is concerned.[6] It remains a widespread belief in China that prisoners can become exemplary citizens. Republican criminologists propagated the blessings of the single cell, where nothing bad could seep into the mind of the inmate, although internationally the efficiency of the solitary confinement system had been called into question by the second half of the nineteenth century. The themes of educability are undercurrents in the scholarly debate today as well.

Part of the influence from abroad came from Western Europe, but another strong influence came from Soviet thinking, even during the republican period. Some penologists spoke with awe of the prison system in the Soviet Union and thus anticipated later debates in Chinese socialist criminology.

Work became a central theme of penology. Critics agreed on the redemptive virtues of prison work. Work, even forced labor (*laoyi*), was intended to instill values of thrift, discipline, and industry, contributing to the moral reformation of offenders. Again the benefits for the nation were stressed. The desire to turn deviant individuals into productive citizens was a central consideration in the moral rhetoric on prison labor. It is important to note that this debate already took place during the republican period, as documented by Xu and Dutton. They show that although the Chinese system was influenced by Soviet practices, the Chinese system was no mere replication of the Soviet penal system. Most Chinese penal cadres seem to have regarded the Soviet system as deficient in so far as it paid too little attention to the transformational role of labor in the program of reforming criminals.

Contrary to penal officials in some European countries, penologists in China continued to stress the moral benefits of work. Model prisons became a microcosm of an exemplary society in which the emulation of models—whether in the school, the factory, or the army—was seen simultaneously as a mission of educative transformation and a project for social discipline as well as a strategy for national power. It is important to bear in mind that these educative elements of reforming the prisoner are living traditions that long precede the PRC. The emphasis on moral education has to do with the ways in which Chinese society remembers and reproduces its past. History thus aids us considerably in our understanding of present Chinese thought patterns and practices.

Dutton and Xu contrast two diametrically opposite viewpoints on labor in the Chinese prison system, represented by American-Chinese crusader against the Chinese *laogai*, former prisoner Harry Hongda Wu, and Chinese criminologist Li Kangtai. Harry Wu likens the Chinese system of labor reform to the Stalinist Gulag and Nazi extermination camps, emphasizing its "brainwashing" and ruthless economic exploitation of prisoners for economic gain.[7] Li Kangtai, in contrast, highlights the proletarian nature of the educational effect of labor discussed by Dikötter. For Li, labor reform illustrates the superiority of the socialist system, not its exploitative nature. Violently opposed to each other politically, Wu and Li share a common belief in the centrality of "thought reform" in the Chinese penal system.

Xu and Dutton question both Wu's and Li's positions. They instead focus on the indigenous historically sanctioned methods that set the Chinese system apart from both Western and Soviet experiences. They emphasize the importance of Chinese culture in framing the response to crime and suggest that the Chinese prison system is not so much a "socialist new thing" as an "amalgam of traditional methods and values wed to a Marxist framework." They also suggest, like Dikötter, that the Chinese system is much more closely aligned with Western penal ideas and practices than Wu would care to admit. The contemporary Chinese penal system has drawn on a legacy that is both traditional and indigenous, modern and imported. The Chinese concept of labor has many sources, but partly emanates from the combination of a strongly authoritarian "legalist" tradition and a more reformist but no less authoritarian Marxist one.

Although not all prisoners in present-day China work, inmates undergoing either imprisonment or labor reeducation are required to work. Of course, prisoners elsewhere in the world, including many incarcerated in various parts of the United States, are required to work. The American "chain gang" is certainly no tea party, and in China the conditions of work can be extremely harsh, and "reeducation" labor is sometimes harsher than "reform" labor. The economic value of prison labor, however, is not great, and Seymour points to the same problem as Xu and Dutton in chapter 5; that a modern national economy cannot (and he strongly adds should not) be built on a foundation of forced labor. He insists that forced labor is today in sharp decline in China.

While the labor and thought-reform programs were crucial in defining the Chinese penal system in the early period of the People's Republic, the present reforms have radically changed the social landscape. Modernization and economic liberalization not only transformed the social fabric, but the classic symptoms of high mobility, rising unemployment, social inequality, instability, and rising crime rates appeared. The result was what Chinese police have described as the most serious "crime wave" in China's contemporary history. While possibly correct, an international comparative perspective still reveals that China is a country with relatively low levels of crime.[8] Reforming the police and the prison system to cope with the new conditions has been very much on the agenda in recent years.

The concept of *ganhua* is still important, but the society in which *ganhua* operates has changed, making individual reform even more difficult.[9] Prisoners resist reform efforts, and the "mutual surveillance" and self-criticism meetings among prisoners, used with some success in the 1950s, appears to be a thing of the past. Modern criminology has discussed the effects of "reintegrative shaming," most notably in John Braithwaite's work.[10] His discussion of a "moralizing social control" in many ways seems to fit the realities of the Chinese debate. In the Chinese example we can observe the practices of shaming in a thick cultural context. Xu and Dutton argue that it is too simplistic to dismiss such processes as "brainwashing." Shaming processes, however, to be effective require a cultural milieu conducive to shaming. The problem is that "reintegrative shaming" strategies are culturally specific and cannot be applied easily to societies that lack the collective customs and traditions that inform them. At least urban China is no longer living in a climate of all-embracing "reciprocal ethics."[11] Chinese modernization makes the positive effects of such shaming more and more difficult since the very culture in which *ganhua* and shaming operated is waning. As a result of economic reform, there has been a break-up of the collective vision of society. Structurally the changes are also dramatic in terms of prison reform. The state plan is gone, and with it also the community network and cadre power needed for practical rehabilitation. Dutton and Xu look at the wide-ranging consequences of this new situation.

In prereform China, an extremely low recidivism rate was achieved, and the Chinese could boast one of the lowest recidivism rates in the world. One reason for this was the tight demographic policing of the population. In post-reform China, the conditions for such tight demographic policing have evaporated. The police force is no longer able to institute tight demographic controls as it was formerly in controlling moving targets. Instead they employed a policy of "targeting" populations more likely to commit crime. Police authorities now talk about the need to concentrate on a "focal population" (*zhongdian renkou*) and "key areas of society" (*shehui kongzhi mian*) where criminals are reputed to gather. The targets were, apart from the obvious ex-inmates and people who had formerly been in conflict with the police, youth groups and vagrants among the millions of laborers huddling together in the cities to find work. Certain groups of minority people also seem to be targeted according to Seymour. Such targeting is strikingly similar to the practices of the nineteenth-century London police force. They too established specific targets of police discrimination, focusing on the vagrants, the agricultural laborers, gangs of youths, and the Irish.[12] The London police, who had been immensely unpopular among the working class, in fact gained popularity through this targeting. The Chinese police might similarly cash in on city dwellers' prejudice against the "floating population," as this group is more and more made the scapegoat for all of China's crime problems.

Legalist theories of government posit the idea of a strong, strict state and suggest that the strength and endurance of good rule lies in its ability to force compliance. This traditional discourse finds many parallels in the socialist notions of "people's dictatorship" and Party rule. Face, in this context, becomes the ability of the state to ensure not only adherence to its rules and laws but also to its dreams and imaginings. Crime not only disrupts the rules and laws of the state; it even threatens its dreams since the development of socialism presumed a declining rate of crime and, indeed, its final eradication. The current rising crime rates, and above all, instances of official corruption, gravely embarrass the Party and rob it of its legitimacy. It is interesting to note that the anti-crime campaigns of 1983 were in fact started, not as a result of rising crime rates (which had actually decreased in 1982), but because of a feeling of loss of face owing to some highly publicized crime cases that had shamed the police. Delegates at the National People's Congress in 1982 in particular pointed to the case of the *er Wang*—the two brothers Wang—who shot and killed police, Bonny and Clyde–style, as they escaped the authorities through several provinces. The two brothers were finally killed in a shoot-out involving the army.

The penal regime might have changed considerably since the days of dictatorship, but the new regime nevertheless offers flexibility to the police. Among other factors, such flexibility is offered by the widespread use of detention.[13] Incarceration in China is divided into two forms: the detention sector and the prison sector. In Chinese law, there are two types of detention: one is administrative detention, where the detainee receives labor education in a "reform-through-education" institution, while the other is criminal, and the prisoner undergoes labor reform within the prison sector proper. Although the first type is considered as an administrative measure, and not a form of punishment, its "education" is clearly used as a form of penalty for vagrants, prostitutes, drug addicts, etc. The irony is that the overcrowded centers do not in the least give opportunities for education. The ideals of *ganhua* seem to be confronted by the harsh reality and practices of ad hoc solutions and strained finances. So-called shelter and investigation centers proved particularly useful in the period of economic reform. Firstly, as detention centers they were under police and not Ministry of Justice control. This meant the police had far more discretionary power and flexibility over their operation than they would have had with reform through education. The detention centers were also particularly well suited to dealing with some of the mentioned key target groups of the reform period. In many ways the renewed stress on shelter and investigation is a direct response to the new mobility caused by the economic reforms. Again we see historical and structural parallels to the reactions against vagrants during the Industrial Revolution in Britain.

The highly published case of Sun Zhigang, a twenty-seven-year-old man from Wuhan who was beaten up and killed by the police while in detention in March 2003, led the National People's Congress to focus on the failings of detention. Many Chinese legal scholars and others have recommended the full abolishment of the system of shelter and investigation, and laws restricting the discretionary powers of the police in this field are already in place. The new rules went into effect on 1 August 2003, and in principle will abolish the 1982 shelter and investigation rules, banning the police from detaining people without trial and court hearings.[14]

Despite recent legal improvements, the authorities have moved from the embrace of persuasion and *ganhua* to the harsh and brutal solutions offered within the tradition of classical legalism, a legalism that "dreams the dreams of socialism" as Dutton puts it. These rules in particular turn upon those who are socially marginal, another trend of "normalization" of the Chinese legal system. The former success of *ganhua* and reintegration lay in the cultural and structural context rather than in the mere technologies of control.

CRIME AND INCARCERATION DURING THE REFORMS

From a global perspective China still has low to very low crime rates, but official crime rates can never be trusted as they reflect the needs of a bureaucratic record-keeping process rather than give an accurate picture of crime. This is of course a universal phenomenon. I argue that the "crime problem" is partly a socially and politically constructed phenomenon, and that official data in fact present a *systematically biased* picture of crime in any system.[15] Three of the chapters (Bakken, Tanner, Dutton) describe the specific Chinese ways in which crime rates are constructed by Party, police, bureaucracy, and even the anonymous contract.

In China, the "crime wave" of the early 1980s has now more than quadrupled in terms of numbers of crime cases if we are to believe official statistics. Overall crime now stands at an official rate of around 360 per 100,000 population. The figure may seem alarming for the Chinese observer, but is considerably lower than the UN (1997) world median crime rate of 2160. Demographic factors explain part of the Chinese figures, since young males of any country are the most likely segment of the population to be committing crime, and China has seen a youth boom resulting in a peak with as many as 272 million of the population between fourteen and twenty-five in the late 1980s. The numbers in that particular age group have since decreased to about 225 million today, but crime rates have continued to grow. Problems of transition explain much of this increase. Internationally, however, the Chinese problem of common crime is still minor. The officially reported crime rates are, however, quite clearly too low. The problem of nonreported crime is an international phenomenon but also has some specific Chinese characteristics as the incentive structure for the police encourages nonreporting. This problem is discussed in more detail in the following chapters. Modern criminology gives us methods to trace the "hidden numbers" of crime, and such alternative methods have been implemented in China, something we will also discuss in more detail. Despite rising crime rates, the real problem perhaps lies in the future as there are trends in today's Chinese society pointing in the direction of an enhanced opportunity structure for organized crime and corruption. Such problems might be more serious than traditional crime and are not easily rooted out by sheer punishment and anti-crime campaigns. Legal and social reforms must instead be implemented to prevent a future scenario of increased crime.

If crime rates are low, then what about the figures on incarceration? Internationally, criminology has found no apparent connection between the rates of crime and the size of the prison population. James D. Seymour addresses the issue of prison reform in more detail. The chapter, which examines the changes seen during recent decades, addresses the difficult task of determining the size of the prison population. In the 1980s, Maoist concepts of thought reform went out of favor, and the authorities began to rethink the *laogai*, with its heavy social and economic costs. The new official mind-set was first reflected in changing terminology. Beginning in the first half of the 1980s, some provinces began to use the hitherto little-used term "prison." Since around 1960 the prisoner population has declined dramatically but stabilized in the 1990s. One reason for this is the growing practice of reducing sentences. It is useful to employ a comparative perspective on prison populations, and Seymour estimates the rate of imprisonment to be considerably higher than the official Chinese figures. Still, the figures compare favorably with the extreme figures of the United States and Russia with relative prison populations four to five times higher than in China.[16] They also compare favorably to China's own recent past, and most certainly that of the former Soviet Gulag. The estimated Chinese prison rate is even well below those of Taiwan and Singapore. In the mid-1990s the Chinese prison population seemed to stabilize, whereas in the United States it was growing steadily, mostly owing to stiff penalties for drug crime. By the turn of the century, however, the numbers began to increase in China too.

One important change in China is that the prison population has to a certain extent been "normalized." The vast majority of prisoners are by now presumed to have committed a crime in the international sense of the word, and this development stands in contrast to the early 1950s, when most of China's inmates were people who were deemed "counterrevolutionaries."[17] While in 1958 nearly half of all reported cases were termed "counterrevolutionary crimes," the number faded to less than half a percent in 1984, and the concept was officially replaced in 1996 with a new prohibition against "jeopardizing state security."[18] This terminological change, Seymour points out, was not accompanied by any real easing of restrictions on expression or association. Both terms are vague, and can include everything from nonviolent political activity to violent activism and espionage. A significant increase in political arrests took place around 1999 and 2000 due to the crackdown on the China Democratic Party and the Falungong movement. These groups, however, are no longer termed "political," and their alleged wrong-doings are thus by definition not of a political character.[19] Minority groups under suspicion of "separatism" are particularly frequent targets. In general criminology we find that police authorities almost everywhere target ethnic minorities more frequently than the average population. In China this is particularly the case in terms of "security" crime.

In general Seymour argues that arrests seem to have a stronger legal basis than in past decades. Indeed, in the 1990s the procuracy often denied police requests to arrest suspects, and commented critically on the excessively long detention of prisoners. Chinese legal experts have raised their voices against the all-embracing power of the state. They have further attacked the administrative and political control of the judiciary, arguing for a more independent judiciary. At the same time one should not forget the discretionary power of the police to ignore the procuracy. In the power struggle between public security (*gong*), procuracy (*jian*), and the courts (*fa*), public security and police still call the shots. Here it is worth focusing on the system of administrative detention. The most severe variety of this system is "reeducation through labor" *(laojiao)*, intended for those whose behavior is deemed to have fallen "between crime and error." In the majority of cases such sentences are imposed directly by the police without trial. An administrative detention can mean labor reeducation of up to four years. Authority to impose these sentences is often abused, and Seymour argues that the system is a means for the police to regain some of the discretionary power lost during the shift from the days of proletarian dictatorship to the new system of alleged law enforcement. It remains to be seen what will be done in this field after the Sun Zhigang case of 2003. The very positive signals given by the NPC in terms of proper legislation is not automatically changing the practices of the police.

This is not only a question of lack of control over the police; there is also the additional problem of scarce resources. Shortage of capital makes the transitional process even more difficult. Underpaid and overworked policing institutions are not effective. The low salaries and poor training and equipment provided to police and judicial personnel create instead a climate that enables corruption to thrive and threaten the stability of the state. Even the practice of extorting confessions by torture has partly been linked to problems of scarce resources.[20] Many human rights critiques fail to recognize police shortcomings as an expression of a weakened rather than a strengthened state capacity.[21] The establishment of effective policing institutions and their role in state legitimization is crucial, and a corrupt and ineffective police force is a much greater threat to stability than the marginal rise in common crime seen over the last two decades. If poorly trained policemen pose a problem, so do poorly trained judges, ineffective legal counsel for defendants, and the highly politicized nature of the judiciary. In court cases the adjudication committee simply does not hear the defense lawyer. Official and judicial authorities have wide and discretionary power and flexibility to reverse or reconsider judgments based on changing circumstances or policy, and courts are simply seen as a part of the bureaucracy.[22]

STERN BLOWS: THE EFFECTS OF CAMPAIGN-STYLE POLICING

Murray Scot Tanner focuses in chapter 6 on what has been called "campaign-style policing." Campaign-style policing refers to concentrated, fixed-term, special targeting of particular categories of crime for arrest and severe punishment—hence their nickname, "stern blows" (*yanda*) campaigns. Both Tanner and Dutton see these anti-crime struggles as a reintroduction of Maoist techniques of mass campaigning. Tanner explains some of the historical reasons for the return of the nostalgia of past mass-line approaches.

There might be a belief in the blessings of harsh punishment here, but again we encounter the problem of scarce resources. Tanner argues that these campaigns represent a pragmatic and organizational response to China's comparatively low ratio of professional police officers to citizens. At the outset of the campaigns the official ratio between regular police personnel and population was extremely low by international standards. Low ratios forced police to rely heavily on the active cooperation of nonprofessional citizen security activists. It was a firm belief in the political leadership that without mass involvement these struggles would not succeed. We still see traces of that belief although it has faded considerably. There might even be a growing distrust of the "masses" among the police. In recent police manuals the person on duty is asked to immediately disperse the crowd if an incident of disorder occurs in the street. The community policeman of yesteryear was advised to cooperate and seek help from the same masses. The police force is today just beginning its transformation into a professional force, and as explained by Dutton, the mass networks are leaving their base of political or community commitment, gradually evolving into informant networks dominated by ex-convicts rather than "moral citizens."

The anti-crime campaigns have been notable for their brutal methods and their frequent use of the death penalty. Quoting high-level police sources,

Tanner points out that deterrence and the "severity" of punishment are "the most fundamental special characteristics" of the anti-crime campaigns. Deng Xiaoping stated that "only by being severe can we cure crime *for good*." For the legalists of the Qin dynasty of the third century B. C., the effectiveness of the laws was directly related to the heaviness of the punishments imposed.[23] Deng's policy seemed to adopt the most draconian traits of the legalist tradition. During the 1980s, simultaneous with the development of legal reforms, the harshness of punishments increased, and the use of the death penalty quadrupled in just over half a decade from 1979 to 1986. Tanner ventures into the draconian details of this severity and touches in particular on the extensive use of the death penalty that has been a feature of the campaigns.

Contrary to what many outside China may think, the campaigns appear less popular within the police force itself than with the general public. There seems to be a general tendency of accepting harsh punishment in China. A Ministry of Public Security survey of 15,000 people showed that the vast majority thought the state's handling of criminals was either just adequate or not tough enough. Nearly 60 percent of the respondents answered that they found the existing laws "too lenient." Only 2 percent found the laws "too strict."[24] We should not necessarily accept surveys from the Ministry of Public Security, but the tendency is confirmed by other sources. We see the same Chinese preference for strong reactions to crime if we explore attitudes to punishment. Recent international survey analyses of cross-national attitudes to punishment seem to confirm the remarkably strong Chinese punitive culture.[25] People were asked to evaluate a case where a twenty-one-year-old man had stolen a color TV and is found guilty for the second time. The alternatives ranged from imprisonment to community service, suspended sentence, a fine, or other reactions. There were some clear patterns in the responses. People in industrialized nations generally wanted community service rather than imprisonment. The exception from that rule was most notably the United States, Northern Ireland, and Eastern and Central European nations. The developing nations were all strongly in favor of imprisonment. Of the fifty-eight nations where we have sufficient data, China came out as the most punitive of all. As many as 84 percent of the Chinese respondents wanted imprisonment (on average a sentence of nearly two and a half years), followed by Uganda with an 80 percent preference, and Zimbabwe with 79. The only respondents suggesting the death penalty were Chinese. The willingness to use capital punishment finds strong support in China. A five-thousand-person survey undertaken by researchers in Beijing, some of whom were personally against the death penalty, found that less than 0.8 percent of the respondents wanted to abolish such punishment. Only 3 percent held that it was "used too often." There were no significant differences in terms of gender as found in most other nations.[26]

Numerous police officials have criticized the tendency for authorities in many regions to turn the anti-crime "special struggles" into a routine and almost constant state of affairs. Police personnel are worn out by constant campaigning. Even criminals know when the campaign is turned on, choosing their strategies on the basis of that knowledge. At the same time, the pressure to catch large numbers of criminals can even negatively affect the case-cracking rate as the police are then no longer in a good position to select the best cases for prosecution. Internal police journals time and again show resistance to the constant campaigning, and many feel that professional policing suffers from the approach. What is more, the campaigns do not reduce crime. Instead they brutalize the crime scene, making the job of policemen even more dangerous. The trend of brutalization as an effect of capital punishment has long been pointed out by criminologists. Illustrative of the brutalized crime scene is the fact that the number of policemen killed on duty increased tenfold from around a total of one thousand during the period 1949 to 1981, to over six thousand in a twenty-year period since 1981.[27] In 2001 alone, 443 policemen were killed on duty, "reflecting the increasing number of violent crimes," according to one police report.[28] The critique of death-penalty abuses in campaign-style policing found in Amnesty International reports has even begun to show signs of gaining a foothold in Chinese legal circles. Chinese scholars themselves have recently reported the same effects of brutalization previously identified in international research.[29]

Within the public security system, however, the criticisms that have shown the most political power have been those pointing out the lack of "professional" policing. Such criticisms claim that the effect of campaigns has been exaggerated, that their effects are not sustainable, and that they undermine efforts to improve police professionalism. Among public security analysts, then, probably the most powerful critique of campaign-style policing is that, over the long term, it simply does not work. Even official crime statistics quickly resumed their rapid upward trends almost immediately after the campaign was ended.[30] Again, such findings are confirmed in the general criminological literature. In particular we observe an upward trend in major crimes such as serious theft, homicide, rape, robberies, and serious assault. While such crime made up well under 10 percent of the total crime rate just before the start of the *yanda* campaigns, it now constitutes well over 30 percent of the total rate.[31] This brutalization of crime is what some think is worth the price of keeping up the impression among the general populace that something is being done to uphold order. The recurring waves of anti-crime campaigns might boil down to the fact that the regime needs legitimacy in the form of creating the impression that it is able to uphold order. Political bodies thus seek to show that something is being done at a time of deteriorating public order in the era of reform.

Although some police officials and scholars have begun to argue that campaign excesses are corroding police relations with citizens rather than strengthening them, there is also ample evidence for support from below. Mass support is a crucial part of the explanation of why the campaigns linger on, and it should be remembered that the regime is gaining popularity and legitimacy by being tough on crime. The harsh methods of deterrence have support from below, reflecting the policies of the authoritarian state pushing for deterrence from above. One important finding of the UN international criminal victimization survey is worth noting here. One of the general conclusions was that public attitudes to punishment seem to reflect and support established sentencing traditions.[32] The fear of crime is a very important factor in explaining the phenomenon. Such fear is obvious in China today despite the internationally low crime rates they experience. The media obviously plays an important role here, and it is well known to criminologists that the media overdramatizes the most serious types of crime.[33] The introduction of modern, market-oriented forms of communication and organization and the subsequent fading of community bonds are among the by-products of modernization. As community deteriorates, the fear of crime is rapidly increasing, as is shown in numerous surveys of attitudes towards public security in China. Again we know from criminology that the mere fear of crime may be perceived as a greater threat to quality of life than actual criminal incidents. Popularity is gained both for the regime in general and the police force in particular if they are able to create a sense of order in society. Legitimacy flows from the regime's ability to uphold order, and there is much popular support for tough policing in China. Reactions against crime in Chinese society, in other words, are not limited to the wish to solve the problem of crime as such. The reactions against crime have to be seen in terms of defending the social and moral order in a society undergoing rapid transformation.

The campaigns should make us particularly aware of the general problem of inaccurate crime statistics. Campaign figures have innumerable hidden agendas, political as well as practical, and it is of course of enormous importance for some to show that the campaigns really deliver. It is clear from Tanner's, Dutton's, and my own research that official statistics and preparation of reports on crime leave the real figures in absolute darkness in order to create images favorable to police performance. Where Tanner tends to see the Party committees and the police bureaucracy as the main culprits in this regard, Dutton argues that these problems are mainly the structural effects of the contract system itself. Both, however, report an inbuilt tendency to fabricate positive campaign reports. Official police sources demonstrate that in addition to simply falsifying statistical reports, local police have developed a vast array of "rational" tactics to manipulate the data. For example, three of the key statistical goals during a campaign are the lowering of the overall number of criminal cases, increasing arrests, and increasing the percentage of officially opened case files that are solved—the famous "case-cracking rate." It is indeed interesting to look closer at the striking symmetry between reported crime rates and the case-cracking rate, indicating a more or less constructed crime rate based upon police report practices rather than real existing crime.

COMMERCIALIZING CONTROL: THE PARADOXICAL EFFECTS OF CONTRACT POLICING

Michael Dutton in chapter 7 goes on to show how such rationalities and incentive structures are dictated by the contract. If you do not report crimes you do not think can be solved, it might benefit your income since the percentage of solved cases will then be higher. The responsibility system in policing, it seems, had produced a decrease in police reporting, but not in the actual number of crimes committed. The reasons for such a low rate of reporting related principally to the performance criteria of the security responsibility system. Police were simply defending their bonuses by not recording crimes reported to them. Reporting a crime to the police does not mean that the report is listed in the crime statistics. It depends on whether or not the police find it beneficial to record those reports. For instance, it has been difficult to have rape reports recorded by the police, something that might reflect the attitude towards women in the police force in general, but also the complexity of such cases in terms of the difficulty in finding evidence that would produce convictions. Every criminologist is familiar with the problem of estimating the true incidence of crime from statistics of offences "known to the police." It is established beyond doubt that the official crime rates reflect only the tip of the iceberg of crimes known to those instigating them (as well as among those investigating them) and their possible victims. Most crimes undoubtedly go unreported in any country.[34] There is one important difference in the Chinese case, however, as criminologists generally list "an inactive police force" as one of the main causes for reporting crime rates which are too low.[35] In contrast, today's China reveals a very active police force with clear incentives for embellishing crime statistics by reducing the number.

Reformist police officials and scholars have warned against the corrosive effect these fraudulent campaign reporting practices have on police professionalism and the state's capacity to gather accurate social order data needed to make criminal policy. Once these statistical abuses have started, they become politically difficult to stop because any official who ignores the exaggeratedly good crime statistics of the past and begins reporting more "honest" higher figures is open to a charge that "social order has deteriorated" on his watch. The logic resembles that of former political campaigns, like that of the Great Leap Forward which led to massive falsification and inflation of production figures and equally massive miscalculations of policy implementation, again leading to severe famine in the late 1950s and early 1960s.[36] I have previously defined a campaign as a phenomenon standing between a craze and a career, where campaign instigators have their careers as the incentive of activism, while the enthusiastic mass of followers or believers of the campaign form part of a craze.[37] Together these forces can lead a campaign into a frenzy of irrational behavior. An official declaration of the campaigns' ineffectiveness is unlikely to be forthcoming according to Tanner. Campaigns compensate for inadequate local funding and staffing and cater to political needs of legitimacy. Popular support for the campaigns should perhaps be added when we try to explain why they are still in fashion.

By looking at the paradoxes involved in policing the market reforms, Dutton challenges the conventional wisdom of the necessary causal connections between markets and the rule of law. Police as law enforcement agencies only began to arrive in China after economic reform. From this time onward, police increasingly claimed to be operating on the basis of the law. It was no longer the "tool" of proletarian dictatorship it used to be under the "rule of man" of the Maoist era. Dutton focuses on the contract and the way police work has been commercialized and commodified as the main basis for explaining what goes on in Chinese policing. Rather than getting rid of the old forms of police "flexibility" and "elasticity" seen during the "dictatorship of the proletariat," the contract seems to give such practices new life. Max Weber insisted that the spread of money and market mentalities requires law and the law of the contract. We deal here with the great divide that took place during the force of the Industrial Revolution described by classical sociology as a divide between value rationality (*Wertrationalität*) and purposive rationality (*Zweckrationalität*), a move from *mechanical solidarity* to *organic solidarity*, or the development from community (*Gemeinschaft*) to society (*Gesellschaft*), or as a historical change from *status* to *contract*. Other theorists than Weber, Durkheim, Tönnies, and Sir Henry Sumner Maine have struggled with similar concepts. Dutton indirectly questions such notions of a "great divide" and argues that in terms of Chinese policing—contrary to many explanations about how law and the market strengthen each other—the growth of the contract paradoxically led to the revival of organs that in different ways challenge substantive law.

Law was central to economic reform because it was through law that stability and prediction could be achieved. Economic reform required stability but far from producing it, created a new type of disorder. In relying upon the market, the old social ills of capitalism seem to come back to China. There is no reason to paint the old community in rosy terms of idyllic comradeship, as *Gemeinschaft*, according to Ferdinand Tönnies, comes both as egalitarian comradeship (*Genossenschaft*) as well as authoritarian domination (*Herrschaft*). *Herrschaft* operated as a communal form of authoritarian domination as in vassalage, contrary to the contract defining a *Gesellschaft*.[38] There is also no reason, however, to hide the fact that the new *Gesellschaft* brought new problems to people. New crimes began to emerge; drug addiction, prostitution, economic crimes, and an increasing number of troublesome "floaters" became scapegoats for the negative side effects of the reform program. The entire policing system was itself caught up in the spread of monetary incentives.

The contract becomes a very important concept in Dutton's analysis. Begun in 1978 with the announcement of the "responsibility system in agriculture," the contract would soon spread to other domains. As the economy filled with "responsibility systems," "bonus systems," and "contract systems," other, more socially oriented areas of life were infected with such language and logic of economic reform. The spread of the contract into noneconomic domains such as policing was an effect of its stunning success in agriculture where it was introduced at the beginning of the 1980s. Police stations, police beats, and even police informers were all put on contract. Economic reform fundamentally reshaped the nature of policing in China. China metamorphosed into the land of the economic contract; social order became the "product" that police are contracted to supply.

In Maoist times, any discussion of law presupposed the centrality of legal elasticity. Without such legal elasticity, everything from the "mass dictatorship" of the 1950s to the "all-round-dictatorship" of the 1970s would have been impossible. In the late 1950s legal circles talked freely of the need for the "rule of man" (*renzhi*) rather than the "rule of law" (*fazhi*) and advocated something I would call a "norm enforcement agency" rather than one of law enforcement. Three decades after the "rule of man" seemed to dominate, the "rule of law" made a comeback. In the debates that followed, legal reformers overturned the left view that law was a mere reflection of the will of a dominant ruling class. The Western history of policing, however, was retold with "Chinese characteristics." A series of novel approaches to policing was dictated by the contract, and we can discern the emergence of a special form of structural corruption based on contract policing. Other links to corruption also became evident. The former mass-line organizations were replaced with an informant network recruited from the criminal community. International criminology regards it as a clear indication of increased corruption in the police force when police cooperate with the criminal community in this way. China would be no exception to that rule.

Security companies (*bao'an gongsi*) are another way public security is being commercialized. The companies represent a rapidly growing sector in China today. Chinese private security companies differ from those in the West, however, in that they are all wholly owned subsidiaries of the local branches of the Ministry of Public Security and it is their bureaus that directly own and operate these businesses. It is estimated that these companies now cover about one-third of all police work in the cities; and it is in guarding banks, restaurants, and serving as security guards in factories that they derive most of their profits. In many instances security companies and security guards do not provide security. In some cases they operate as vigilantes, controlling and mistreating workers in prisonlike factories.[39] While authorities recognize the problem of unauthorized so-called black security companies (*hei bao'an*),[40] the main point is that security has become commercialized, and like any other commodity, it can be bought and sold. A large number of retired servicemen work for the companies. It is worth noting that the number of retired army personnel in a society is as a rule positively correlated with violence and violent crime.

Police have more and more become law enforcement agencies and are themselves increasingly subject to the law. But the main law they are subject to, Dutton argues, is the law of the contract. One might argue that the extensive use of the contract described by Dutton has seen its worst excesses and that the system is about to be moderated. The police have pared back the contract system in recent years as its negative effect upon policing has become more and more evident. The trend is likely to be moderated even further, but the description here might be seen as the "form" of the entire social system of reform momentarily revealed in China.

PARADOXES OF THE ENGINEERING STATE

The paradoxical effects of commercialization and economic reform are reaching their climax in today's rampant corruption. Corruption has been defined as a relationship of power and influence existing within, and taking its form from, specific environments of opportunity.[41] We have seen how the crimes of the weak and the marginalized have been handled in today's China, but the largest problem is perhaps the crimes among the strong and the well connected. Several chapters show the difficulties linked to official crime statistics. The difficulties in interpreting the statistics of crime are greatly magnified when we move from crime in the streets to crime in the suites. The change in the environments of opportunity during reform makes corrupt practices within the police force far more profitable than before. Huge profits were derived from the coexistence of government-set and market-led prices, so-called official profiteering, or *guandao*. The second boom of this development was ignited by Deng Xiaoping's "southern tour" in 1992 and expanded the environment of corrupt opportunities for the police. It has a profound and disastrous effect on the whole society when "the forces of order" are instead turned into "forces of disorder," operating to a great extent through corruption. The damage inflicted by this type of crime probably entirely dwarfs that of "ordinary" crime, and corruption in the police and the armed forces in particular is much more damaging to the long-term stability of the regime.

The Chinese Communist Party (CCP) has seen the writing on the wall, and stricter control has been implemented. The widespread use of the police contract has been significantly limited. The opportunity for setting up business ventures within the police and the armed forces has likewise been made much more difficult. In mid-1998, the central government issued an order, trying to disconnect state apparatuses from all business organizations set up *spontaneously* and run *informally* by them before a specified deadline. This is an important input in order to curb corruption, but to what extent the disconnection order functions in practice remains an open question.[42]

The Chinese investment in sheer punitiveness is a futile strategy, more bent on gaining political legitimacy through creating the appearance of "order" than actually reducing crime as such. The massive social and legal problems associated with the rapidly widening gap between rich and poor will have to be addressed before crime can be reduced significantly. The administration and police force still appear to maintain a large amount of discretionary power, which makes corruption a growing problem. There is a need to focus on this "crime of the strong" rather than lashing out at the weak and the destitute "floating" masses. The international experiences are that the lack of a rule of law is closely correlated with corrupt practices.

Corruption on its side is closely linked to organized crime that is again correlated with violent crime. We might see a spiral of violence and counterviolence and a situation that creates an ideal climate for organized crime and corruption instead of a situation with continued low crime rates. The experiment with market socialism is applied to policing and punishment as well, and this book reveals that the experiment is far from successful. What China has gained in legal reforms might be lost in a counterproductive strategy of harsh punishments and commercialized policing. The stability of the country is not secured by such an approach, and the experiences of international criminology and international crime trends should be examined more seriously in Beijing.

We do right in not assuming an "evil empire" when we deal with control in today's China, or in any other country for that matter. For Zygmunt Baumann, not even the Holocaust was a pure irrational outflow of barbarism but in its own horrific logic a "normal" and "legitimate" resident in the house of modernity.[43] The questionable developments we see in the regimes of control should rather be linked to the history and the processes of modernization, the patterns of culture in thinking about control and punishment, the bureaucracy of the Party state and its career and incentive systems, the economy with its problems of scarcity and its novel structures of opportunity, the norms and the fears of the public, and the structures of power and needs for face and legitimacy on the part of the regime. Deng Xiaoping's stern manifesto that "only by being severe can we cure crime *for good*," and his understanding of legality as synonymous with the draconian Chinese tradition of legalism, follows the logic of the "engineering state" where social engineering provides the answers to all kinds of social problems. Or perhaps we should rather talk of a "gardening state" where society becomes an object for design, cultivation, and weeding.[44] Its logic is that spiritual pollution (*jingshen wuran*) should and could be eradicated for good, exemplary behavior is possible to achieve, and the control system with its policing and its prisons is seen as a means to achieve this aim. The educative becomes a logical element of what Foucault has coined the *carceral*. We clearly discern this line of thinking about modernity and control from the ideas of the republic to those of the present Chinese regime.

NOTES

1. *The Criminal Law and the Criminal Procedure Law of China, China (Zhongguo renmin gongheguo xingfa, Zhongguo renmin gongheguo xingshi susong fa)* (Beijing: Foreign Languages Press, 1983), 32 (English) and 86 (Chinese).

2. From Europe we see widespread mafia stereotypes encouraged in the reporting of crime, particularly in Russia, Poland, and the former Soviet bloc in Eastern Europe. See Freedom Forum, *The*

Media versus the Mafia. Critical Issues in Covering Organized Crime, quoted from Mark Findlay, *The Globalization of Crime* (Cambridge: Cambridge University Press, 2000), 28. Since the 1980s the Chinese press has been full of accounts of gruesome crime, and the Western press preys on such accounts, often presenting stories of particularly sensational crimes accompanied by alarmist accounts of soaring crime rates in China. See for instance, *Far Eastern Economic Review* (November 2, 2000): 72–75. Real existing crime in China does not justify such accounts which in large part are a product of changing media practices. China is not the only society in which sensational crime reportage sells.

3. See my discussion on the links between control, discipline, and education in Børge Bakken, *The Exemplary Society: Human Improvement, Social Control, and the Dangers of Modernity in China* (Oxford: Oxford University Press, 2000).

4. See Kanishka Jayasurya, "Corporatism and Judicial Independence within Statist Legal Institutions in East Asia," in *Law, Capitalism and Power in East Asia: The Rule of Law and Legal Institutions,* ed. Kinishka Jayasurya (London: Routledge, 1999), 173–204.

5. Still, the rise in crime is often seen as caused by modernization and socioeconomic development. Increased crime and development is not seen as a one-to-one relationship but is more often explained in the picture of social integration. Weakened social bonds are often seen as a product of the modernization process. See Mark Findlay, *The Globalization of Crime,* 27.

6. For a glimpse into the debate of Western views on "rehabilitation," see Don C. Gibbons, "Review Essay: Changing Lawbreakers: What Have We Learned since the 1950s?" *Crime and Delinquency,* no. 2 (April 1999): 272–93. In China rehabilitation is a core theme of penology, and among mainstream penologists the issue of *ganhua* education is still very central in discussions of rehabilitation. See for example, Jin Jian, ed., *Jianyuxue zonglun* (General theory of penology) (Beijing: Falü chubanshe, 1997), 541–65.

7. Harry Hongda Wu, *Laogai: The Chinese Gulag,* translated by Ted Slingerland (Boulder, Colo.: Westview Press, 1992). In the climate dominating the debate in the aftermath of the Korean War, the paradigm of "totalitarianism" dominated the scholarly debate. The classic work within this paradigm of analysis concerned with Chinese prisons is Robert Jay Lifton, *Thought Reform and the Psychology of Totalism: A Study of "Brainwashing" in China* (London: Victor Gollancz, 1961). The paradigm of totalitarianism is now being replaced by other theoretical approaches better equipped to explain a China in rapid transition. For an overview of such approaches, see Flemming Christiansen and Shirin Ray, *Chinese Politics and Society: An Introduction* (London: Prentice Hall, 1996), 1–24.

8. The anti-crime campaigns of 1983 were started after two years of declining crime rates after the peak in 1981. At least there were other reasons than mere rising crime rates that triggered the onset of the campaigns. Despite the increase in crime in China, we should not forget the perspective that "crime waves" may be manufactured when government legitimacy is weakened. See an account of such phenomena in Stuart Hall et al., *Policing the Crisis: Mugging, the State, and Law and Order* (London: Macmillan, 1978).

9. Fieldwork among Chinese prisoners has shown that the strategies of faking reform can be quite cunning and widespread. See Dang Guoqing, "Laojiao renyuan jiehuo fan gaizao wenti de pouxi" (Analysis of the problems of ganging up and faking reform among inmates of reeducation-through-labor institutions) in *Zhongguo qingshaonian fanzui yanjiu nianjian 1987* (Beijing:

Chunqiu chubanshe, 1988), 406–11. See also my general discussion on "ways of lying," simulation, theater, deception, and "fake reform" in Børge Bakken, *The Exemplary Society*, 411–42.

10. See John Braithwaite, *Crime, Shame, and Reintegration* (Cambridge: Cambridge University Press, 1989).

11. Zhu Xiaoyang uses the expression in his account of village punishment, where the cultural practices of face (*mianzi*) and personal networking (*guanxi*) informed the realities of punishment. Among other methods, the performance of shouting abuses in the street (*ma jie*) could cause effective shaming and sanctioning in the village community. See Zhu Xiaoyang, "Punishment in a Chinese Village in Yunnan," (Ph.D. dissertation, Department of Anthropology, Macquarie University, Sydney), 209.

12. Barbara Weinberger, "The Police and the Public in Mid-Nineteenth-Century Warwickshire," in *Policing and Punishment in Nineteenth-Century Britain*, ed. Victor Bailey, 65–93 (London: Croom Helm, 1981), 75.

13. For a more thorough account on arbitrary detention (*shourong qiansong*), see Human Rights in China, *Not Welcome at the Party: Behind the "Clean-up" of China's Cities: A Report on Administrative Detention under "Custody and Repatriation*," Human Rights in China, HRIC Arbitrary Detention Series, no. 2 (September 1999), http://www.hrchchina.org/reports/cleanup/html (10 January 2000).

14. *Xinhua News Agency*, Beijing, in English 1024 gmt 27 June 2003. See also *Beijing Review*, no. 25, 19 June 2003, 22–26.

15. International statistics on crime, such as the figures supplied by Interpol, leave us uninformed about national differences with respect to reporting practices, laws, methods of calculation, or definitions of crime. The Interpol data thus provide a rough indication only of where China stands internationally in terms of crime. Reports from 113 countries in the late 1980s on crime rates rank China 111th. See Organisation Internationale de Police Criminelle, *Statistiques Criminelles Internationales*, 1985–1986 (International Criminal Statistics, 1985–1986) (Lyon: Le Secretariat Géneral de l'O.I.PC. Interpol, 1988 and 1990). The figures quoted in this chapter are based on 1985–1986 and 1987–1988 statistics, thus supplementing the ninety-seven countries in the 1985–1986 statistics with an additional sixteen countries from the 1987–1988 statistics. Only two countries—Mali with 11.08 per 100,000 population, and Nepal with 33.29 cases—have a lower reported crime rate than China's 51.9 cases per 100,000 population in 1986.

16. See Nils Christie's "maps of pain" in Nils Christie, *Crime Control as Industry: Towards Gulags, Western Style*, 3rd. edition (London: Routledge, 2000), 25–39.

17. See Børge Bakken, *The Exemplary Society*, 377–79.

18. In 1997, 2026 people officially served sentences for jeopardizing state security, totaling 0.46 percent of the prison population. *Xinhua News Agency* (31 March 1997), in *SWB-FE/2881* (1 April 1997): G3.

19. It is thus a matter of definition when Du Zhongxing, head of China's prison system, during a recent visit to Australia claimed that "there are no political prisoners in China because in China every person can give his political views." See *Sydney Morning Herald* (13 August 2002): News, 2.

20. According to Zhou Guojun, a professor of the Chinese University of Politics and Law, the now-illegal use of torture by the Chinese public security forces can partly be explained by a flawed police mentality and partly by the lack of material resources. He advocates stricter control of the police, better funding, and legal reforms. See Zhou Guojun, "Yanjin xingxun bigong ruogan wenti tantao" (Inquiry into several issues concerning the prohibition of extorting confessions by torture), in *Jujiao faxue redian* (Focusing on the hot topics of law), ed. Zhao Xianglin (Beijing: Falü chubanshe, 2002), 417–32. For a detailed account of the current use of torture in China, see the Falun Gong Human Rights Working Group, *The Falun Gong Report* (Buford, Ga.: Golden Lotus Press, 2002).

21. A similar argument is used in the case of Cambodia. See Roderic Broadhurst, "Lethal Violence, Crime and State Formation in Cambodia," *The Australian and New Zealand Journal of Criminology*, no.1 (2002): 7.

22. Jayasurya, "Corporatism and Judicial Independence," 196–97.

23. See chapter 2 in Geoffrey MacCormack, *Traditional Chinese Penal Law* (Edinburgh: Edinburgh University Press, 1990), 26–48.

24. Zhonghua renmin gongheguo gonganbu, ed., *Nin ganjue anquan ma?* (Do you feel safe?) (Beijing: Qunzhong chubanshe, 1992), 46, 60, 250ff.

25. Pat Mayhew and John van Kesteren, "Cross-National Attitudes to Punishment," in *Changing Public Views of Punishment*, ed. Julian Roberts and Mike Hough (London: Villan Publishing, 2002). Draft dated 8 May 2002. See also the Beijing survey in Ugljesa Zvekic and Anna Alvazzi Del Frate, *Criminal Victimization in the Developing World*, publication no.55 (Rome: United Nations Interregional Crime and Justice Research Institute, 1995), 78–79.

26. Hu Yunteng, ed., *Cun yu fei: Sixing jiben lilun yanjiu* (Survival and abolishment: Basic discussion on the research of capital punishment) (Beijing: Zhongguo jiancha chubanshe, 2000), 342–43. The information about some of the researchers was given to me by people involved in the survey.

27. Estimates based on Shuliang Feng, "Crime and Crime Control in China," in *Crime and Social Control in a Changing China*, Jianhong Liu, Lening Zhang, and Steven F. Messner, eds., (Westport, Conn.: Greenwood Press, 2001), 125.

28. China says 443 policemen died in the course of duty in 2001, *BBC Monitoring Asia Pacific—Political* (25 January 2002).

29. See my discussion in Børge Bakken, *The Exemplary Society*, 397. See also William J. Bowers and Glenn Pierce, "Deterrence or Brutalization: What is the Effect of Executions?" *Crime and Delinquency*, no. 26 (1980): 453–84. Researchers at the Chinese Academy of Social Sciences have found similar effects. See several issues on public security in Jiang Liu, Lu Xueyi, Shan Tianlun, eds., *Zhongguo: shehui xingshi fenxi yu yuce* (Analysis and forecast of the social situation in China) (Beijing: Zhongguo shehui kexueyuan chubanshe, annual edition).

30. I found clear indication of this myself. See Børge Bakken, *The Exemplary Society*, 392–93.

31. See more details in Børge Bakken, *The Exemplary Society*, 393–94.

32. See Pat Mayhew and Jan J. M. van Dijk, *Criminal Victimisation in Eleven Industrialized*

Countries: Key Findings from the 1996 International Crime Victimisation Surveys (London: Home Office Publications, 1997).

33. See "Official Crime Statistics and the Media," in Graeme Newman, ed., *United Nations Global Report on Crime and Justice*, New York: United Nations Office for Drug Control and Crime Prevention, Centre for International Crime Prevention (Oxford: Oxford University Press, 1999), 14.

34. Mike Maguire, "Crime Statistics, Patterns, and Trends: Changing Perceptions and their Implications," in *The Oxford Handbook of Criminology*, ed. Mike Maguire, Rod Morgan, Robert Reiner (Oxford: Clarendon Press, 1994), 233–91; and Roger Hood and Richard Sparks, *Key Issues in Criminology* (London: Weidenfeld and Nicolson, 1970), 15–18.

35. Mark Findlay, *The Globalization of Crime*, 144.

36. For an excellent account of the unfolding of the Great Leap Forward, see Frederick Teiwes with Warren Sun, *China's Road to Disaster* (Armonk, N.Y.: M. E. Sharpe, 1999).

37. Børge Bakken, *The Exemplary Society*, 424–25.

38. The concepts are discussed in more detail under "social relationships" in Ferdinand Tönnies, *Einführung in die Soziologie*, vol. 2 (Stuttgart: Ferdinand Enke, 1931), 34–73.

39. See Liu Xinhua, "Zhaojie Footwear Company: Mistreatment of Workers under Investigation," in Anita Chan, "The Conditions of Chinese Workers in East Asian–Funded Enterprises," *Chinese Sociology and Anthropology*, vol. 30, no. 4 (Summer 1998): 58–61. See also Anita Chan, *China's Workers Under Assault: The Exploitation of Labor in a Globalizing Economy* (Armonk, N.Y.: M. E. Sharpe, 2001).

40. Yang Kezhong, "Bao'an fuwuye de fazhan yu sikao" (Reflections on the development of the security service industry), *Zhongguo bao'an*, no. 7 (2001), 14.

41. Mark Findlay, *The Globalization of Crime*, 34–35.

42. X. L. Ding, "'Special Business Ventures' by 'Special Apparatuses' of the Chinese State: The Seed-Bed of Corruption and Crime," (unpublished manuscript); and Børge Bakken, "Norms, Police and the Problems of Control," in *China Today: Economic Reforms, Social Cohesion and Collective Identities in China*, ed. Taciana Fisac and Leila Fernandez-Stembridge (London: Routledge-Curzon, 2003), 123–48.

43. Zygmunt Baumann, *Modernity and the Holocaust* (Cambridge: Polity Press, 1989).

44. See Børge Bakken, *The Exemplary Society*, 50–81, and Nils Christie, *Crime Control as Industry*, 179.

I

RECENT DREAMS, PRESENT TRENDS, AND FUTURE SCENARIOS

2

Penology and Reformation in Modern China

FRANK DIKÖTTER

The prison today is often condemned as a form of brutal deterrence, but it was viewed as a product of benevolence and a producer of goodness across the globe during most of the nineteenth and twentieth century. A cathedral of modernity, the prison was embraced by local notables, county magistrates, government officials, legal experts, and political elites around the world from Paris to Rio de Janeiro and Auburn to Tokyo. Changing sensibilities towards pain, new representations of bodily integrity, humanitarian values heralded by Enlightenment thinkers, utilitarian ideas about punishment as a corrective measure, growing dissatisfaction with existing legal penalties, and revulsion at the conditions of existing jails combined towards the end of the eighteenth century in England and France to create a new conception of the prison as a total institution in which the bad criminal could be reformed into a good citizen. While commitment to social improvement and faith in the malleable nature of humankind pervaded these early debates, the single most important factor in the emergence of the prison was the political revolutions of the late eighteenth and mid-nineteenth century. During the French Revolution, the fall of the Bastille symbolized the defeat of an entire ancient regime of punishment widely perceived to be cruel and arbitrary. A post-revolutionary mode of governance, in which legitimacy was vested in the nation rather than in a king, based its authority to punish on a code of law. Moreover, as the social hierarchies specific to traditional regimes were theoretically swept away by a new ideology of equality and fraternity, the state proclaimed a duty of care over its subjects: criminals were part of a new political order and should be punished in a humane way before being restituted to the social body. The idea of the prison—producer of obedient citizens for a moral community based on the rule of law—paralleled the rise of the modern state and the extension of political rights. Russia, for instance, opted for rehabilitation over corporal punishment during the era of Great Reforms, undertaking to redeem the nation's criminals in a new prison system, while prison reform was embraced by the Meiji reformers in Japan after 1868. These global developments were dynamically interrelated: portraying their mission as a fight against "barbarism" and "inhumanity," prison reformers around the world operated within a comparative framework in which prison reform was seen as an indicator of a nation's "progress." The dungeon stood as an embarrassing reminder of backwardness, while the prison epitomized civilization. Corporal punishment, arbitrary justice, and corrupt jails were remnants of an old world, while reformed judicial systems, legal codes, and modern prisons were indicative of a new political order.

The ideas of Beccaria, Bentham, Locke, Montesquieu, and other philosophers were appropriated across borders, as modernizing elites dispersed around the globe identified with and shared in the Enlightenment concepts of law and government. With the rise of evolutionary theories in the last third of the nineteenth century, the prison became one of the most discussed indicators of a nation's capacity to survive in a context of struggle for survival. Where modern states proclaimed their duty to provide adequate social protection for all their citizens and construct a united national community—building hospitals, schools, and prisons—they also acted within a global frame of reference in which emulation and competition led to ever shifting standards, innovations, and expectations: modernizing elites in Peru, Russia, Japan, or China posed as vanguards of a new world who were instrumental in helping their country to "catch up." The prison was a prestige symbol that exerted fascination around the world as governments enthusiastically invested vast amounts of money in cells and walls—often well beyond their financial capacities—in order to join the privileged group of "advanced nations." In London, Pentonville Prison opened its doors in 1842, the most expensive and modern building of the capital besides Parliament. Similar prestige prisons would appear in the world's capitals, from Lima and St. Petersburg to Tokyo and Beijing.[1]

The history of prison reform, in short, is a global history. A comparative approach to the history of the prison highlights the extent to which common knowledge is appropriated and transformed by very distinct local styles of expression dependent on the political, economic, social, and cultural variables of particular institutions and social groups. As ideas move across borders, they are adjusted to specific local conditions: inculturation, rather than acculturation, characterizes a modernity that is inflected in a multiplicity of ways by different modernizing elites. The emergence of the prison in Latin America, Russia, Japan, China, or India cannot so much be interpreted as a belated replication of a European model—and even less as a uniform imposition by "world capitalism" or "cultural imperialism"—but as the local appropriation of global ideas. As internationally circulated discourses and practices of punishment intersected locally with concrete ideological and political configurations, they engendered new varieties of incarceration: underneath an overarching rationale based on the idea of humane and reformative punishment, the prison was multivalent, capable of being adopted in a variety of mutually incompatible environments, ranging from the congregate system at Auburn to the agricultural colony of Mettray. The very flexibility of the idea of the prison allowed it to be transplanted widely around the globe as it not only adapted but also adopted existing notions of crime and punishment. Its modernity, in other words, was more a matter of aspiration than of actuality: in England, for instance, arguments against corporal punishment had been aired frequently well before the Enlightenment, while older religious notions immediately invested the moral space of the prison. The very term "penitentiary" defined the cell as a place of penance, while the evangelical movement and its concern with moral decay, sin, forgiveness, prayer, and redemption—the prison chaplain was a central reformative figure—played as important a role in the new conception of the prison as secular developments in the eighteenth century.[2]

Ideas and things have multiple uses: prisons, too, can remain in place while fundamentally changing their purpose. In China, the prison was a modern tool appropriated to pursue a more traditional vision of an ordered and cohesive social body governed by the rule of virtue. One of the most fundamental ideas in traditional penal philosophy was that punishment should be designed to educate people in ethical norms (*mingxing bijiao*): the law was an instrument of moral education. Confucian scholars believed that the *jiao*, or ethical norms, should be brought about by education. The appearance in modern China of a model of imprisonment based on the idea of reformation was part of both a global movement towards penal reform, drawing on an international repertoire of ideas and institutions, and a local reconfiguration of a more traditional faith in the transformative capacity of education. Based on a Mencian view of human nature as inherently good, the notion of *ganhua* further sustained the belief that even criminals could achieve individual self-improvement through proper institutional guidance. *Gan* meant to feel, to sense, to move or touch a person emotionally, while *hua* indicated a meaningful transfiguration forward, "to change something or someone for the better," a process of moral transformation.³ The element *hua* appeared in other composite terms which were current in modern China: *jiaohua* was a "civilizing process" by which individuals were transformed via the inculcation of ethical norms in education, while *jinhua* was a term used to translate the Darwinian notion of "evolution": contrary to Darwin, however, *jinhua* did not mean random change but a directional process of evolution forwards. *Ganhua* referred to moral reformation by an emotional appeal to the feelings of a criminal. The protean term *ganhua*—a core value of penalty in republican China—anticipated repentance and moral reformation: to affect (*gandong*) a criminal and obtain change (*zhuanhua*) by exemplary words or acts, to admonish and guide by providing a model, to "change by persuasion."⁴ Punishment, in other words, was meant to educate, and reformative education was the inculcation of correct ethical norms of behavior within the therapeutic isolation of the prison.

Education was designed to consolidate the social bond between the individual and the collective. Selfish behavior, either sexual or criminal, should be eliminated in the interests of social unity, as the ultimate interests of society and the individual were seen to coincide like a biological cell contributed to a living body. Within this vision of the collective whole, the contradictory goals of the person and the community and the diversity of interests of various social groups were rarely envisaged: law reflected a general consensus or collective will that was based on shared customs and national interests. The social, the moral, and the legal overlapped, as correct behavior was the ability to follow prescribed ways in society. As all persons were thought to have the ability to follow correct behavior through moral education, widespread education was seen as a key to achieving national unity, social cohesion, and economic prosperity. Good behavior stemmed from moral education, which provided the people with the rules of proper conduct. The *li*, or "rules of proper conduct," was a core concept of Confucian ethics that lay at the heart of personal identity. As James Watson has underlined, "to be Chinese was to understand and accept the view that there was a correct way to live one's life."⁵ Practice, in other words, was seen to be more important than belief, an observation that is also valid for modern China. The responsibility of the state was to provide clear rules of proper conduct, which would discipline and bind all individuals into a cohesive social entity.

As correct behavior was of paramount importance in the moral education of subjects, the emulation of models was a dominant pedagogical strategy. As much as the sages of the past were upheld as models of virtuous behavior to be emulated by the people in imperial China, models pervaded the institutional landscape of republican China: model schools, model villages, model cities were all designed to encourage correct moral behavior and promote standards to be emulated by the rest of the country. Model education was not only found in schools or prisons, but also pervaded the institutions designed to promote correct behavior. Administrative culture in republican China was dominated with the expectation of model behavior, as benevolent rule was seen to have a transformative effect on the rest of society. The promotion of strict rules of behavior was part of this "exemplary society," in the words of Børge Bakken.[6] Where health manuals instructed pregnant women how to sit, stand, walk, eat, and drink, sex handbooks detailed the precise etiquette to be followed behind curtains, from the initial kiss to the final orgasm. Slogans appeared on prison walls enjoining prisoners to behave correctly, while rules of proper deportment were propagated to the rest of the population in mass campaigns like the New Life Movement: lack of national unity and social cohesion was believed to be a moral and spiritual problem rather than a political one. In many cases, of course, the rigidity inherent in prescriptive culture could engender precisely the opposite effect, namely complete disregard for the collectivity and cynical use of the prevailing rules. As we will see, prisons should theoretically inculcate repentance but often succeeded merely in producing recidivists. Moral reformation was designed to foster socially responsible individuals who obeyed authority and controlled selfish desires for the benefit of the collectivity: in republican prisons, many prisoners learned how to manipulate the prison rules and to fight for their own survival in a harsh milieu of ruthless competition over scarce resources. The prisoners who were most gifted in faking contrition, displaying repentance, and expressing regret benefited from early release: they were also the ones most likely to apply their talents to a life of crime. Where a model failed to achieve its goal, however, it was not necessarily adjusted to shifting circumstances but shored up with yet more rules and regulations deemed to be capable of correcting a slipping model and channeling it into the desired direction. The promulgation of numerous prison rules in republican China, for instance, reflected the administrative belief that more prescriptive norms could control and mold rapidly changing situations.

Inherent in the prescriptive culture of modern China was a system of rewards and punishments. Already in imperial China, ledgers of merit and demerit promoted good deeds while discouraging incorrect behavior. These moral account books listed all the good and bad deeds and had a point system whereby the reader could precisely evaluate his or her moral conduct.[7] The progressive system used in republican prisons was also based on a reward system whereby the prisoner could gain certain privileges or even conditional release when adhering to the standards of good conduct. Intricate point systems were used to evaluate a prisoner's progress, including points for good behavior and hard work. Prison administrators themselves were enmeshed in an administrative culture that revolved around the constant evaluation and monitoring of government officials. Evaluation encouraged virtuous behavior, promoted the exemplary norm, and integrated the individual to the collectivity: in prisons, detailed knowledge of individuals was produced in efforts to measure and quantify repentance. The constant evaluation of individuals in prescriptive cultures, some critics have argued, produced an outer social ethic at the expense of an inner personal morality.[8] As public regulations, norms, and standards controlled individual behavior, many individuals constructed their sense of self in relation to other people. More importantly, the techniques of evaluation that pervaded the prescriptive culture of republican China closely tied the individual to a state in charge of moral education.

Education, in short, was intrinsically linked to discipline. The prison was part of an educative mission that placed faith in the malleability of human beings while it was also a disciplinary project aimed to instill respect of social norms. Modernizing elites in republican China viewed the reformation of criminals as a constitutive part of a project of national regeneration in which social cohesion, economic development, and state power could only be obtained by molding obedient subjects. This chapter explores the importance of the idea of *ganhua* in the penological philosophy of modern China.

PENOLOGY IN REPUBLICAN CHINA

Patricia O'Brien notes that prison systems in Europe developed in a similar way in the nineteenth century, reflecting a commonly held penal philosophy that placed great faith in the reformative prison. Towards the end of the nineteenth century, however, imprisonment was increasingly criticized, as many states introduced noncustodial sentences, including the suspended sentence, supervised parole, and probation.[9] The shrinking size of prison populations after 1865, following decades of growth, was a reflection of new punitive sanctions, although this trend was not characteristic of countries that were relatively late to embark on prison reform, such as Italy, Spain, and Russia. Penal philosophies started to diversify substantially in Europe in the early twentieth century, leading in some cases to the partial obsolescence of the prison as a method of punishment. These innovations were presented at international conferences: the parole system, established in France in 1885, was approved throughout Europe at the International Prison Congress of 1910. In the 1930s, a growing reliance on fines marked the penal system of some countries in Europe, in contrast to Italy and Germany, which drastically increased their prison populations, a trend advanced by the accession to power of authoritarian figures like Adolf Hitler.

The penal philosophy dominant in republican China, with its emphasis on the moral reformation of the prisoner, was proposed in Europe during the early nineteenth century but came under increasing criticism from the 1850s onwards. In England, for instance, the widespread building of new prisons that followed the opening of Pentonville in 1842 was followed by public skepticism not only in the efficacy of model prisons, but also in the very possibility of reformation through imprisonment. The appearance of a broad range of critical voices, from one end of the political spectrum to the other, marked the end of the second wave of prison reform in England as the prison was viewed with increased revulsion. By the end of the nineteenth century, the debate against prisons was further fuelled by the experiences of those who had seen the prison from the inside. The model prisons of the Victorian era were now subject to the same virulent attacks as the old jails had been by the eighteenth-century prison reformers like John Howard. Although prisons continued to be used on a widespread scale, they were seen in a very different light and used for a different purpose: deterrence, rather than reformation, justified the continued use of a system drained of all purpose.[10]

Faith in the capacity of prisons to instill moral reformation in prisoners was undermined by the huge gap between articulated goals and observable realities. In the United States, the Elmira Reformatory, which offered vocational and academic education to youthful offenders and was considered a model prison by advocates of the movement for prison reform during the late nineteenth century, never quite lived up to its own proclaimed ideals of humane treatment and reformation. As an investigation in 1894 revealed, guards on occasion resorted to severe corporal punishment, while the reformatory as a whole suffered from grave overcrowding, eroding the effectiveness of rehabilitation programs. Despite these shortcomings, Elmira remained a model for many prison reformers, inspiring imitators across the United States who themselves were equally unable to resolve the problems that had undermined Elmira.[11]

The failure to narrow the gap between institutional realities and proclaimed goals, due largely but not uniquely to severe underfunding and overcrowding, also marred the prison reform movement in republican China. Contrary to other countries, however, the idea of reformation thrived in modern China, where few voices appeared to echo the critical reflections on the prison. While the emphasis on reformation migrated from the carceral universe to juvenile reformatories in Europe, where young people were still viewed as malleable entities open to moral transformation, belief in the perfectibility of human beings and faith in the capacity of institutions to reform depraved minds continued to hold sway in republican China, where even critics of the prison never questioned the educative mission of punishment.

Penologists in republican China, however, were thoroughly conversant with the various legal principles and penal philosophies that circulated internationally in the global movement for prison reform. While penology was initially restricted to the legal institutions set up during the late Qing, it developed rapidly during the 1920s to become an established field of knowledge to which a variety of professional groups contributed during the Nanjing decade. Lawyers, judges, magistrates, wardens, procurators, and sociologists were the carriers of new knowledge and penal modernity as they participated in international conferences and introduced important innovations from abroad in talks, lectures, articles, and books. Many of the penal principles they advanced, moreover, were disseminated by less noted writers, in particular in the form of simple textbooks used for the preparation of examinations in the fields of law and politics. Wang Yubin's textbook, which was part of the *Encyclopaedia of Explanatory Tables in Law, Politics and Economics*, compressed in sixty pages of tables all the knowledge deemed necessary for the study of penology.[12] Another example is the textbook by Zheng Aizou, entitled *Outline of Penology:* part of the *Series on the Preparation for Examinations in Political and Legal Studies*, it provided simple questions and answers that ranged from international norms in prison architecture to the treatment of juvenile delinquents.[13] In a similar vein, the "Examination Series" packaged the necessary knowledge to succeed in examinations in a concise *Essentials of Penology.*[14]

Although the field of penology was characterized by divergent approaches, opposed political opinions, and contradictory values, a certain unity of outlook existed as it attracted modernizing elites who shared a nationalist outlook, expressed faith in the educative mission of the prison, and believed in the fundamental malleability of human nature. Penologists chose the reformative model of imprisonment from an international repertoire of diverse and often contradictory prison systems. This model was part of a widespread voluntarist worldview embraced by modernizing elites who believed that the potential of each and every citizen could be developed in order to construct a powerful nation. In search of wealth and power, these elites viewed the reformation of criminals as one aspect of a project of national reconstruction in which social cohesion and national wealth could only be obtained by forging disciplined and productive citizens. The diversity and unity of penal philosophy in republican China will be illustrated on the basis of the work of Zhao Chen, Sun Xiong, Rui Jiarui, and Li Jianhua, who will be gradually introduced in the following section.

THE EDUCATIVE MISSION OF SUN XIONG AND RUI JIARUI

One of the most influential prison reformers in republican China was Sun Xiong (born in 1895). Contrary to other penologists in the republican period, he spent his entire career in the prison service. Born in Hunan province, he graduated from the Hunan School of Law to work as a warden in such places as Changsha, Ningyuan, and Qingpu. Sun was gradually promoted to higher offices within the prison administration, becoming a Section Chief in the Jiangsu Number One, Number Three, and Number Four Prisons, among other penal institutions, to finally assume the headship of Shanghai Special District Number Two Prison and of Jiangsu Number Four Prison. Sun Xiong used his vast experience in prison work to lecture at a number of universities in Shanghai, a commitment that culminated in his nomination as professor at Fudan University in Shanghai. Sun wrote a number of works related to prison work, including an extremely influential textbook on penology and a practical handbook on prison administration that found widespread application in republican prisons.

A government official trained as a prison administrator before contributing more formally to the shaping of penal philosophy, Sun wrote his textbook in the wake of a request in 1933 from the Ministry of Justice to the Ministry of Education to systematically promote the teaching of penological principles in all the country's legal institutions of higher learning. According to Sun Xiong, the purpose of prisons was deterrence and reformation. While prison acted as a warning to people who would think twice before turning to crime, the rehabilitative virtues of the prison, on the other hand, would turn criminals into useful citizens.[15] Sun represented the prison as an instrument of punishment against offenders used by the state to ensure law and order. Like his contemporaries, Sun believed that criminal rates increased with the advance of civilization, although a failure to implement prison reform was seen as another contributing factor: unreformed prisons produced criminality like poorly managed hospitals spread disease. They were the "organ which spreads crime" (*fanzui zhi chuanbo jiguan*), turning the thief into a robber and the assaulter into an assassin. Prisons were spaces where the criminal could be confined to prevent the spread of evil to the rest of society: "Like a doctor confronted with the carrier of a transmissible disease, he is ordered to be confined to a segregated hospital in order to prevent him from infecting other people." Similarly, the rehabilitative function of the prison was stressed in medical language: "The prison is to the criminal what the hospital is to the sick. The main task of the hospital is to diagnose and cure the roots of the illness, bringing back the sick to health. The main task of the prison is to eliminate evil inclinations (*huachu exing*), bringing the criminal back to goodness, either by fostering his morality by lectures, or by enhancing his knowledge via education."[16] Zhao Chen, to be introduced below, observed that "the state has built prisons for criminals in the same way as it has constructed hospitals for the sick: the goal of the hospital is to cure the sick, while the goal of the prison is to reform the criminal."[17]

Many penologists in the republican era pursued the ideal of a benevolent government (*renzheng*) put forward by reformers since the early nineteenth century. The benevolent relationship between the state and the offender was described like one of care between an educative father and an obedient son. The prison was to a criminal what a family was to a son: fed and clothed, the criminal was also educated in prison, which would naturally foster a sense of respect for the state: "Men are not made out of wood or stone, and patriotism can only well up in the criminals' heart."[18]

Another example of the importance of education appears in the work of Rui Jiarui, a government official who joined the Research Centre for Prison Administration (*Yuwu yanjiusuo*), founded by the Ministry of Justice in 1933, to write a handbook on prison rules widely distributed by the Commercial Press as part of its series entitled *New Age Legal Studies*. Rui Jiarui, like most republican prison reformers, placed great faith in the capacity of education to transform the erring individual. Education was paramount to penologists in China: schools taught children as much as prisons educated criminals. Rui believed that the prison was to the offender what a school was to the child with special needs: like the deaf and dumb, criminals had special educational needs that the prison should address.[19] The very verb *jiao* meant to educate and to transform, while *jiaohua* literally meant to civilize by way of education. As education was the inculcation of moral norms of correct behavior, it was endowed with a transformative and civilizing potential that benevolently included in its embrace the marginal categories of society, including the poor, the handicapped, the criminals, and ethnic minorities. The closely linked notion of *ganhua*, which meant reformation by following superior moral examples, was common in penological literature, although it easily migrated to other fields of moral government: Sun Yatsen, for instance, hoped to amalgamate a disparate country into a cohesive nation by virtue of propaganda and reformation, which he called *ganhua*.[20] Reformative imprisonment and moral improvement were thus two facets of a penal philosophy that stressed the educative mission of incarceration as much as its punitive dimensions.

In their educative mission, republican penologists differentiated between moral instruction (*jiaohui*) and basic education (*jiaoyu*). Basic education should be provided according to the individual circumstances of the prison, although the curriculum, derived from the official curriculum used in schools, should include Mandarin, mathematics, calculation with the abacus, and physical exercise. Tests should be part of the education of the prisoner, and those who performed well should be rewarded accordingly: merit and motivation were key values that would push the worthy towards self-improvement. Following the example of modern prisons in Europe and the United States, the library should contain three categories of books, namely religious and morally instructive material, educational books on geography, history, science, technology, agriculture, and other practical topics, and leisurely publications, although novels depicting "sexual matters" (*nannü zhi shi*) were to be strictly forbidden.[21] Lack of education was analogically linked to a lack of morality. Republican penologists believed in the natural depravity of the great unwashed: poverty, idleness, and ignorance bred criminality that popular education could eradicate, while vocational training and mass education would ensure social order and economic growth. Education in the prison not only implied the inculcation of moral instruction and vocational skills, but a paternalistic relationship of care. According to Rui Jiarui, the warden's attitude towards his prisoners was ideally described as a caring father towards his sons, while the teacher in charge of moral lectures should be like a "loving mother" towards her youthful children.[22] Benevolence and education were not only core values of reformative imprisonment proposed by prominent penologists: the *Anhui Number One Prison Journal*, published by the Anhui Number One Prison with a very limited circulation, devoted an entire article to the need of prison staff to treat prisoners "like parents their children," some criminals effectively having the intelligence of mere children.[23] Trust was central to a relationship of pastoral care, as a prison director, according to Rui, should win the confidence of the prisoners in order to further the goal of repentance. An admission of guilt was part of the process of reformation, although the teacher should respect the confidentiality of minor confessions: in the case of more serious revelations, the prisoner should be convinced to approach the prison authorities voluntarily. Moral transformation, in short, should come from within the individual, a task that could be facilitated by the adoption of the single cell.

ZHAO CHEN AND THE VIRTUES OF THE SINGLE CELL

Zhao Chen (1899-1969) was an equally noted expert in the field of penology who stressed the educative mission of the prison. Contrary to Sun Xiong and Rui Jiarui, he started his career outside the civil service as a successful lawyer and teacher. Born in Dongyang, Zhejiang province, he studied law in Japan. Zhao Chen returned to China in 1924 to lecture in a number of universities, including the Shanghai Law University (*Shanghai Fake daxue*), where he also served as head of the Law Department. He joined the Guomindang in 1925. Working as a lawyer in Shanghai, he became involved in a number of legislative initiatives in the ten years preceding his nomination as a professor at the Central Police School in 1936, where he specialized in the problem of juvenile delinquency. Zhao Chen eventually became a Supreme Court judge, finally joining the Ministry of Justice in 1948 before fleeing with the Guomindang to Taiwan, where he died twenty years later.[24]

Zhao Chen's most influential book was entitled *Penology* (*Jianyuxue*), first published in 1931 and reedited in 1948. Zhao Chen gave three goals that had motivated him in writing a book on penology: fair principles in the administration of punishments (*xingxing*), in which prisoners could be reformed into good citizens; the establishment of penology as a "science" related to legal studies and fundamental to the rule of law of any modern nation; and, finally, prison reform and the abolition of extraterritoriality. Zhao Chen acknowledged a number of influential books in the field of penology, out of which only two were written in a European language, namely *John Howard and the Prison World of Europe* by William Hepworth Dixon[25] and *The Crofton Prison System* by Mary Carpenter:[26] both emphasized the use of the progressive system in a reformative model of the prison that dated from the mid-nineteenth century. The most influential author, however, was Ogawa Shigejirô, the influential prison reformer recommended by Shen Jiaben and appointed by the court during the legal reforms of the late Qing.

Zhao Chen, like many of his colleagues, believed that most criminals suffered from a weak morality, having been pushed onto the path of crime by the cultivation of evil habits or by the pressure of adverse circumstances. Morality was not so much absent in criminals as a potential that had been hidden (*yanbi*): it was the task of the penal system to uncover that dormant morality in order to bring the criminal back to full humanity.[27] As offenders themselves had to real-ize the full import of their crimes, psychology was deemed to be an indispensa-ble tool in penal philosophy: each criminal had a unique character, habits, and social background, and psychology could help to adapt penal treatment to the prisoner's individual profile.

Individual treatment, in Zhao Chen's view, implied individual incarceration. Zhao deplored shared cells (*zaju*) as schools of crime where partners in vice were cherished like family members, a paradise (*letu*) to be enjoyed rather than a hell to be feared, a place of endless dissolution and depravity rather than a disciplined institution dedicated to moral reform. Lewd practices in crowded dormitories targeted young offenders at night, while ceaseless opportunities for social inter-course during day-time weakened the impact of penal discipline only to strengthen criminal passions: "Despite the close surveillance of guards, it is very hard to prevent prisoner A becoming acquainted with prisoner B, prisoner B be-coming intimate with prisoner C. Obscene practices spread throughout the cell, preventing handsome young prisoners from sleeping at night. Swindlers consider learning how to thieve, as thieves learn how to rob, while robbers go even further and investigate the ways of the most insidious and cruel criminals."[28] The system of shared cells created an environment of deviant sexuality and rampant crimi-nality as vice and evil spread like germs through the prison population, contam-inating each and every inmate. Zhao Chen pointed at four problems associated with the use of shared cells: it destroyed the morality of the prisoner and thus posed a threat to state laws and social order; it stripped the idea of custodial pun-ishment of any meaningful purpose by allowing prisoners to rebuild criminal links inside the prison; it was insufficiently severe to instill a sense of fear of the state in prisoners; it was unfair as it created an environment viewed with delight by the hardest criminals but dreaded by occasional offenders with some "social status and moral conscience" (*shenfen yu liangxin*). Zhao mentioned the silent system (*chenmozhi*) as an improvement on the system of shared cells, as inmates slept in single cells but worked together in silence. Severe discipline, however, was necessary to impose a strict observance of the rules of silence, eliminating even the subtle body gestures and secret codes that acted as so many conduits of vice. Zhao Chen viewed financial duress as the principle obstacle to the widespread adoption of the single-cell system in China.

Although the efficiency of the solitary system had been called into question by the second half of the nineteenth century—statistics collected by penologists re-vealed much higher rates of suicide, death, and madness—it continued to be viewed with awe by prison reformers in China. According to Zhao Chen, solitary confinement could reform the moral character of the prisoner and prevent the spread of evil. The crushing solitude within the bare walls of a single cell could break the malignant passions of the most hardened criminal: his resistance to virtue broken by penal discipline, quiet contemplation and cathartic reflection would lead to moral transformation. Purged of evil thoughts, the lonely mind of the prisoner would be opened to a remembrance of the past: nothing less than a veritable rebirth (*susheng*) was envisaged, to be induced by the appearance of repentant thoughts and the germination of good intentions (*mengdong shannian*). Confinement was envisaged as a process of purging and breaking criminal instincts indispensable to the emergence of a new sociable being guided by higher motives.

Solitude promoted virtue as it frustrated vice. The silent weight of prison architecture, analyzed separately in a section below, contributed to this process of moral renewal, as the iron windows placed high in the cell and the massive door and concrete walls isolated the prisoner from all outside sounds and sights, leaving him the lonely inhabitant of his own conscience. The salutary dread of solitary confinement was also underlined by Zhao Chen as it would help the prisoner understand the true value of liberty and the full power of the state. Protracted seclusion, moreover, would cut off all nefarious intercourse with fellow inmates and place the prisoner entirely into the therapeutic hands of the prison staff, who would gradually subdue his will and mollify his moral character, to be guided into the right direction by a series of small incentives, such as family visits and edifying reading material, as the prisoner showed improvement on the path towards redemption. In resonance with the views proposed a few decades earlier by the French penologist Raymond Saleilles in his highly influential work entitled *L'individualisation de la peine* (1898), Zhao Chen upheld a penal philosophy that recognized the moral responsibility of society and the free will of the criminal: as both were accountable for deviant behavior, the punishment should be tailored to the special needs of individual criminals. Imprisonment should be treatment, and solitary confinement should isolate the criminal like a patient in the clinic: "The separate system is not only compatible with the principle of individual treatment, but it is the only one which can be expected to carry it through: the fierce can be restrained, the past misdeeds of the cunning can be severely exposed, the timid can tactfully be given guidance, the obdurate can be admonished, so it is suitable to the idea of taking into account the personality of each convict."[29]

The only reservation Zhao Chen harbored against solitary confinement was masturbation, although it was a practice he judged to be relatively easy to investigate and control. Shared cells, moreover, could hardly be claimed to be free of this evil habit: not only was masturbation performed in front of others, undermining a sense of shame, but there was another unnamed "licentious and obscene habit" (*weixie yinfeng*) that was all too common. Another common objection against the separate system was that absolute isolation led to higher rates of madness among prisoners, an argument Zhao Chen countered by pointing out that only the solitary system could offer total observation and control over the prisoner, which would result in a much earlier diagnosis of mental disease than if he were to share a cell with other inmates. As to the practical costs of building prisons structured around the principle of solitary confinement, Zhao believed that the long-term benefits associated with the true conversion of criminals would amply compensate for the initial investment.

Similar views were expressed by other penologists, including those working directly under the auspices of the Ministry of Justice: Rui Jiarui, for instance, underlined that solitary confinement at the start of a sentence would suitably impress the power of the state and the discipline of the prison onto the criminal's mind, who would be shocked by social isolation into a full contemplation of his evil past.[30] Segregation led to reformation, although the psychological shock induced by solitude was too strong for vulnerable categories of people, including the elderly, the mad, the epileptic, those suffering from neurasthenia, the handicapped, and those inclined to contemplate suicide. Solitary confinement, in his view, was strong medicine reserved for sturdy criminals, although a medical opinion was necessary to ascertain who suffered from a psychological disorder, as some prisoners might plead illness in order to evade the ordeal. Rui Jiarui underlined that prison rules and regulations stipulated that the offender should "repent and improve" (*gaihui xiangshang*) in order to "adapt to social life" (*shiyu shehui shenghuo*). He proposed a strict taxonomy of criminals that would distinguish, for instance, between opportunistic offenders and heavy criminals. His typology was not merely the result of a desire to rank and classify pathological cases into modern taxonomies, to impose order and meaning onto the seemingly random manifestations of crime, or to treat social deviance as a dangerous field demanding a medical nosology in order to be effectively managed and treated. It had practical implications, in particular in a context of poor financial resources that forced prison authorities to make difficult choices as to which prisoners should receive what kind of treatment. As most prisons had insufficient single cells, penologists recommended the use of criminal typologies to prioritize penal treatment. Rui Jiarui, for instance, recommended occasional offenders for strict discipline, opportunists for rehabilitation, and habitual criminals for perpetual seclusion: first offenders thus deserved a harsher treatment for their own good, as solitary confinement would prevent them from further contamination by hardened criminals.[31]

THE PROGRESSIVE SYSTEM AND THE SYSTEM OF REWARDS

The contradiction between official demands for financially viable solutions to imprisonment and the penological insistence on the use of singles cells was partly resolved by the adoption of the progressive system. Zhao Chen, for instance, praised the merits of the single-cell system, but also recognized the need for a progressive rehabilitation of the prisoner. The progressive system (*jiejizhi*), based on inducements and threats, was seen as an intermediary system that allowed the prisoner to work his way out of a single cell into a shared dormitory before being granted parole. The system was first devised in the mid-nineteenth century by Captain Alexander Maconochie, who proposed that convicts be sentenced to a certain amount of labor, to be measured in a system of marks, rather than a period of time in the colonies. Marks could be earned for work and good behavior. Encouraging personal responsibility and mutual trust, Maconochie envisaged the prison as a small universe that would reform the prisoner and prepare him for the larger society outside. He was allowed to institute his scheme as an experiment on Norfolk Island in Australia, where he advocated the use of small jails and large personal discretion for prison personnel, emphasizing moral power over prisoners by guards rather than physical coercion. Although his scheme was a success, Maconochie was dismissed by the Colonial Office. His system had no impact on the penal regime in England, although it was largely adopted by Walter Crofton, an administrator in charge of Irish prisons. In an emphasis on reformation, the 1870 Declaration of Principles of the American Prison Association was also partly inspired by Maconochie's work.[32]

One of the two books in English included by Zhao Chen was specifically on the Crofton system: Zhao praised the progressive system implemented in Ireland during the 1850s, which consisted of four stages, namely single cell, shared cell, intermediary prison, and probation, in which the intermediate prison was described as a filter to freedom, an open institution suspended between custody and liberty, a microcosm for prisoners entirely managed by prisoners, a miniature version of society resembling a disciplined guesthouse more than a coercive jail. According to Zhao Chen, the progressive system was capable of instilling a sense of hope that could spur moral betterment in the prisoner: he proposed the use of differential treatment in clothing, housing, and work, in the quantity of food allotments and the quality of food served, in access to letters, books and family visits, and even in the salary paid for labor. Zhao's emphasis on the individualization of punishment was consonant with the progressive system as moral hierarchy based on individual behavior undergirded his penal philosophy. Prisoners who were incapable of moral improvement would linger at the bottom of a harsh system that penalized the unrepentant in every minute aspect of daily life, from the quality of clothing to the quantity of food. The progressive system effectively extended the custodial sentence by imposing a whole range of petty deprivations on the prisoner: differential treatment rather than legal equality lay at the heart of the reformative prison. Self-interest and self-motivation were seen as keys to individual repentance as the progressive system liberated hidden forces and potentials from within the individual himself: unbound reason would smother criminal passion. A sense of emulation among prisoners further encouraged individual betterment as those at the bottom of the system would fear to stay behind and "spontaneously work in a diligent and assiduous way to achieve sincere reformation."[33]

A remarkable degree of convergence existed between different penologists in republican China. In his discussion of different prison systems, Sun Xiong, for example, equally viewed communal cells as contaminated spaces promoting the spread of crime. He praised the use of single cells and fully supported the progressive system. Sun Xiong also provided long lists with all the details of the point system used in Ireland. He even copied the section on the progressive system used in Japan from Rui Jiarui's handbook on penology, including blank forms used for giving marks to prisoners. Sun also illustrated the progressive system with an example from China, giving a detailed account of the marking system he used as director of the Shanghai Number Two Special District Prison after its retrocession from France in August 1931.[34] Four different forms were used to separately mark achievements in behavior (*xingzhuang*), work (*zuoye*), moral teaching (*jiaohui*), and basic education (*jiaoyu*). Behavior was further divided into obedience, words, and deeds, sensibility, thrift, and hygiene, while labor included marks for learning, meticulousness, diligence, parsimony in using material, and respect of machinery. Each form allocated points ranging from zero to one hundred, poor (*buliang*) being rated under fifty, unsatisfactory (*shao buliang*) from fifty to sixty, average (*putong*) being sixty to seventy, fair (*shao liang*) from seventy to eighty, good (*liang*) from eighty to ninety, and excellent (*shan-liang*) as ninety or above. The total was calculated on a monthly basis and divided to obtain an average figure locating the prisoner on a scale of excellence: that single figure had the power to add or remove a variety of privileges which shaped the life of the prisoner. Each prisoner was allocated to one of six groups on the basis of his behavior, each stage corresponding to a different treatment within the prison hierarchy. Small inducements to reward good behavior consisted of greater access to visits, mail, food, payment, and reading material. New prisoners entered the lowest stage on arrival, benefiting only from the minimal treatment allowed by prison rules. If they were found eligible on the basis of good behavior for promotion to the top stage, they could gain up to three times more visits and mail, one extra meal every fortnight, six times better pay for labor, and free access to the library. Release on parole could be obtained after satisfactory performance in the top group.

THE CONCEPT OF SELF-GOVERNMENT AND THE USE OF PAROLE

The concept of self-government, based on the belief that a sense of responsibility could be instilled in prisoners if they were allowed to participate in limited democratic practices such as voting and office-holding, was first introduced into the penitentiary by Thomas Mott Osborne in 1913 at Auburn prison. Appointed warden of Sing Sing Prison the following year, he organized a Mutual Welfare League composed of elected prisoners and introduced various measures giving greater powers of decision to the prisoners. Although his experiment came to an end in 1929 in the face of widespread political opposition, his approach was different from other penal practices by taking its model from the community rather than from the hospital, representing the prisoner as a responsible person to be prepared for a free society by fostering communal bonds rather than a diseased element to be cured by confinement. Many penological treatises in republican China reported the experiments in prisoner self-government in great detail, stressing the rehabilitative virtues of a system that gave a sense of responsibility and self-respect to the downtrodden elements of society. The concept of self-government also circulated widely outside the field of penology as modernizing elites attempted to devise a viable way of integrating the individual within participatory politics. Experiments in student self-government, for instance, appeared in the 1920s as students were allowed to self-regulate a limited number of administrative tasks under the pastoral care of college authorities. We have seen how the prison was shaped by an educative mission that took its model from the school and the training center. In the case of self-government, we have another example of a notion that migrated from the school to the prison: Rui Jiarui himself wrote a handbook on student self-government, demonstrating how new notions of self-discipline could move from one discursive field to another.[35]

Limited self-government would teach the offender how to become a responsible person socially engaged in the broader community: it undermined the egocentric tendencies (*ziwo zhongxin*) of criminal elements, transforming them into sociable individuals capable of exerting self-control. Sociability and productivity were central notions as a range of incentives in the self-governing system would lead to much higher financial gains in prison labor. Heralded as the latest breakthrough in penal philosophy by some penologists like Zhao Chen, others like Sun Xiong expressed caution and reserved the experiment for the last stage in the progressive system. The generally positive reception of the idea of self-government, however, is indicative of a profound faith in the perfectibility of humankind: discipline was a means rather than a jail in an educative mission which underlined the social potential of each human being.

Noncustodial sentences were presented by most penologists as the last stage in the progressive stage system, and referred to the Maconochie experiments on Norfolk Island and the Crofton system in Ireland as the origins of supervised parole. Provisions for parole were included in all the prison regulations and criminal codes passed since the foundation of the republic. The first prison to start using parole was Beijing Number One Prison, which released Jia Wanhe shortly after the promulgation of the New Criminal Code in 1912: condemned to death by beheading in 1902 for robbery, his sentence was delayed many times after the autumn assizes before being commuted to a twelve-year sentence with the advent of the republic. Having completed nine-tenths of the sentence and shown due repentance, the Parole Board of the prison invoked Article 253 of the new code to release him on parole under the supervision of the Number Four District's self-governing association of his home county at Wanping. Jia Wanhe had learned to work with cane and bamboo in prison, successfully applying these skills after his release to make a living and soon becoming an example of the merits of rehabilitation combined with early parole. From 1912 to the middle of the 1930s, over 5,000 prisoners were released on parole, with less than twelve committing a new offence. According to Sun Xiong, such huge success could only be maintained if scientific principles were rigorously applied: the role of science was vital in assessing the physiology, temperament, intellect, education, religion, social background, and other personal factors of prisoners at the time of admission in order to properly gauge their progress as they approached eligibility for release on parole. The tools of psychology were particularly invaluable, and careful examination by an experienced prison administrator was required, as true remorse and genuine repentance might be difficult to distinguish from the fake contrition displayed by sly prisoners trying to secure early release: the heart of the prisoner was to be scrutinized in order to distinguish between sincerity and hypocrisy.[36]

PENAL DISCIPLINE AS A PRODUCER OF SOCIAL RESPONSIBILITY

The educative mission did not rigorously distinguish between criminality, vagrancy, and even poverty, as lack of education contributed to a lack of sociability in different categories of undesirable elements. The goal of reformation demanded strict discipline because prison rules and regular habits would instill social responsibility into the prisoners. Poor behavior and indolent appearance (*duorong*) would be corrected (*qiaozheng*) thanks to a regime of order structured by prison rules since criminals were for the greatest part undisciplined individuals (*bu jilü zhi ren*) who had habitually acquired vagrant manners conducive to crime. Strict regimentation would imbue prisoners with a sense of discipline: elaborate routines, strict schedules, and fixed habits would maintain order inside the prison while producing socially responsible behavior necessary for civil life in a modern society. The vocabulary of charity, furthermore, was appropriated to represent coercive regimentation as a merciful act: "Those prisoners who by ordinary disposition or natural tendency have dissolute habits and cannot comply with the rules when abruptly restrained by this type of severe action should be adjusted by the principles of charitable, equitable and individualized treatment: stern demeanor (*yansu*) is the core of the law of the administration of punishments."[37] Compassion (*ci'ai*), according to Rui Jiarui, was another central value of the penal system: compassion in the midst of discipline had the power to inspire reformation.

Like other penologists, Rui Jiarui also reconciled the concept of equity (*gongping*), which emphasized the need of the law to be impartial, and the concept of individualized treatment, which saw each prisoner as a special case in need of differential treatment. These two concepts were not seen to be incompatible: the idea of equity was based on the assumption that all the special circumstances of a criminal would be taken into account in order to apply the most effective "treatment" that might transform him into a socially responsible individual. All individuals were equal in as far as they were held capable of exerting a sense of responsibility: individuality was extensive with responsibility because the mad and the bad were declared irresponsible for their acts and not considered to be individuals in their own right. Explained Rui Jiarui, "Individualized treatment is one of the most important conditions of the law of the administration of punishments. Looking at it superficially, it may seem that the aim of equity stands in contradiction to it, but in reality that is not so."[38] In the penal philosophy of reformation, the criminal rather than the crime was the center of attention, an approach that commanded a close scrutiny of a whole range of individual characteristics, from age and profession to social status and family background: all these differences were to be carefully evaluated as part of a complex taxonomy of the criminal that would ensure that the appropriate "medication" (*yaoji*) was dispensed.

LI JIANHUA AND THE EXAMPLE OF THE SOVIET UNION

Few alternatives to the penal philosophy of reformative imprisonment were considered by penologists in republican China. Where critical voices appeared, however, they were generally sympathetic to communist regimes and discovered in the Soviet Union a superior social system that punished more humanely and effectively. One influential admirer of the Soviet Union was Li Jianhua. Born in 1900 in Sichuan province, he studied sociology in Tokyo from 1921 to 1925 before assuming various positions in Shanghai universities, including a professorship at Fudan University, specializing in labor law. Li Jianhua also published influential books in criminology, penology, and general sociology. In the preface to his penological treatise, Li Jianhua remembered how as a child he had been shocked by the discovery of the local prison in his county's *yamen*. Li rhetorically asked the reader why prisons should be reformed for the benefit of convicted criminals in times of economic depression when law-abiding, hard-working citizens in regions struck by floods, drought, or famine were obliged to eat the bark of trees or dig for white clay to appease their hunger. The tragedy of the Chinese nation, in his opinion, was precisely captured by this dilemma. Prison reform was justified as a step intrinsically linked to the reform of the nation: only a nation with empty prisons could claim to have been truly liberated from the specter of a feudal past. Law, in this utopian vision, was a temporary means rather than a necessary measure as schools would replace prisons in a crime-free future where moral sanctions would replace all legal punishments. Writing on the hundredth day after the death of his mother, Li Jianhua explained crime as an "unfortunate" reality for which penology was an "unfortunate" science: he took up the pen in order to ensure its disappearance in a modern world that in future would be governed by a shared morality.[39]

Writing at the height of the political purges under Stalin, which claimed the lives of millions between 1934 and 1939,[40] Li Jianhua spoke with awe of the prison system in the Soviet Union. As the class system had not yet been completely annihilated and remnants of capitalism still survived, prisons remained a temporary necessity. Penologists in the Soviet Union, Li Jianhua observed, denied the existence of crimes because only mistakes (*guoshi*) could be made by people, and such mistakes had accumulated as the result of hundreds of years of capitalism.[41] A new society should use education and the "various methods of medical science" to change "faulty" behavior, while individuals whose "faults" could not be improved should be segregated from society in order to preserve social order and peace. Li Jianhua reported on experiments with penal reform in the 1920s mainly initiated by Anton Makarenko, a key figure in Soviet pedagogy who used group pressure as a means of moral reformation in a commune for young offenders.[42]

Historians have observed how a progressive policy in the treatment of common prisoners coexisted with the more brutal approach pursued by the Cheka, which gained a predominant position after 1929 only. The first concentration camps, later called labor camps, were established by the Cheka for political prisoners in 1918 and foreshadowed the brutal and severe treatment that would characterize the following decades. Common prisoners, on the other hand, benefited from much more lenient practices that stressed noncustodial sentences and rehabilitation. Contrary to the "coercive work" (*prinuditel'ny trud*) imposed on "class enemies," common criminals were requested to perform "corrective work" (*ispravitel'ny trud*). Minor offenders were required to continue their own work in full liberty or to perform an assigned task at a reduced level of payment. Agricultural colonies and "places of confinement" replaced the prisons that were marked by negative political connotations of a past regime, while penal philosophers like M.A. Makarenko replaced the notion of "crime" with "social protection" and stressed reeducation rather than repression.[43] By the summer of 1929, however, Stalin started to systematically subordinate penal policy to the goal of economic transformation. The penal system, in the meantime, was converted into a state instrument used against political enemies: these two shifts account for the disintegration of the progressive penal philosophy pursued during the early 1920s.[44]

Anton Makarenko's main work, translated into English as *The Road to Life*, had a huge influence in Europe,[45] while positive impressions from foreign visitors, in particular the popular writer Maurice Hindus, did much to popularize the appeal of communism in the West. The work of Maurice Hindus was also conveyed in Li Jianhua's work. Hindus, a personal friend of the liberal intellectual Hu Shi, was a Russian educated in the United States who had returned to his home country for a year in 1923. Like many of his contemporaries, he was "bursting with a new faith" and ecstatic at what he interpreted for his many readers as an unprecedented attempt to build a civilization based on an entirely new pattern.[46] Such enthusiastic accounts found a favorable reception in China, where many intellectuals had followed the construction of a communist regime very closely since the October Revolution.

Positive impressions from Chinese visitors were also quoted at length by Li Jianhua, including the observations made by Tan Zhen (1885–1947), the vice president of the Judicial Yuan, after a six-month tour of judicial systems in England, France, Germany, Italy, and the United States in the summer of 1934.[47] Although the delegation did not visit the Soviet Union, the report submitted by Tan Zhen included a few comments on the commune system for young offenders.[48] Tan, who had himself been imprisoned for his participation in the failed uprising at Changsha in 1908, praised the Soviet system of moral improvement in state communes as well as the abolition of all traditional penal systems of surveillance, observing that common prisoners in the Soviet Union could hardly be distinguished from ordinary citizens. Such favorable comments on the Soviet penal system were all the more striking as Tan Zhen was widely known to have little sympathy for the Chinese Communist Party (CCP). Elected a member of the Central Executive Committee of the Guomindang in 1924, Tan participated in the rightist Western Hills Conference that called for the expulsion of all communists from the Guomindang. His interest in the Soviet Union demonstrates the extent to which leading judicial figures were receptive to penal innovations from abroad despite particular political proclivities.

Well after the subordination of the penal system to the politics of terror by Stalin, sympathetic observers continued to report favorably on the Soviet Union. The first number of the *China Prison Journal* (*Zhonghua jianyu zazhi*), for instance, carried an article signed by Chen Jianwu that focused on moral rehabilitation after the October Revolution: open communes stood in contrast to the secretive dungeons of the old regime and were hailed as a "harmonious and dignified paradise."[49] Throughout the republican period, the Soviet Union would be perceived as a viable alternative by critics of the prison system, although ironically they replicated the malleable vision of humankind and the educative mission of the prison which precisely lay at the heart of dominant penal discourse. Critics also agreed on the redemptive virtues of prison work.

THE VIRTUES OF INDUSTRY: WORK IN THE PRISON

If sloth was a vice, industry would cure it: idleness, indolence, and languor were direct causes of crime which supervised work in the prison would dispel. Work, or forced labor, (*laoyi*) instilled values of thrift, discipline, and industry, contributing to the moral reformation of offenders. Besides moral considerations, the economic benefits of prison labor were also highlighted by penologists. Not only would prisoners acquire a trade that would steer them away from a life of crime, but industry inside the walls could make a contribution to the purse of the state, paying for the costs of imprisonment: why would the state penalize obedient citizens by allowing offenders to sit idle and eat the fruits of the people's labor, wondered Rui Jiarui?[50] Rui Jiarui compared idle prisoners to parasites who sucked the blood and fat of the common people, laggards who dissipated the state's precious resources, loafers who burdened the nation. In his view, moreover, labor was not so much a duty as a right. In the utopian vein shared by many other penologists, Rui even considered work in the prison to be a pleasure rather than a chore, a favor bestowed on bored prisoners by the state, which allowed them to pursue a useful trade. Redemption thus lay in discipline, while profit also guided hard labor. The need to turn the prison into an economically viable institution in times of financial restrictions, the desire to reduce recidivism when crime rates were perceived to grow to unprecedented rates, the wish to turn deviant individuals into productive citizens were some of the more central considerations in the moral rhetoric on prison labor.

Contrary to some countries in Europe, penologists in China continued to stress the moral benefits of work. Widespread during the nineteenth century, the principle of reformation in work continued to be actively supported in the republican era, while few penologists queried the morality of supplying prisoners with productive labor when free workers were suffering from unemployment. Most prison reformers, moreover, agreed that the operating expenses of penal institutions should be met by prison labor, organized under penal administration, or contracted out to private companies. Three distinct systems of organized work were envisaged: (1) official management (*guansiye*), in which the state was entirely responsible for investment, management, and distribution; (2) commission business (*weituoye*), in which an outside company was commissioned to organize production and supply the machinery and raw material; (3) contract work (*chenglanye*), in which either a part or the entire business was contracted out to a local company. In practice, these three systems were not always clearly distinguishable, and most prisons joined with a regional company in a variety of arrangements dictated by local circumstances as much as by personal links between the prison authorities and local business leaders. Such arrangements were often more the result of ad hoc arrangements with local entrepreneurs contacted by prison authorities than a response to directives from the central government: considerable leeway was given to the director of a prison to adapt to local conditions, a bargaining process that necessarily emphasized labor productivity at the expense of vocational training or educational value. Adaptability to local conditions was not only the result of economic necessity, it was promoted as good practice by penologists, who portrayed the prison as an institution embedded within and contributing to a local economy. Responsiveness to regional conditions, moreover, was seen to be a positive factor in helping the prisoner prepare for a return to the free society lying outside the prison walls. Regionalization of the overall organization of work thus prevailed over the proclaimed necessity to individualize labor to fit the offender: prisoners were not so much allowed to choose the trade in which they wished to be trained as the local business culture defined the occupational practices that could be profitably pursued. In Nantong, for instance, cotton production was a dominant trade, while the bamboo craft was popular in Hangzhou.

While debates about pay, bonuses, and fixed allotments for prisoners' work in Europe were closely followed, most penologists upheld the right of the state to appropriate the benefits of productive labor. Many referred to the Fifth International Penitentiary Congress held in Paris in 1895, where representatives concluded that prisoners had no legal claim to a salary. Some sort of pecuniary reward was generally described as a positive form of "encouragement" and "reward" by penologists, in particular those who favored the progressive system in which a bonus was seen as a spur to reform: in the language of rehabilitation, token payments rewarded industry while preparing the prisoner for a return to free society. Such payment was referred to as "pecuniary reward" (*shangyujin*) rather than a salary. Although different modes of payment to prisoners were used throughout the modern world, ranging from a fraction of the benefits of productive labor in France to a fixed third of the income in Sweden, few penologists contested the official system in China. One notable exception was Li Jianhua, an admirer of the penal system of the Soviet Union who praised the full payments meted out to prisoners in a communist system. Li Jianhua even recommended the labor camps set up in Siberia by Joseph Stalin: in contrast to imperialist countries who used convict labor to exploit their colonies, the Soviet camps relied on human labor rather than slave labor, alleviating the overcrowding characteristic to most prisons, showing prisoners the right path to a decent living, and enabling them to productively contribute to the national economy.[51] Work, then, was seen to be an essential part of punishment by different penologists in republican China, and prison architecture took into account the needs for labor by allocating generous space to factories and workshops.

WALLS AND BARS: THE SILENT WEIGHT OF PRISON ARCHITECTURE

Architecture molds the life that takes place inside the prison walls as the design of the buildings imposed constraints on the prisoners.[52] The radial design, for instance, enforced total separation of the prisoners with a number of wings radiating from a central tower because prison architecture was meant to assist the goal of reforming the character of prisoners. The very symmetry of prison design, based on regularity and fixity, was a reflection of the sense of order that the prison was meant to inculcate. Transparency and impermeability were two commonly articulated goals in republican China: on the one hand, prisons should be designed to allow the guards to observe prisoners at all times, while thick walls and iron gates should prevent all escapes. Bricks and iron symbolized the impermeable nature of the modern prison in which inmates were cut off from the rest of society, while centrifugal towers and long corridors made sure that no prisoner could escape from the vigilant gaze of the prison administrators. As much as the cells were sealed off from each other, the prison was hermetically isolated from the outside world: bastions defending civilized society against depredation, they were also engines designed to produce morality in industrial quantities. As much as the gaze of the guardian should "permeate" all cells under surveillance (*tongguan*), air should be let "through" all the cells (*tongfeng*): *tong* encapsulated the values of openness, interconnectedness, and permeability that should characterize the modern prison. On the other hand, steel plates and reinforced concrete should be "strong" (*jiangu*), much as the prison itself should be "well-made and sturdy" (*wangu*), a vision in which *gu* stood for impermanence, strength, and solidity. Power was thus attributed to the walls of the prison, capable simultaneously of containing evil and instigating virtue.

Prisons, moreover, were designed as palaces of reason, monuments to science, temples of hygiene: the modern principles of hygiene were paramount in prison architecture as prisoners should be protected from germs and microbes as much as society at large ought to be defended against criminal elements. Modern technologies such as a ventilation system, water plumbing, and electricity network run like blood vessels through the building, the lifelines supplying all the essential nutrients of air and water to the capillary cells. Plenty of fresh air should be inhaled by the prisoners, and thorough ventilation should drive infectious particles from their cells.[53] Bolstered by popular ideas of *qi* ("gas," "breath," "odor," or "air") still current at the time, the atmosphere itself was thought to be prone to infection, spontaneously generated and spread in miasmas and foul effluvia. Although these more traditional conceptions were superseded by the germ theory of contamination in the first decades of the twentieth century, notions of disease breeding in dark, murky, and humid places continued to hold sway on many minds.

Prison building thus took place in a period marked by an increased concern over cleanliness, bolstered by scientific notions of infection, contamination, and septicity. Within the coastal citadels, public bathhouses, water distribution networks, and sewage systems were increasingly installed: "public hygiene" (*gonggong weisheng*) as a social practice gradually spread. With the creation of the Ministry of Health by the Guomindang in 1928, social regeneration and national strength became official slogans used in campaigns of public education, prominent for example during the New Life Movement (1934–1937).[54] With the framing of bacteria as agents of ill health, a military terminology of "assault," "invasion," and "bodily defenses" started to pervade medical representations of disease in republican China.[55] Official organs became responsible for waging a war against disease with government money: in theory, at least, public hygiene became a prerogative of the state. In the collective campaigns for hygiene and sanitation under the Guomindang, disease was portrayed as the enemy within upon which fantasies of social decay and contamination could be projected. The principle of segregation (*geli*) played on these wider fears of social and medical contagion (*chuanran*): prisoners should be separated into individual cells with sound-proof walls to avoid communication, the prison itself should have high walls to segregate it from the outside world, while the sick should be segregated from the healthy in special wards: even individual toilets ought to be designed in such a way that foul odors would not travel from one cell to another.

Prisons should be ample and spacious, while crowded locations in big cities ought to be avoided. The noise and tumult from a busy city would be within the reach of the prisoners, frustrating the aim of reform as their feelings would be stirred and some might attempt to escape. Building on the ideas of segregation and contamination, penological discourse held that no sight or sound from the outside world should come to interfere with the quiet reflection of the prisoner. The clamor from the streets, moreover, would also prevent prisoners from fully absorbing the teachings dispensed by prison lecturers, while silence prepared the mind to absorb the message of change offered by the prison regime. Sun Xiong advanced another argument against cities, again based on the idea of social contamination: with the construction of a prison in a busy part of the city, the land surrounding it would gradually become cheaper, attracting workers and paupers who would inevitably have a negative influence on the hygiene and discipline of the prison.[56] The best location was envisaged to be a quiet spot a few miles out of the city near a major transportation axis, out of sight but within easy reach, socially separated from the outside world, but technically integrated with society at large. The lecture hall, finally, should be both hygienic and majestic: cleanliness was not only next to orderliness, but public hygiene and penal education were both thought to converge with the principles of science in this modern temple built for the redemption of the guilty.

A variety of prison designs emerged in the modern world, some highly idiosyncratic in their adaptation to local circumstances, others relatively standardized and common across different countries. Prisons converted from older buildings, for instance monasteries, temples, or even private houses, could vary significantly as they incorporated older buildings within new structures. Even newly built prisons were vastly different in architecture, ranging from concrete fortresses divided into steel cages to agricultural colonies laid out in open space. Over a dozen designs were relatively common internationally, ranging from the "telephone pole" model with multiple cell blocks at right angles of a central corridor, to the radial design with wings spreading out from a central watchtower. Out of this international repertoire of forms, only a few found a favorable reception in China. Although writers on prison architecture were drawn from a variety of backgrounds, ranging from journalists to procurators, they were confronted by similar economic problems and financial pressures, operated in the same political climate, and often shared common ideas in penal philosophy, thus restricting the number of solutions that were actually envisaged in prison architecture. The most popular models were the radial design, called "fan-shaped" design (*shanmianxing*), and the cruciform design (*shizixing*): both had been recommended by Shen Jiaben and the Board of Justice by the end of the Qing and retained their popularity throughout republican China. Zhao Chen, for instance, judged the radial and the cruciform designs to be appropriate respectively for large and for small prisons. An example of the cruciform design was the Anhui Number Two Prison, which had four wings radiating out of a central control tower and a separate administrative building, a system that was praised by penologists for its better circulation of air and light. The fact that prisoners could not secretly communicate via the windows of their cells was also singled out as a distinct advantage. The radial design, used in Beijing Number One Prison, was described as a variation of the cruciform shape, although it could accommodate extra wings running out from the center. Finally, the "ray of light" design (*guangxianxing*), with five or six wings radiating out of the central tower, was also mentioned by some penologists, as it was seen to be particularly suitable for confined spaces. Represented by the Hunan Number One Prison, it was believed to be less convenient from the point of view of surveillance and hygiene.[57]

As much as thrift was a core value to be inculcated into the restive prisoner, economy should preside over prison architecture. Unnecessary decorations, ornaments, or other frivolous additions were to be rigorously avoided, as the calm austerity of penal architecture ought to inspire respect, while the silent weight of brick walls should encourage reflection. Here too, cultural values and economic choices were consonant because a "plain" (*pusu*) architectural design would also be more affordable for underfunded prison departments. Sun Xiong provided many examples of possible savings, underlining for instance that showers should to be designed in the most economic way possible in order to save time and water.[58] Architectural visions of ordered space, in other words, rarely prevented a more detailed examination of concrete financial realities. Leading penologists never simply expatiated on international prison norms that remained elusive even to the judicial authorities of wealthy provincial capitals: they provided much detailed information on how to minimize construction costs, from the ways of mixing a local variety of cement to the most cost-effective way of building a shower system. The most detailed comparison of national and international standards in penal architecture was compiled by Bei Shoutong, a government official attached to the Ministry of Justice, and his study was incorporated in Sun Xiong's widely circulated manual on penology.[59] The study provided a comprehensive list of international standards and measurements of prison cells, showers, bathrooms, sick wards, kitchens, factories, toilets, lecture halls, offices, and even storage rooms: here too, a central value was thrift. The single most important figure was the average surface occupied by prisoners and the average number of cubic meters of air needed in different types of cells, and precise calculations were made to gauge the extent to which local prisons could deviate from international practice without jeopardizing either the security of the prison or the health of the inmates. Thirty percent of valuable space could be saved on European standards by restricting the size of single cells to sixteen or eighteen cubic meters of air. Shared cells that were occupied by three to ten inmates could be reduced to ten or twelve cubic meters per head, while an average surface per prisoner of 7.14 square meters, including corridors, was sufficient by local standards. Larger cells in Jiangsu Number Two Prison reduced the average space per prisoner to 4.42 cubic meters, an example of thrift and economy for cells that were used only for prisoners on short sentences: more space was condemned as an inconsiderate expense and a waste of valuable resources. On the other hand, class A prisons, considered the largest and most progressive, were obliged by regulations of the Ministry of Justice to provide twenty-two cubic meters of air for single cells, eleven cubic meters for cells reserved for single occupancy during the night, and ten cubic meters per head in shared cells. Shared showers were recommended, although the Japanese style of collective bathing was seen as a model for emulation, being both economical and hygienic. Big jars of water next to the pool would allow prisoners to rinse and rub the body down (*chongca*), saving water, time and space. Economic and hygienic principles were invoked even to lower the ceiling of the kitchen, as it would save prison authorities money and would prevent steam from cooling down in temperature, impeding its full flow. Order and cleanliness, on the other hand, prevented any excessive thrift in the realm of the toilet: neither too narrow in size nor too simple in design, solid toilets were an unmistakable sign of modernity that would not tolerate any savings.[60]

As much as the toilet was a highly visible sign of cleanliness that ought to be held in awe, reinforced concrete was judged to be an excessively expensive material: visible technology rather than hidden strength was emphasized, and reinforced concrete, used for the prison foundations in Europe for reasons of security and fire prevention, was recommended for staircases and corridors only.[61] All the rage with architects in Europe in the 1930s for combining the tensile strength of steel with the compressive virtues of concrete, reinforced concrete was often replaced by bricks and mortar. Cement (*yanghui* or *shuimenting*), a modern product whose long-lasting properties stood in contrast to the frailer materials like wood used in traditional architecture, was essential for the foundations and the walls of the prison. Designed for practical use, some handbooks in penology provided concrete details on the actual construction of prisons in which every measurement was provided, including ways to prepare lime, make cement, or mix a local version of concrete on the basis of lime, earth, and sand (*sanhetu*).

CONCLUSION

Penal reform was not merely talk, and its strong institutional basis can only be studied on the basis of archival evidence. Recent research based on a broad range of municipal, provincial, and national archives demonstrates that the penological principles proposed in republican China were widely applied in penal institutions, from the model prisons of provincial capitals down to local county jails.[62] As in other countries, of course, prison reform was only one task among many others set by the central government. Prison reform alone was a huge project that demanded vast administrative and financial resources that even economically developed countries did not command. While financial and institutional constraints impeded the actual implementation of penological principles proposed by authors like Zhao Chen and Sun Xiong, many local and regional authorities nonetheless strove to adhere to agreed prison rules, often using local human and financial resources when insufficient funds were provided by the Ministry of Justice. Prison reform, moreover, was deeply enmeshed with existing cultural values, economic systems, institutional frameworks, political configurations, and competing individual aspirations. Conceived as a benevolent project which upheld the promise of repentance, it was inevitably transformed by these different factors, leading to accommodations and compromises that strayed from the initial vision of rehabilitative incarceration. As elsewhere, benevolent intentions were subverted by practical constraints as the custodial sentence started to engender as many problems as it had been designed to solve.

More importantly, however, the penological principles which revolved around the notion of *ganhua* were never seriously challenged in the republican period. Imprisonment in republican China was a new tool of law used to pursue a more traditional vision of an ordered and cohesive social body governed by the rule of virtue. Modernizing elites viewed the reformation of criminals as a constitutive part of a project of national regeneration in which social cohesion, economic development, and state power could only be obtained by molding obedient subjects. Based on the idea of reformation, the custodial sentence was part of a global movement towards penal reform and a local reconfiguration of a more traditional faith in the transformative capacity of education. In resonance with the Mencian view of human nature as inherently good and profoundly malleable, the notion of reformation sustained the belief that criminals could achieve individual self-improvement through proper institutional guidance. As correct behavior was of paramount importance in the moral education of subjects, the emulation of models was a dominant pedagogical strategy in the republican period. Model prisons were thus the microcosm of an exemplary society in which the emulation of models—whether in the school, the factory, or the army—was seen simultaneously as a mission of educative transformation, a project for social discipline, and a strategy for national power. The conformity inherent in this worldview suited the political elites who wielded the power to define models in the first place. It also corresponded to a particular social structure in which a highly educated elite viewed the rest of the population as illiterate, backward, and superstitious. This strong elitist bias was reflected by a paternalistic approach that aimed to reform, correct, guide, and educate the paupers who had strayed on the path of crime: the exemplary prison director should act towards his prisoners as a caring father towards his obedient sons. Punitive yet benevolent, like the state, he reformed while he punished.

NOTES

1. A very useful study which goes beyond the common focus on Europe and the United States is Ricardo D. Salvatore and Carlos Aguirre, eds., *The Birth of the Penitentiary in Latin America: Essays on Criminology, Prison Reform, and Social Control, 1830–1940* (Austin: University of Texas Press, 1996).

2. David Taylor, *Crime, Policing and Punishment in England, 1750–1914* (London: Macmillan, 1998), 146–47.

3. Wang Gungwu, *The Chineseness of China: Selected Essays* (Oxford University Press, 1991), 147.

4. The term found an early use in the *Hou Hanshu* (History of the Later Han); see *Hanyu Da Cidian*, vol. 7 (Shanghai: Hanyu da cidian chubanshe, 1990), 609.

5. James L. Watson, "The Renegotiation of Chinese Cultural Identity in the Post-Mao Era," in *Popular Protest and Political Culture in Modern China: Learning from 1989*, ed. Jeffrey N. Wasserstrom and Elizabeth J. Perry (Boulder, Colo.: Westview Press, 1992), 73.

6. My thinking has greatly benefited from Børge Bakken, *The Exemplary Society: Human Improvement, Social Control, and the Dangers of Modernity in China* (Oxford University Press, 2000); see also Harald Bøckman, "China's Development and Model Thinking," *Forum for Development Studies*, no. 1 (1998), 7–38.

7. Cynthia J. Brokaw, *The Ledgers of Merit and Demerit: Social Change and Moral Order in Late Imperial China* (Princeton, N.J.: Princeton University Press, 1991).

8. Børge Bakken, *The Exemplary Society*, 245.

9. Patricia O'Brien, "The Prison on the Continent: Europe, 1865–1965," in *The Oxford History of the Prison: The Practice of Punishment in Western Society*, ed. Norval Morris and David J. Rothman (Oxford University Press, 1995), 199–200.

10. See Robin Evans, *The Fabrication of Virtue: English Prison Architecture, 1750–1840* (Cambridge: Cambridge University Press, 1982), 387.

11. Edgardo Rotman, "The Failure of Reform: United States, 1865–1965," *The Oxford History of the Prison: The Practice of Punishment in Western Society*, ed. Norval Morris and David J. Rothman (Oxford University Press, 1995), 174.

12. Wang Yubin, *Jianyuxue Biaojie* (Explanatory tables on penology) (Shanghai: Shanghai kexue shuju, 1933).

13. Zheng Aizou, *Jianyuxue Gaiyao* (Outline of penology) (Shanghai: Shijie shuju, 1929).

14. Xu Langrong, *Jianyuxue Gangyao* (Essentials of penology) (Shanghai: Faxueshe, 1929).

15. Sun Xiong, *Jianyuxue* (Penology) (Shanghai: Shangwu yinshuguan, 1938), 2nd ed. (1st ed. 1936), 3.

16. Sun, *Jianyuxue*, 7.

17. Zhao Chen, *Jianyuxue* (Penology) (Shanghai: Shanghai faxue bianyishe, 1948), new edition (1st ed. 1931), 259.

18. Sun, *Jianyuxue*, 8.

19. Rui Jiarui, *Jianyu Falun* (On prison rules) (Shanghai: Shangwu yinshuguan, 1934), 141.

20. Sun Zhongshan, "Xuanchuan Zaocheng Qunli" (Propaganda can forge unity), in *Sun Zhongshan Xuanji* (Selected works of Sun Yatsen) (Beijing: Renmin chubanshe, 1956), 556–70; he also used the term *ganhua* in his *Three Principles of the People*; see Sun Zhongshan, *Sanminzhuyi* (Three Principles of the People), *Sun Zhongshan Xuanji*, 620.

21. Rui, *Jianyu Falun*, 147.

22. Rui, *Jianyu Falun*, 141.

23. Xia Lanqing, "You Zhishi Wu Zhishi Zhi Qiuren Jianyu Dangju Ying Zhuyi Hezhong" (The types of literate and illiterate inmates prison authorities ought to pay attention to), *Anhui Diyi Jianyu Yuekan* 1, no. 3 (May 1926), 8–9.

24. See Guan Guoxuan, "Zhao Chen (1899–1969)," *Zhuanji Wenxue* 45, no. 4 (October 1985): 134–35; Zhao Chen found a model of impartiality in the fictive figure of Heilian Baogong (Black-faced Judge Bao), or Bao Xiaoxiao, who was reputed to have been personally helped by the emperor. Zhao Chen liked to think that he was assisted in his judicial duties by the support Jiang Jieshi lent to the administration of justice. The high point of his career was the sentencing to death of the collaborator Zhou Fohai, a controversial decision that was much criticized by his opponents, who described him as self-willed and incapable of coordinating his approach with national policy. Despite these criticisms, Zhao was generally recognized to have been a fair and just person, popularly called the "living Judge Bao"; Cheng Deshou, "Zhao Chen Xiansheng Ersashi," *Zhongwai Zazhi* 6, no. 5 (Nov. 1969), 22–24.

25. William Hepworth Dixon, *John Howard and the Prison World of Europe: From Original and Authentic Documents*, third edition, with additional illustrations (London, 1850).

26. The correct title is Mary Carpenter, *Reformatory Prison Discipline as Developed by the Right Hon. Sir Walter Crofton in the Irish Convict Prisons* (London: Longman, 1872).

27. Zhao, *Jianyuxue*, 18.

28. Zhao, *Jianyuxue*, 282.

29. Zhao, *Jianyuxue*, 294.

30. Rui, *Jianyu falun*, 55.

31. Rui, *Jianyu falun*, 62.

32. John Hirst, "The Australian Experience: The Convict Colony," in *The Oxford History of the Prison: The Practice of Punishment in Western Society*, ed. Norval Morris and David J. Rothman (Oxford University Press, 1995), 290–92.

33. Zhao, *Jianyuxue*, 302.

34. Sun, *Jianyuxue*, 129–37.

35. Rui Jiarui, *Xuesheng Zizhi Xuzhi* (Basics of student self-government) (Shanghai: Shangwu yinshuguan, 1921).

36. Sun, *Jianyuxue*, 140–43.

37. Rui, *Jianyu Falun*, 9.

38. Rui, *Jianyu Falun*, 11.

39. Li, *Jianyuxue*, 2–3.

40. See Michael Jakobson, *Origins of the Gulag: The Soviet Prison Camp System, 1917–1934* (Lexington: University Press of Kentucky, 1993).

41. Li, *Jianyuxue*, 14–18.

42. James Bowen, *Soviet Education: Anton Makarenko and the Years of Experiment* (Madison: University of Wisconsin Press, 1962).

43. Ralf Stettner, *Archipel Gulag: Stalins Zwangslager-Terrorinstrument und Wirtschaftsgigant: Entstehung, Organization und Funktion des Sowjetischen Lagersystems, 1928–1956* (Paderborn: Schöningh, 1996), 44–48.

44. Peter H. Solomon Jr., "Soviet Penal Policy, 1917–1934: A Reinterpretation," *Slavic Review* 39, no. 2 (June 1980): 208.

45. Anton Semenovich Makarenko, *Road to Life*, translated by Stephen Garry (London: Stanley Nott, 1936).

46. Maurice G. Hindus, *Broken Earth* (London: Jonathan Cape, 1931) (orig. 1926), preface.

47. Positive reports on labor camps in Siberia also appeared in the daily press, for instance in the *Dagongbao* on 22 November 1934.

48. Li, *Jianyuxue*, 17–18.

49. Chen Jianwu, "Banli Yuwu Buke Hulüe Xingshi Zhengce" (Penal policies cannot be ignored in prison administration), *Zhonghua Jianyu Zazhi* 1, no. 1 (May 1934), 27–33.

50. Rui, *Jianyu Falun*, 102.

51. Li, *Jianyuxue*, 64.

52. On the crucial role of prison architecture, see the superb studies by Robin Evans, *A Rational Plan for Softening the Mind: Prison Architecture in the 18th and 19th Centuries* (Colchester: University of Essex, 1975), and Robin Evans, *The Fabrication of Virtue: English Prison Architecture, 1750–1840* (Cambridge University Press, 1982); also of interest is Norman Bruce Johnston, *The Human Cage: A Brief History of Prison Architecture* (Philadelphia: Walker, 1973).

53. Zhao, *Jianyuxue*, 282.

54. Ka-che Yip, "Health and Society in China: Public Health Education for the Community, 1912–1937," *Social Science and Medicine* no. 16 (1982), 1197–205.

55. See Frank Dikötter, *Sex, Culture and Modernity* (London: Hurst; Honolulu: Hawaii University Press, 1997), 123–25.

56. Sun, *Jianyuxue*, 193.

57. Sun, *Jianyuxue*, 196.

58. Sun, *Jianyuxue*, 193.

59. Sun, *Jianyuxue*, 227.

60. Sun, *Jianyuxue*, 218–27.

61. Sun, *Jianyuxue*, 227.

62. Frank Dikötter, *Crime, Punishment and the Prison in Modern China* (London: Hurst; Chicago: Chicago University Press, 2002).

3

Comparative Perspectives on Crime in China

BØRGE BAKKEN

Accounts of crime and policing in China have generally been isolated from the vast literature on international criminology and the growing research on international and comparative statistics on crime trends. There has been a tendency to see China exclusively in light of its own history, thereby missing out on the interesting developmental and historical comparisons that could be made with the many different experiences of crime and policing in the rest of the world. In the process China has become more or less mystified as a "special case." Rapid change defines the present development of crime and control in China, and in the wake of that development alarmist accounts of the frequency of crime and general confusion regarding the state of affairs in China are common. Of course, China is full of interesting cultural and developmental particularities which should not be slighted. However, it is also time to include China as part of the picture of international knowledge on crime and policing. It is time to demystify China when it comes to crime and control. This is of course a vast task that cannot be solved by a single chapter, but the examples presented here are indicative of where this approach might take us and of the problems inherent in including China within this international research agenda.

Let us look briefly at the overall crime rates in China since the year of the "crime wave" of 1981. That year was significant because it represented a peak in crime never before seen in the People's Republic. From reported crime rates as low as in the twenties per 100,000 people in the 1950s, the rate increased to over eighty in 1981, triggering a debate over soaring crime. Since then, there has been a vast increase in the number of crime cases reported, and the latest statistics from the

Ministry of Public Security report that cases have more than quadrupled over two decades, and now stand at approximately 360 per 100,000 population.

Let us look closer at the reports on soaring crime rates in China over the last few years. In particular we see a more violent crime scene in China if we choose to rely on the statistical material coming from public security sources. In relative terms the figures are indeed alarming as shown by data on violent crime in figure 3.2.

Both figures 3.1 and 3.2 appear to reveal an explosion in crime in China at the turn of the millennium. The most dramatic increases we see are in reported cases of robbery, where the numbers went up from 22,266 in 1981 to 352,216 in 2001. This represents a startling, almost sixteenfold increase in twenty years, and a decisive "take-off" seems to have occurred around 1998. The rate of assault was more or less unchanged from 1981 to 1988, just over 20,000 reports per year, but by 2001, 138,100 cases were reported. Reports on rape increased from around 30,000 in 1981 to a peak of nearly 50,000 in 1991. Since then the number of rapes decreased to about 35,000 in 2001, the only example of violent crime to record a decline. Homicide figures seem to have followed a more stable path, and more or less equal the population growth over the last twenty years.

Before we analyze the data in more detail, let us briefly refer to Adolphe Quetelet, who had as early as 1831 warned against the limitations of official crime data.[1] His warning is still valid. In crime statistics it is important to note

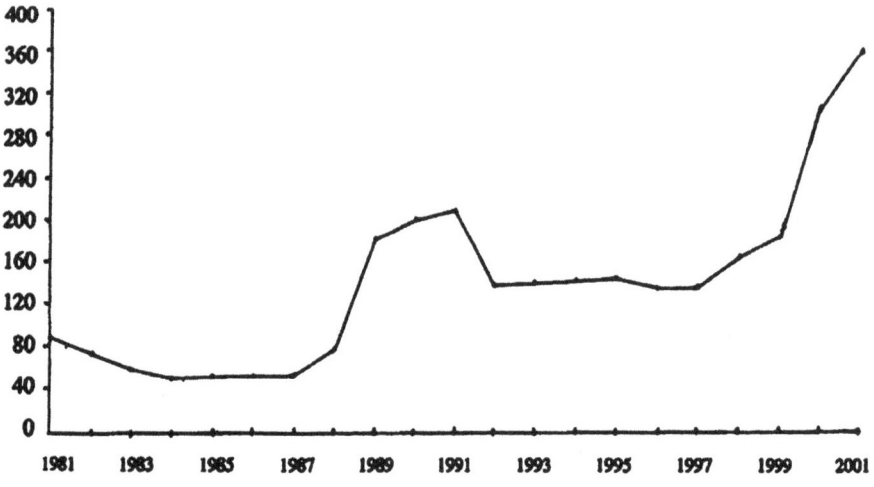

FIGURE 3.1
Officially Reported Overall Crime Rates in China (per 100,000 population), 1981–2001.
Source: From data in Zhongguo falü nianjian (Law Yearbook of China) 1988–2002. See also note 6.

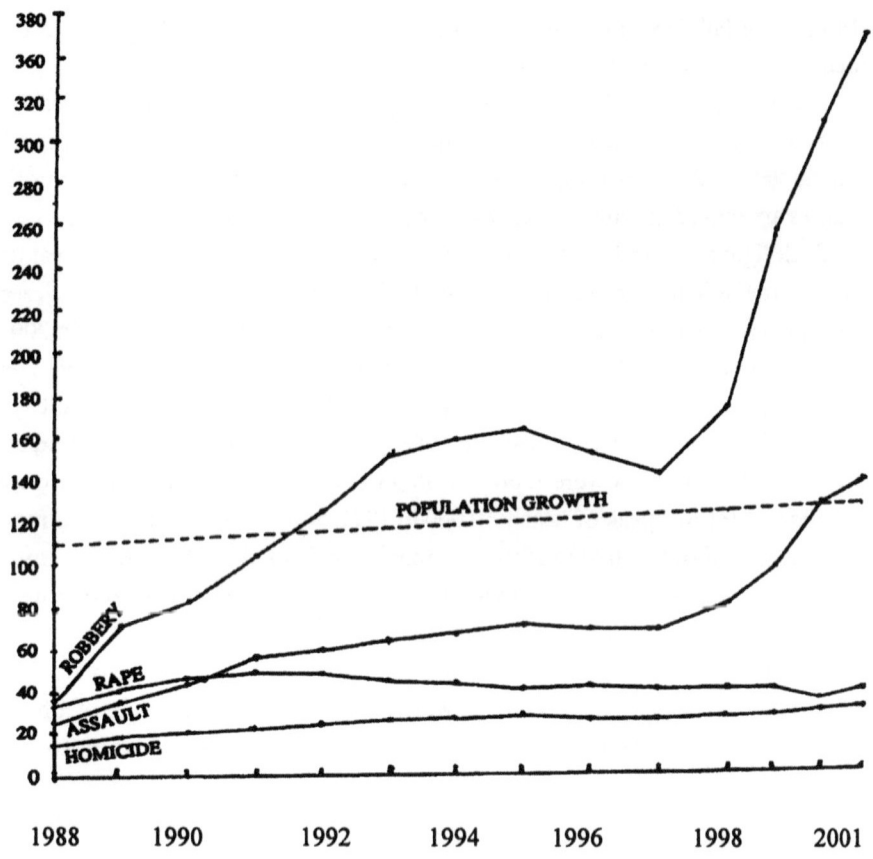

FIGURE 3.2

Violent Crime Cases in China in Absolute Numbers, 1988–2001. (Cases given in thousands; population given in ten millions).

Source: Table based on official crime rates in *Zhongguo falü nianjian* (Law Yearbook of China) 1989–2002.

that we do not deal with "objective reality" since data is often derived from official police and court records. Such records reflect a bureaucratic record-keeping process linked to the needs of those organizations, being used and misused for political means. In other words, the "crime problem" is partly a socially and politically constructed phenomenon. It is hardly controversial any longer to state that official data not only creates an incomplete picture of crime, but it even presents a *systematically biased* picture of crime.[2]

Judicial descriptions of "the facts" are partial reconstructions of "what really happened," partial in the sense that only part of the truth is told, and partial in the sense of being biased. Such figures do not lend themselves to international comparative analysis since they simply do not compare apples with apples. United Nations statisticians have taken this into consideration, and improvements have been made in terms of standardizing figures and improving the comparability of data. Nevertheless, they urge us to use such data with care. The "hidden figure" of crime is also due to the fact that people frequently do not report crime to the police. We should have this in mind when we look at the official Chinese statistics presented and commented upon here and elsewhere.

Internationally, we are currently able to find reasonably reliable data when we compare countries that are grouped together (in terms of level of development, etc.), while comparisons between individual countries are in many cases more problematic owing to more inaccurate figures in some nations and for some categories of crime.[3] I will venture into the difficult task of comparing the People's Republic of China with crime trends in groups of other countries and occasionally with particular countries. I think there is enough evidence in the gradually more standardized international data to make some conclusions about crime in China, but we first need to look at alternative ways to measure and compare crime on an international basis.

CHINESE OFFICIALLY RECORDED CRIME FROM AN INTERNATIONAL PERSPECTIVE: THE UN DATA

What do the alarming increases in reported crime tell us? Is China really a society of high crime? I have earlier used international official statistics from Interpol as rough indications of crime levels in a society, asking readers to handle the data with caution. I presented data from the early 1980s indicating that the Chinese reported crime rates were about 1:140 of a selected number of industrialized Western nations used for comparison. Some years later I concluded that official Chinese rates had increased but were still at the level of 1:60. I advocated looking at the homicide rates since the definition of such crimes would not differ as much as most other crimes and therefore represent a better basis for international comparison. By that comparison I found Chinese crime rates to be closer to international crime rates but concluded that they were still remarkably low.[4]

The United Nations regularly publishes data on international crime. Table 3.1 lists the Chinese crime rates and the country's placements on the UN list. I have estimated overall median and mean values for a number of crime categories in the UN survey. We have to conclude from UN statistics that China's officially reported crime rates range from fairly low to very low when compared internationally.

Table 3.1. Officially Reported Crime Rates in China in the UN Survey of Crime Trends, 1995–1997 (rounded figures)

	China	China's Placement	UN Median	UN Mean
Total crime	132	67 of 67 countries	2161	3569
Theft	86	56 of 62 countries	633	1030
Major theft	37	22 of 33 countries	87	350
Robbery	12	53 of 68 countries	46	276
Assault	6	57 of 59 countries	99	222
Rape	3	47.5 of 66 countries	6	14
Homicide	2	37 of 64 countries	3	7

Source: Derived from data in draft of sixth United Nations survey of crime trends and operations of criminal justice systems covering the period 1995–1997

Many alarming reports of crime in China still continue to appear, giving the impression that crime rates are extremely high rather than relatively low.

This trend is evident in the Chinese as well as in the international press. The country has even been compared to Russia and other nations in transition with high levels of crime. The comparison seems misleading. In terms of completed intentional homicides, Russia has one of the highest rates in the world with a reported 15.3 per 100,000 population in 1996, a number later increased to more than twenty.[5] In the aftermath of the fall of the Berlin Wall, we have seen extraordinary high increases in recorded crime in countries such as Russia, Poland, Hungary, and Estonia, particularly during the 1989–1995 period. In some of these countries recorded crime has stabilized at a relatively high level, while in others it continues to increase.[6] Is Chinese transition really plagued by the same trends of high crime rates as in post-Soviet Russia?

In principle it is appropriate to compare the obvious increases in Chinese crime with figures from other nations in transition experiencing rapid increase in crime rates. However, Chinese crime levels are rising from a much lower basis, making the relative increase look more dramatic. During the crime wave of the early 1980s, we noted that the overall crime rate was about eighty per 100,000 population. The rate went down to just over fifty per 100,000 in 1984, but then reached a peak of 210 in 1991. The overall crime rate was listed as low as 132 in the UN statistics. The UN material thus compares the lowest rates given in China for many years. According to the UN material, China had the lowest recorded grand total crime rate among the sixty-seven nations quoted. Only India was close to the Chinese reported crime rates with 179 in 1997. Do these official Chinese crime rates really provide an accurate picture? Does China still have less crime than perhaps any other country in the world, or do official crime rates play games with us? To answer this question, let us first look more closely at the officially recorded crime rates. At first appearance there seems to have been two "crime booms" since the early eighties, one in 1989 and a more serious one in 1998–1999.

Let us first look at the grand total reported crime rate. This measure is a very unreliable measure of crime. The grand total is very much dependent on the reported theft rates, since they constitute the vast majority of recorded crime in any country. When it comes to theft, the numbers are very complicated indeed. We generally know little about international definitions and ways of recording theft, and it is simply impossible to base any type of international comparison on such flimsy data. China's rate of total recorded thefts of 86 per 100,000 population seems unbelievably low. The apparent fall in theft rates (and thereby in total recorded crime) during the 1990s is due to the fact that several types of petty theft were omitted from the statistics in 1992 and no longer termed "criminal," making the comparison difficult. Different recording practices were also introduced from 1992.[7] The 2001 material records major theft at about 320 per 100,000 population. This is a dramatic increase from 1997, but still well under the UN mean and median figures. Since the theft rates make up most of the grand total of recorded crime, and theft is defined in totally different ways, it would seem more or less meaningless to compare grand totals of recorded crimes at all. The picture of China at the bottom of the UN statistics thus has little meaning in terms of comparative significance.

"Major theft" is potentially a better indicator, although still inadequate in our case. When we compare "major thefts" with "overall theft," we see just how greatly international statistics differ in terms of what is recorded. It is illustrative of the problem that major thefts make up well over 40 percent of the total number of thefts in China, while only about 0.3 percent in countries like Canada and Finland, 0.8 percent in Poland, and 97.3 percent in Belgium! Each country has its peculiarities in recording crime. We see from this that the vastly different figures are the product of equally vastly different definitions of crime and recording practices. The problem of unreported crime also has some specific Chinese characteristics as the bonus incentive structure for the police force encourages non-reporting. This is a problem discussed later in more detail.

I mentioned that homicide is a better indicator for comparison, and although the increase is less dramatic here, the homicide rates nevertheless present a picture of a more serious crime problem in China. Reported homicide in China nearly tripled in absolute numbers from 1981 to 1998, from 9,576 in 1981 to 27,501 in 2001. There has only been a slight increase in the homicide rates since the late 1980s, however, and the rate of "completed intentional homicide" in 2001 stands at 2.0 per 100,000 population as compared to 1.9 in 1990 and 2.3 in 1998.[8] South Africa resides at the top of the UN list with the extreme figure of 60 homicides per 100,000 population, while the United States currently experiences about 6 (Washington has 50). The U.S. figure has gone considerably down since 1992 when more than 10 homicides were recorded per 100,000 population. The present figure is still only surpassed in the developed world by Russia and some Eastern European nations.[9] Although a lot of the recent increases in violent crime are due to more accurate reporting, the officially reported homicide rate has remained on the same level. According to recent evidence, however, the Ministry of Public Security, despite issuing one set of "official figures," might have withheld the real homicide figures for internal use only. A Public Security publication where researchers were allowed to use the "not yet officially issued" (*hai wei zhengshi gongbu*) homicide rates for 2000–2003 in several tables comparing homicide with population statistics and GNP data shows that the real numbers might be up to twice as high as the official yearbook figures. Figures derived from these tables showed a peak of about 52,500 homicides in 2002, exactly twice the official number. These figures would give the substantially higher homicide rate of 4.2 per 100,000 population. The new figures give the estimated number of 48,500 homicides in 2003. We are clearly operating in what could be called the fog of national official statistics. There are, however, other ways of reaching more accurate estimates of crime.[10]

FINDING THE "DARK FIGURE" OF CRIME BY ALTERNATIVE MEASURES

Measuring the actual extent of crime in the world is a task beyond the capacity of current measurement techniques, and the challenge of accurately mapping the dark figure (*hei shu*) of Chinese crime remains particularly challenging. The lack of uniform definitions of offences and the lack of a common methodology to measure crime has led criminologists to develop alternatives to complement and challenge official statistics. Instead of relying on unreliable official police records on crime, we should rather explore the experiences of victims and criminals themselves. Two major efforts have been made in this regard: that of international comparative victimization studies and international comparative self-report surveys. Let us first look at the International Crime Victims Survey (ICVS). Since the late 1980s the ICVS has proven to be a formidable international standardized instrument in monitoring crime and perceptions of crime and criminal justice on a comparative basis without running into the problems of different recordings, definitions, and practices done by the police.[11] One important contribution of the ICVS has been to focus on crime reporting. It has for instance been found that victims in industrialized countries are much more likely to report to the police than those in poor agrarian nations.[12] The ICVS is based on interviews where representative samples of people in each country are asked about crimes they have experienced, regardless of whether or not they are reported to the police. Crime rates computed from representative surveys of the population are universally higher than those of official records.[13] One important finding is that Asian cities have the lowest overall victimization rates in the world as well as some of the lowest report rates, China included. According to the sample data, only one out of five cases of violence is ever brought to the attention of the police.[14]

China agreed to take part in the International Crime Victims Survey in 1993, and it was conducted in Beijing in May 1994.[15] Although four urban districts and one suburban district in Beijing (Chaoyang) are far from representative of all of China, the standardized random sampling process and extensive interviews with 2,000 residents gives a fascinating and arguably in many ways more accurate picture of crime trends and experiences of crime in China than those given by police-reported data. One obvious and serious weakness of the survey is its reliance on official household registers. This method leaves out the vast "floating population" (*liudong renkou*) who make up several million of those presently living in Beijing. These are people without a residence permit and are thus not included in the survey. The bias is all the more serious because there is anthropological and criminological evidence that this part of the population is far more likely to be victimized by all kinds of crime, including crimes committed by the authorities.[16] By the late 1980s this group already made up more than 20 percent of the population in Beijing, and at the time of the 1994 survey it was even higher.[17] The Chinese survey was part of a larger report on criminal victimization in the developing world and included selected countries and cities from Asia, Latin America, North Africa, and Sub-Saharan Africa. The ICVS method has now been tested out in a standardized way in about sixty different countries, and similar surveys have been done in a number of industrialized countries as well as in developing countries.[18]

The results of the survey showed that the victimization rate in China was 12.6 percent in one year, meaning that 12.6 percent of the respondents experienced the types of crime mentioned in the survey at least once during the preceding year.[19] This is a rate much higher than the crime rate based on official statistics, but this was found to be the case in all countries surveyed. The numbers do confirm that the Chinese crime rate is still low by international standards. China, represented by Beijing, had the lowest overall victimization rate found in the developing nations survey at 12.6, and it was lower than any of the countries surveyed in the industrialized nation survey. The lowest victimization rate found in Europe was Portugal with 15, equal to the Japanese rate, while Australia had the highest victimization rate of 30 percent.[20] Compared to almost any other participating country in the ICVS, Beijing, with the exception of bicycle theft (a category now taken out of the Chinese theft statistics), has the lowest crime victimization rates in all other categories. In terms of violent crimes against the person, or so-called contact crimes (robbery, assault, sexual crimes), incidents in the Chinese survey are mostly reported to be of a less serious type. The victimization rate was significantly higher in urban areas than in the rural areas in Beijing. If more rural dwellers had been part of the survey, indications are that the victimization rates would also be lower. Again, the bias resulting from omitting "floaters" could represent quite a serious flaw in the material, and although it gives a much more accurate picture than the official crime statistics, the ICVS might lose some of its credibility because of such omissions. Let us look at the overall victimization risks in some industrialized (1999) and developing (1994) countries based on the ICVS in table 3.2. Despite the bias of the survey, there are many interesting traits and valuable findings in the Beijing survey that I will comment upon in more detail. When we look at robbery, the 1994 figures of approximately 160,000 reported cases seemed to represent a serious crime boom in China. If we use robbery data from the International Crime Victims Survey, we find that a mere 0.5 percent of the population in Beijing were the victims of such crimes during a year. The figure was by far the lowest in the study of developing nations and ranges at the absolute bottom levels of all nations taking part in the ICVS.

Even in 2001, where the rates doubled, it still remained very low by international comparison.

The ICVS includes questions regarding "sexual incidents" experienced over the past year.[21] Such incidents were reported by 2.4 percent of the Beijing respondents. This was a higher rate than in Manila, Bombay, and Rio de Janeiro, but considerably lower than in Dar es Salaam, Cairo, or Kampala. Overall the Asian rates were much lower than those of Africa and Latin America. In addition, three-quarters of the sexual incidents reported in Beijing were defined as "offensive behavior" of a

Table 3.2. Overall Victimization Risk in Some Countries—Persons Victimized Once or More in Twelve Months (in percentage)

Australia	30	Denmark	23	Spain	19
England and Wales	26	United States	21	Switzerland	18
Sweden	25	Belgium	21	Portugal	15
Canada	24	France	21	Japan	15
Poland	23	Finland	19	P.R. of China	13

Source: John van Kesteren, Pat Mayhew, Paul Nieuwbeerta, *Criminal Victimization in Seventeen Industrialised Countries: Key findings from the 2000 International Crime Victims Survey,* and Ugljesa Zvekic and Anna Alvazzi Del Frate, eds., *Criminal Victimisation in the Developing World.*

less serious type, and only one-quarter represented cases of sexual assault. There was no rape, and only one attempted rape reported. There was, however, an alarming fact in the Beijing figures. Among sexual incidents regarded as crimes, only about one in ten was reported to the police. These report rates were among the lowest in all cities, and only in Jakarta and Cairo were the report rates lower than in Beijing. Beijing women were apparently extremely reluctant to report sexual incidents, even those they regarded as a crime. Again, the omission of the "floating population" from the survey represents a serious bias. This group is likely to experience far greater risks in terms of sexual assault, rape, and sexual harassment than the registered population. While the official reports and the victimization survey both show China as being low on the scale of occurrences of rape and sexual crime, it is not justified to say that they are among the lowest in the world. The lack of willingness to report sexual incidents to the police and the bias represented by the omission of part of the population from the survey could indicate a considerably higher incidence of sexually related crimes in China. The lack of willingness found in China to report crimes to the police in general is somewhat puzzling since the ICVS found high degrees of satisfaction with the police force in general. The data, however, showed that people who had been victimized and had been in contact with the police were less willing to evaluate the police in a positive way. The low rape rates might have to do with the fact that rape cases are difficult to solve, therefore providing little incentive for the police to report.

Let us move on to yet another method constructed in order to find more reliable crime data for international comparison, the self-report survey. Such data are based on self-reports about crimes and deviant behavior committed over one year regardless of whether they have been reported to the police or not. Instead of the victim talking, this method is based on the perpetrator talking about his or her experiences. From a survey of twelve Western countries (including city surveys), the percentage of respondents who reported that they had committed theft over the last year was lowest in England and Wales at 16 percent and highest in the city of Helsinki at 38.6 percent. The mean value of that survey was 26.8 percent for property crime, 29.1 percent for violent acts (defined as vandalism, carrying weapons, group fights, rioting, and beating up of nonfamily), and 14.1 percent were involved in drug-related crime of some sort.[22]

We do have some scattered evidence from self-report studies in China. A comparison based on a large-scale survey of self-report data from China (Shanghai), Japan, and the United States in 1987 showed highly significant differences between the rates of deviant behavior was much more common in America than in

Japan, while Japanese adolescents on their side reported far higher participation rates than did the Chinese sample. In one category, theft, 20.7 percent of the Americans reported some act of stealing, while 6.6 percent of the Japanese and a mere 0.9 percent of the Chinese admitted having taken part in such illegal activities during the last twelve months.[23]

Internationally, the overall "ever" rates for all kinds of crime (did you *ever* commit) ranged roughly between 80 and 90 percent, while the rates for "last year" typically range between 50 and 80 percent.[24] A recent study based on self-reported delinquency data from Shanghai showed that only 29 percent of adolescents in the city reported some involvement in delinquent behavior "last year" compared to 65 percent for a corresponding group of adolescents in Brisbane, Australia.[25] The survey showed increases in crime among the Shanghai respondents compared to 1987, but still the self-reported crimes are exceptionally few in number. In conclusion we should note that both the International Crime Victims Survey and international self-report surveys seem to confirm the generally low crime rates in China.

THE SOCIAL CONSTRUCTION OF CRIME RATES

We have established that China does not experience internationally high crime rates, although the relative increase in China might seem dramatic for those involved. Crime has increased considerably over the last two decades. One mystery, however, is the more recent dramatic peak in the crime rates. The rise does not seem to be reflected on the street level or in society at large. The explanation of this apparent sharp rise in crime given by Chinese public security spokesmen focuses on statistical corrections and better policing.[26] Although there is much truth in both explanations, we need to look at them in more detail.

The problems of estimating the true incidence of crime from statistics of "offences known to the police" is something every criminologist would be familiar with. It is established beyond doubt that the official crime rates reflect only the tip of an iceberg of crimes known to those instigating them and their possible victims. Most crimes undoubtedly go unreported in both China and the rest of the world.[27] In one example, research from England showed that official crime statistics listed only between 15 and 25 percent of the estimated real number of cases.[28] There is one important difference in the Chinese case, however, as criminologists generally list an "inactive police force" as one of the main causes for reporting too low crime rates.[29] In China we have rather seen a very active police force with clear incentives to "improve" crime statistics by reducing the number of cases, indicating order and a higher efficiency in solving cases. Cases that are not easy to solve are often not reported by the police. Sometimes the police also do not accept cases reported to them by the victim. I already mentioned the general problem of getting the police to accept rape cases. This problem was the focus of the so-called Xiao Li case in the Women's Federation newspaper, *Zhongguo funübao*. The paper focused on the rights of migrant women by using the case of Xiao Li, a pseudonym for a migrant woman who was raped by her employer but was refused by the police to file a case against the perpetrator.[30] The police focus instead on the easy-to-crack cases that add to their bonuses. Reformist police officials and scholars have decried the corrosive effect these campaign reporting practices have on police professionalism and the state's capacity to gather accurate social order data and make predictions needed to implement criminal policy.

The Chinese anti-crime campaigns should make us particularly aware of the problems linked to inaccurate crime statistics. The Chinese figures have many hidden agendas, political as well as practical, and it is of course of enormous importance for some to show that the campaigns really deliver. Scholars, discussing the reliability of crime statistics in China, have focused on the tendency to fabricate positive campaign reports. Police salaries, budgets, personnel hiring, and promotion are all largely determined by local Party committees, and some (see Tanner in chapter 6) blame fraudulent statistics on a tendency among Party secretaries to report the most favorable numbers. Others (see Dutton in chapter 7) argue that these problems are mainly structural effects of the police contract responsibility system.

Three of the key statistical goals during a campaign have been lowering overall numbers of criminal cases, increasing arrests, and increasing the percentage of officially opened case files that are solved—the "case-cracking rate" (*po'an lü*). Policemen have been led to look for the "easy to catch," and local police have had an incentive to artificially inflate arrest rates by rearresting past offenders for alleged "new offences," or by focusing their attention on arresting petty criminals rather than the hard-core criminals meant to be targeted in campaigns. The crime rate (*fanzui lü*) seems to be very closely linked to the case-cracking rate; in fact, in many ways it is directly constructed by the latter. One effective way to increase the case-cracking rate is of course not to open or report cases that are not easily solved.

Michael Dutton has shown in this volume how such rationalities and incentive structures are dictated by the contract. When police are paid by the rate of solved cases, massive underreporting of crime is a rational response closely linked to the maximization of wages and bonuses. A study of police station records nationwide revealed that a huge gap had developed between the number of known or "real" crime cases and the number of cases reported. The reasons for such a low rate of reporting related principally to the performance criteria of the security responsi-

bility system. Police were in danger of missing out on their bonuses and even incurring a penalty for failing to reach the allotted targets. As a result they dealt with
reports on crime in inventive ways and would gain their financial bonuses because
under- and nonreporting meant high case-cracking rates.

A nationwide study of the problem undertaken in 1997 discovered that 80
percent of known cases were reported to the police and only 30 percent of these
were actually recorded by the police. In other words, the official number of cases
used in crime statistics would be only 24 percent of cases known.[31]

Only 37 percent of this 24 percent were actually solved, giving us the number
of 8.88 percent. In China the number eight still counts as a lucky number, and in
this case 8.88 seems to define the criminal lucky number: lucky because of the
more than 90 percent chance of getting away with the crime committed. Important improvements in statistical recording have been made recently. Chinese
public security scholars have developed the term "degree of accuracy," trying to
map the proportion which official figures make relative to total offences made.
The new statistical measures might explain much of the 1989 peak in crime rates.
The degree of accuracy improved from a mere 29 percent in 1988 to an estimated
51 percent in 1990, a fact manifested in figure 3.1, and repeated in figure 3.3 below.[32] At the same time it was found that many offences listed in international
statistics were omitted from the Chinese data.[33]

The 1989 increase could reflect both strengthened policing as well as more accurate reporting, and the drop in overall crime rates from 1991 was, as already
concluded, mainly due to the redefinition of crime in 1992 when several offences
were no longer listed as criminal. During the early 1990s, however, China also
saw a strengthened emphasis on contract policing, which again led to an increase
in the relative importance of the case-cracking rate. The move boosted police
bonuses, and the case-cracking rate grew rapidly after the dramatic fall of 1989.
To understand the second crime boom, we have to look closer at the functions of
the case-cracking rate.

The uneven crime rates do not closely reflect real existing developments in
crime. The explanation rather lies in internal administrative redefinitions and
not least in structures defining police income incentives. This is best illustrated
in the observed symmetry between the crime rate and the case-cracking rate (figure 3.3). Periods of high crime rates show low case-cracking rates and vice versa.
The case-cracking rate was high and growing in the 1980s, reaching a peak of
81.3 percent in 1987. We find a rapid decline in the case-cracking rate in 1989,
and again from 1997 and onwards. It reaches its lowest level in 2001 when only

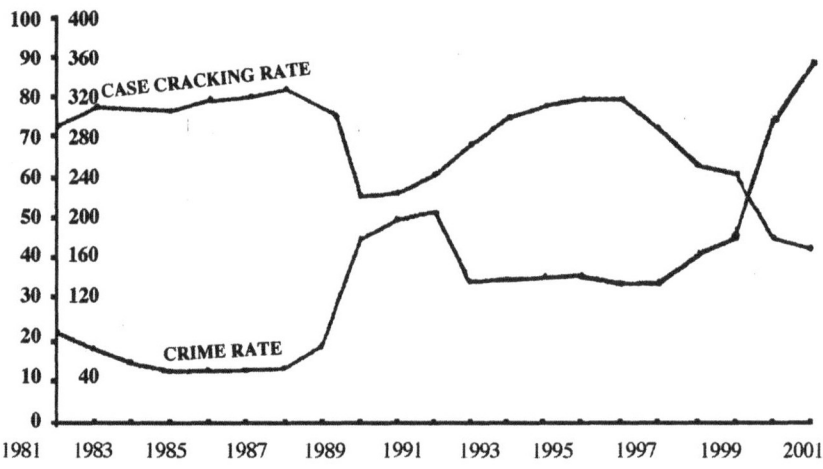

FIGURE 3.3

The Case-Cracking Rate (in Percent of Total Reported Crime Cases) and Total Number of Reported Crime Cases per 100,000 Population, 1981–2001.

Source: Table based on official crime rates and official case-cracking rates in *Zhongguo falü nianjian* (Law Yearbook of China) 1988–2002.

42.9 percent of reported cases were cracked.[34] In some ways it might seem natural that increased crime leads to a lower percentage of cases solved. In years where the overall crime rate is low, the case-cracking rate is high. In years of high crime rates, the case-cracking rate is low.

The reality is not that simple, and the relation between the reported crime rate and the case-cracking rate is not that between an independent crime rate and a dependent variable called the case-cracking rate. The latter instead contributes directly and independently to the way in which the crime rate is reported. In circumstances where case-cracking is important for the bonuses of the police, they naturally do not report crime since high case-cracking rates mean high bonuses. The bonus incentives of high case-cracking rates were particularly high during the 1990s. In periods where there is less emphasis on case-cracking bonuses, we naturally see more crimes known to the police reported in the overall statistics. The case-cracking rate therefore has little to do with the effectiveness of the police as such. The failure of contract policing became increasingly evident, and the fraudulent effects of the bonus incentive became clearer in the late 1990s. In many places the case-cracking rate has now been diminished or abolished as a measure of police effectivity and is no longer linked to salaries and bonuses. As a result we have seen more cases known by the police reported in the statistics. It is also interesting to note that criminological research has found that the relation between crime rates and detection or case-cracking rates in general are linked to corruption. There is some evidence that effective suppression of corruption within the police force tends to inflate reported crime rates while it decreases detection rates. At least this was found in the case of Hong Kong.[35] This is precisely what is happening to those rates in China today, and might indicate that China experiences a gradual increase in the suppression of police corruption.

Despite the indication given by the dramatic increases in official crime numbers, we have to conclude that there has been no explosion in crime around the turn of the millennium. Instead of a seemingly uneven development, there has been a fairly stable increase in crime rates over the last twenty years. Although crime is still most certainly considerably higher than officially reported in China as elsewhere, we have no reason to believe that China gives a lower estimate than, for instance, India. I have pointed out, however, that there exists a particular bias in the Chinese reported crime rates. To a large extent this bias is linked to incentive structures deciding police income, and more generally it is explained by the marketization of policing in China. It is fair to say that contract policing has hampered rather than aided public security and the ability of the authorities to make predictions. Chinese authorities have become aware of this effect, such practices are now being gradually corrected, and we have seen rising crime rates and sinking case-cracking rates as a function of this correction. Chinese crime rates are still relatively to remarkably low seen in an international comparative perspective even if we take the much higher actual crime rates into consideration. Both self-report surveys and the ICVS have confirmed the relatively low crime rates in China. Contrary to popular perceptions in China and abroad, there is no immediate reason to be particularly alarmed by the present Chinese crime rates. This does not at all mean that crime is an insignificant problem in China. For instance, the statistical material which I hold to be the most reliable, the ICVS, still leaves out some of those who are most likely to be the heaviest crime victims—the floating population. In China this group has mainly been targeted as perpetrators rather than as victims. Relative increases may still be dramatic for the Chinese population. What is most alarming about the current crime scene, however, is the very climate or opportunity structure for future crime. There are some indications that Chinese trends point towards a potential dangerous future crime scene.

A SCENARIO OF CRIME: THE CASE OF CORRUPTION

It has been argued strongly in China that harsh punishment is the solution to the rising crime rates. I will not touch upon the matter of punishment here but state in general that deterrence is not a productive approach if one wants to reduce crime. The alleged effectiveness of anti-crime campaigns and harsh punishment does not find much support in criminological literature. The effect of such measures might be a brutalized rather than a stabilized crime scene.[36] There is much more to be found in macro approaches involving legal and social reforms, and I will concentrate on these issues here. We see a pattern of international crime today. Transitional societies with discredited government institutions and a weak judiciary are likely to be victims of organized crime and corruption because of the ripe opportunity structures for crime represented by the lack of a rule of law. It is not modernity in itself that causes crime. Traditional societies are often more violent than well-regulated modern societies.[37] Crime, however, thrives in a climate of transition where the rule of law has not been firmly established.[38] For instance, we see a very interesting pattern in the development of organized crime. Such activities are closely linked to what criminologist Jan van Dijk has called the three main indicators of the rule of law.[39] Van Dijk argues that the rule of law tends to come in a package where the following elements mutually influence each other: *(1) The degree of corruption among politicians and public servants, (2) The relative effectiveness of the police, and (3) The relative independence of the judiciary.*

We have to go beyond the traditional definitions of crime to map the massive problems of corruption—the uninvited guest of the economic reforms. Corruption normally evades the statistics of traditional crime, but the scope of the problem is enormous. One corruption case or massive fraud case can cause billions of dollars in losses and victimize thousands. Because of their complexity, however, such crimes are poorly recorded statistically. Sometimes a few minor cases of petty crime can leave their marks on the crime statistics more than does a single huge corruption case. The traditional targets of crime might not be representative for the real crimes committed in a society, and police targeting often gives a flawed and biased profile of crime, typically leaving out a large number of white-collar crimes and corruption. According to the International Crime Victims Survey, nearly one in five people in developing countries reported experiences with corruption during the previous year. The biggest problems were seen in Latin America, followed by Africa and Asia and the transitional countries of Central and

Eastern Europe where one in eight had felt victimized by corruption. In comparison, reports of corruption were much more uncommon in the industrialized countries.[40] The ICVS focuses on victimization and is probably less effective in measuring the positive effects some people may privately experience through corruption. The ICVS mainly measures the negative effects of corruption and the perception of injustice experienced. Corruption, however, is a difficult offence to measure both in an individual country and for international comparison, but we do have some indications about the relative scope of the problem in the ICVS data as well as in the figures from the Global Corruption Report.

Corruption has plagued China in particular since the economic reforms started in the late 1970s, and the ICVS results from 1994 show that corruption was already serious, although not experienced on a regular basis in Beijing in the same way as in cities like Jakarta, Buenos Aires, Cairo, or Kampala where as many as 30–40 percent of the population had personally experienced corrupt activities over the last year. Still, close to 6 percent of the Beijing citizens reported having been victimized by corruption during the year preceding the survey.[41] The figure was still relatively low in comparison with some of the most corrupt cities in the developing world, but it was close to the levels of Bombay and Johannesburg, and up to fifteen times as common as in most Western European cities.

The Beijing ICVS, however, is already nearly a decade old, and corruption has grown in China since then. Even according to official statistics, the number of cases tripled from 1993 to 1997 when a peak of nearly 150,000 corruption cases was reported. A Party Central Committee directive from 1998, preventing public security and armed forces from setting up their own businesses, did produce results countering the trend of rapidly increased corruption by attacking some of its most damaging structural causes. The amount of money involved in corruption cases, however, is still twice as high as in 1993, and since inflation is not a sufficient explanation of the figures, it seems larger cases have been singled out for attack.[42] Despite the efforts to prevent corruption, major obstacles are not being removed as the government seeks absolute monopoly on anti-corruption activities. For instance, the Chinese media is not allowed to investigate corruption independently, particularly if the exposés implicate powerful officials. Journalist Jiang Weiping uncovered several corruption scandals involving high-ranking officials. He was charged in September 2001 with "revealing state secrets" and given a nine-year prison sentence in a secret trial.[43] Household surveys like the ICVS do not address corruption in high places, and the picture may be even more serious when reported by groups closer to the "action." This is exactly what the nongovernmental organization Transparency International aims to show in their annual Global Corruption Report.

Corruption is an elusive concept, and there are several major problems in attempting to define it. It ranges from the illegal to the unethical, consists of several distinct but related problems, and differs in legal definitions and public opinion perceptions of corruption all over the world.[44] The Transparency International's Global Corruption Report has tried to standardize and operationalize the concept, and the index is gaining more and more international and scholarly reputation despite the obvious methodological difficulties linked to this effort. It is fair to say that the report gives an indication about the scope and trend of international corruption although accuracy can never be achieved in this field. China was measured on two indexes, the Corruption Perception Index (CPI) and the Bribe Payers Index (BPI).[45] A score from ten (highly clean) to zero (highly corrupt) is used, and 102 countries were listed in the 2003 report. Finland was reported the cleanest of the countries surveyed with a score of 9.7. China shared the fifty-ninth place with Ethiopia and the Dominican Republic, all with a score of 3.5. Bangladesh ended at the bottom of the list with a score of 1.2.[46] Among the twenty-one countries measured on the Bribe Payers Index, China ended up second from the miserable bottom of the list with a score of 3.5, just ahead of Russia at the very end (3.2). This index, however, was dominated by industrialized nations since not many developing nations had been surveyed. For East Asia and the Pacific the report maintains that "China faces the region's greatest challenge in reining back corruption."[47] Although there is disagreement surrounding the figures of the Global Corruption Report, it can still be used as an indication of the situation. Professor Hu Angang at Qinghua University put the cost of corruption in China as high as 13.2–16.8 percent of GDP.[48] He further estimated that 15–20 percent of public project funds "leak" into private hands. Such figures place China somewhere in the middle in terms of cost of corruption on an international scale. These figures may be inaccurate estimates only, but nevertheless give the same indications as those found in the Global Corruption Report. We have over the last couple of years seen notorious petty corruption in the public sector and even large cases targeting people in relatively high political circles. One such case led to the execution of a former National People's Congress vice-chairman, convicted of embezzling over forty million yuan.

POLICE EFFICIENCY: BETWEEN NORM ENFORCEMENT AND LAW ENFORCEMENT

There are very clear data showing an inverse relationship between the level of corruption and the willingness among the population to report crime.[49] In countries where corruption is common, citizens have less confidence in the police, who are seen as corrupt themselves, or they simply do not regard corruption as a criminal act. In some areas corruption has become a habit, something that affects the over-all economy in devastating ways. There have been a lot of reports on corrupt po-lice personnel in China, and this question is crucial for the stability of the country. Let us look briefly at the situation in the police force.

Let us first look at some numbers. In the UN statistics, based on official data from China (1997), the number of police are listed as nearly 1.2 million, or a rate of 96.3 per 100,000 population. The average of the fifty-five nations listed that same year was three times higher at 285.2. More recent official figures operate with a number of 1.5 million regular police in China, or about 115 per 100,000 population, but it is not entirely clear what is included in either these or the UN figures.[50] Most likely the data only gives the number of people's police—the *min-jing*. The Law Yearbook of China ceased publishing police figures after 1991. In 1991 it was 854,000 people's police (*minjing*), and 623,000 armed police—*wujing*—in China. In addition there were 870,000 special function public secu-rity officers in 1990 (e.g. traffic, agriculture, enterprise safety, aviation, railway, and economic security police). Even without a substantial increase in armed po-lice and special function police since the early 1990s, the number should be closer to three million today. This figure would at least make a better basis for in-ternational comparison and bring China up to something around the average world level or over in terms of regular police per 100,000 population.[51] In addi-tion there are people working for security companies (*bao'an gongsi*) and people involved in security work within the work units who are not listed as "police" or "security personnel" in the statistics.[52] We have no figures for the latter category, but we know more about the *bao'an*. By 1995 there were over 200,000 and in 1998 there were as many as 300,000 employees employed by private security companies.[53] The informal "Internet police" are not professionals, but the force adds up to 300,000 controllers.[54] The police force in China is undoubtedly much larger than reported in the UN statistics. For China, however, the most impor-tant issue is not numbers. It should be emphasized that police "effectiveness" does not lie in the weapons they wield or the number of their force. Actually, the number of police is found to be unrelated to total crime rates in any society.[55] Arming the police can even lead to a more brutal crime scene as criminals be-come increasingly armed when confronted with an armed police force.

China is a transitional society and should thus be analyzed in comparison with other countries in their process of transition. Law, norms, and community were linked together in complex ways in European and American history as well. The culture and habits of the police cannot be changed in one day. The formation of a law-enforcing professional police force is a relatively novel story even in our own societies. Established in 1829, the London Metropolitan Police represented the world's first attempt to develop a relatively impersonal, bureaucratic, professional law enforcement agency. The New York "cop" was a citizen with a degree of delegated power who relied very much on his personal authority. During the nineteenth century he was not the impersonal agent of a legal system and was inclined to participate in local community conflicts as a citizen much more than the "Bobbies" of London.[56] The American "cop" in many ways was a far more traditional type of policeman. These basic traditions seem to stick even with present British and American police cultures, although the differences have diminished over the last century.

In traditional societies as a rule, mere "law" had to step down when faced with the ruling morality of the day. In China this had been the basic principle and practice for centuries, and the Chinese legal tradition has succinctly been summed up by Chinese scholars as being "pan-moralist" (*fandaode zhuyi*).[57] Despite the renewed stress on law, morality remains a central theme of law and order. It is enough to consider Jiang Zemin's former remarks that "governing the country by the rule of law (*fazhi*) should be combined with the "rule of virtue" (*dezhi*) in order to build a lofty ideological and ethical foundation for maintaining a good public order and practice."[58] We are required to take into consideration the historical continuities of the Chinese system of law and policing and its embeddedness in social mores and norms. The conflict between law (*fa*) and feelings or human sentiment (*qing*) has been central in Chinese history. The view that *qing* either promotes or distorts justice has been the central Chinese view of justice ever since the days of Qin Shihuang. Traditional culture continued to represent a challenge against substantive law under the "dictatorship of the proletariat." The police's rule of morality and norms came from their close links to power as well as from their power of definition. The police, therefore, formed a forceful part of the community more than they represented a law enforcement agency in the modern and professional meaning of the term. Those in charge of public security were to take care of the moral order rather than the impersonal black letter law. Even in terms of formal legal codes, at least until 1997, the Chinese criminal law was still "policing the norm" rather than the law. What has been termed the analagous application of law, punishing conduct that is viewed as harmful to society even when such conduct is not criminalized by law, was legal practice until 1997. The legality of this principle was established by Article 79 in the 1979 Criminal Code.[59] This article was abolished in the new 1997 Criminal Code, and such analogous application of law is now theoretically seen as unlawful and against the spirit of the law. This is undoubtedly an important achievement in Chinese law, but how is it viewed by lay policemen and policewomen? Policing the exemplary norms provided the police force with a large amount of discretionary power. They became a guarantor of the dictatorship of the proletariat, and it was their duty as the People's Police (*renmin jingsha*) to define the people's interests and uphold the prescribed proletarian norms. They were responsible for their own exemplary quality as well as that of the people. The police largely remained a "norm enforcement agency" rather than one of law enforcement. An effective side of that tradition in terms of crime reduction is perhaps its close community policing. A more modern, mobile, and complex social structure, I would say, however, has made tight community policing increasingly difficult.

Traditional police culture clearly represents a problem, but material resources are probably the main obstacle in attempts to modernize the police. There is still a lack of human and social capital; police are often underpaid and overworked. One report presents a survey showing that 58 percent of the local police force worked from eleven to fifteen hours a day and 15 percent worked even more than that.[60] The low salaries and poor training and equipment provided to the police help induce bribery and corruption. The establishment of effective policing institutions is crucial for upholding order in society and the legitimacy of the state. Due to a reduction of the general budget, however, the police receive less and less from the government. The national government only provides the budget for the Ministry of Public Security, and the public security organs at lower levels are principally financed by the governments at the respective levels. Local government support cannot even cover the basic salaries of officers. It has been widely reported throughout the 1990s that the police in some jurisdictions could not even pay for electricity, phone bills, and police uniforms. Police are forced to rely on so-called extra budgetary funds—a euphemism for corruption—such as fines and fees and sponsorships to make ends meet. Suspects have even been released unpunished after paying off the police.[61] There are growing reports of police engaged in corruption, torture, organized crime, drug trafficking, gambling, and prostitution. There are also problems with the indiscriminate use of detention and fines, activities that severely undermine the authority of the police force.[62] Even the cruel practice of extorting confessions by torture may be linked to the lack of funding, making the modern and more costly approach of investigation far more difficult. The development of a legal culture within the police force should have top priority, but this is a systemic problem and not primarily one of "moral quality" (*daode suzhi*) as is so often used as an excuse in official reports on the problems of deteriorating police discipline.[63] The efficiency of the police is bound to be low as long as basic funding is lacking. Without proper funding, we will see a more corrupt police force with less power to reduce crime and uphold stability.

ON LEGAL REFORMS AND THE INDEPENDENCE OF THE JUDICIARY

The third indicator of the rule of law concerned judicial independence. Judicial independence is important in matters of corruption because it engages the classical question of "*Quis costodiet ipsos custodes*," or "Who guards the guardians?"

The mere existence of laws does not ensure the rule of law, and if the guardian is not guarded, there are no limits to his power. It remains true that power corrupts and absolute power corrupts absolutely. The judiciary faces problems such as poorly trained judges, ineffective legal counsel for defendants and, last but not least, its highly politicized nature.[64] In court cases the adjudication committee simply does not hear the defence lawyer. The principle of "those who try cases do not decide them and those who decide cases do not try them" is being practiced.[65] The committee is free to change any decision given by the judges, and the Party effectively controls the courts. In addition the courts are controlled and supervised by the National People's Congress. Official authorities have wide discretionary power and flexibility to reverse or reconsider judgments based on changing circumstances or policy, and courts are simply a part of the bureaucracy.[66] China lacks a tradition of proper judicial independence. Imperial China did not divide administrative and adjudicative tasks.

Judicial independence (*sifa duli*), however, is not at all alien to recent Chinese legal debate, At the Fifteenth Party Congress in 1997, Jiang Zemin himself announced that China needed an independent judiciary, although it is not immediately clear what he meant by that term. Law is central to economic reform because through law stability can be achieved and calculable outcomes forecast. Economic reform required stability but in reality created conditions of social disorder. In relying upon the market, the Party in fact created what Marx once termed the "double freedom" of the proletariat. They now had freedom to move and sell their labor, and at the same time they had the freedom to sleep under bridges. Disorder increased while the old social control structures waned.

Before looking further at the Chinese debate on legal reforms, we should note the links between the structure of the judicial system and certain forms of crime, including organized crime and corruption. These phenomena are interconnected, and the frequency of crime and corruption not only depends on prevention and deterrence on the micro level, it is very much linked to the structural organization of the police and the judicial system. Public security, procuracy, and judiciary (*gong jian fa*) in that order describe the relative power, prestige, and importance of the different parts of today's Chinese justice system. The police have retained their discretionary powers which often operate in the form of "administrative" powers outside the criminal code. Judges are often still seen as "troublemakers," particularly by the police, and lawyers continue to be arrested for defending unpopular clients or challenging people in high places.[67] Today lawyers are still generally passive at trials. They have no right to question witnesses or the police during the trials, introduce new evidence, or enter a plea of innocence for the accused. Judges and procurators may decide the verdict, and sometimes even sentences, before the trial has begun. There are, however, informed voices arguing for a stronger position of the rule of law in China.

Important suggestions for legal reform and the establishment of a more independent judiciary have been made. Again, Rome was not built in a day, but little by little legal reformers are pushing for reform. Yin Chunli, a lawyer, is not acting alone when he attacks the system of nonparticipant adjudication committees, suggesting that committee members must attend the actual trial and hear the defence.[68] At the same time the *Zhangfanwei*—the Party political legal committee—operates at every level to control the police as well as the prosecutors and the courts. Most participants in the debate readily admit that there is no judicial independence in China but argue that gradual improvements are taking place. Meng Qingguo and Xiang Yong argue that the Chinese system is one of "relative judicial independence" (*xiangdui sifa duli*).[69] The principle they advocate is that judicial and administrative organs are indeed separate, that they have different duties, and that they should not interfere in each others' affairs. The principle might not be one of independence as understood in Western legal terms, but one of "mutual non-intervention" (*hu bu ganshe*). While far from calling for an independent judiciary, they propose a move away from the administrative domination of the judiciary.

Professor Chen Xingliang at the Beijing University Department of Law stresses the necessity of *impartiality* (*gongzheng*) in establishing the rule of law. Professor Chen, a member of the legal establishment, was crucial in establishing the 1997 criminal law, and is influential both in legal and political circles. He lists three key concepts for the establishment of the rule of law and the reform of the criminal justice system: the guarantee of human rights, formal rationality, and procedural justice.[70] The state should be subject to legal restraints, Chen argues. While criminal law is meant to punish crime, it is also meant to ensure the freedoms and the rights of the individual. Without the guarantee of human rights (*renquan baozhang*), the penal code becomes a tool of despotism, Chen holds. Further, criminal proceedings should be based on formal rationality (*xingshi lixing*) grounded in standardized criminal statutes and the presumption of innocence.[71] Nonformal rationality, on the other hand, will lead to arbitrary and irrational proceedings, directly undermining the rule of law. Thirdly, the rule of law for criminal proceedings means procedural justice (*chengxu zhengyi*) based on impartiality and efficiency. Impartiality is particularly important, and Professor Chen argues that it should even take preference over efficiency. He defines impartiality as the life-blood of the judicial process. If justice is not impartial, it becomes despotic, and thus a crime of its own, he concludes.

He calls for a three-in-one structure of police, procuracy, and court where the accused and the accuser are ideally equal, and with the judge serving as an intermediary referee. Chen seeks to strengthen the position of the judge as the impartial voice of the law. In other words, the triangular procedural structure should offer a legal balance of power between the prosecution and the defence. The judge should be impartial and detached, representing pure law. This requires strengthening of both the judge and the defence. In the state-centered criminal justice system, the defendant is a mere passive judicial object. The defendant's rights are not properly guaranteed in this system. The three-in-one system, suggested by Chen, would activate the defence, save the state judicial resources, and at the same time ensure a greater degree of judicial impartiality as well as efficiency.

Chen does not refrain from addressing the main issue of power. In a recent book he elaborates on this theme, starting his discussion with an attack on what he terms the "doctrine of state power," or the "doctrine of statism" (*guoquan zhuyi*).[72] He advocates legal restraints on the punishing power of the state in order to prevent its unrestrained powers (*wuxian quanli*). The Chinese state, he argues, has formerly had its citizens "completely in its power," and this approach should now be replaced by a "doctrine of human rights" (*renquan zhuyi*) or a doctrine of democracy or civil rights (*minquan zhuyi*). Law should restrain the state and the state function within the boundaries of law, he argues, advocating the German *Rechtsstaat* principle—*fazhiguo*, a state ruled by law.

Of course, Chen's principle of impartiality might prove difficult to implement and may not be sufficient to restrain the state adequately if the judiciary is not at the same time independent. Nevertheless, Chen raises a matter of great consequence for the long-term capacity of the state to control crime and social instability. President of China's Supreme People's Court, Xiao Yang, on revealing the draft plan of the new judicial reform, takes care to emphasize that the suggested reform explicitly opposes judicial independence, focusing instead on what he terms judicial fairness.[73] An often-heard argument against the value of an independent judiciary is that it would add another corrupt level to the administrative corruption already existing. There have indeed been problems with judicial corruption, and law enforcement personnel have repeatedly violated the law.[74] One should remember the weak foundation of a legal culture and the legal profession as such. The problem, of course, touches the issue of the "quality" (*suzhi*) and the education of judges and lawyers, but the main question is one of checks and balances. Again it should be emphasized that corruption is first and foremost a systemic problem, not primarily one of morality.

MACRO APPROACHES TO CRIME: THE VICIOUS CIRCLE OF CORRUPTION, ORGANIZED CRIME, AND ECONOMIC INEQUALITY

In opening their economy, China has become part of a global pattern of organized crime. Organized crime is most prevalent in transitional societies rather than in the poorest countries where few opportunities exist to make organized crime a lucrative business. Developing nations of moderate wealth and poverty offer enough opportunities and an ideal climate for organized crime. In Russia, violent crimes have skyrocketed as the country has seen a dramatic increase in organized crime. This trend is not uncommon within nations in transition, as crime is seen as a viable shortcut to affluence and prosperity in a system where the judicial system is in flux and the police force does not function effectively.[75] We have already emphasized the fact that police efficiency is not a function of its numbers or its weapons. It is the structural organization of the judicial system that determines the level of crime. Today organized crime is no longer a local phenomenon of Mafia-style "families" and local crime cultures; transnational crime has also become a major problem. Over recent years we have seen clear evidence that corruption, organized crime, and violent crime, in particular homicide, are closely interrelated.[76] Organized criminal groups use corruption to protect their illegal business activities. The interrelations between organized crime and corruption have prompted expert groups negotiating the United Nations convention against transnational organized crime to include an obligation to criminalize corruption among public officials in the draft convention. Article 294 in the new Chinese Criminal Code from 1997 concerns the crime of forming syndicates in order to carry out criminal activities, recruitment of members by overseas Mafia organizations, and protection and facilitation of criminal syndicates. The last issue is the theme of "*baohusan*," or protective umbrellas, meaning criminal protection from government officials allowing syndicates to operate.[77] The involvement of civil servants, however, is no longer considered vital to define a triad, and Beijing is examining draft amendments to the criminal law to redefine "criminal syndicates" in a bid to strengthen the crackdown on other types of organized crime.[78]

Organized crime has undoubtedly reemerged and increased in China and is said to have preserved some of the traditional forms from the secret society (*hei shehui*). The typical black society syndicates are groups of medium size, up to 50–200 members. They are hierarchically structured and follow strict "house rules." Recent statistics indicate that there are considerable numbers of organized crime groups in many Chinese provinces. Organized crime in China as elsewhere seems to be closely linked to official corruption and violent crime.[79] It is important here to emphasize organized crime's links to corruption. At the same time, however, we should be cautious in assuming high levels of organized crime. Internationally there has been a tendency to overinterpret the organized character of crime, assuming that loosely connected gangs are highly organized. There is no consensus in China about the phenomenon, and criminologists disagree on whether or not an "underworld" is already established. While one of the veterans of Chinese criminology, Kang Shuhua, argues that a criminal underworld already exists in China, Professor Jiang Lihua claims that an "underground system" has not yet been firmly established. They both agree that so far a large criminal underworld such as the Mafia in Italy or the Jakuza in Japan is not likely to appear in China in the near future. The picture is still that of small-scale gang crime.[80] The latest anti-crime "hard strike" (*yanda*) campaign is particularly focused on serious crime with special emphasis on "gang and Mafia organizations."[81] Analysis of existing global data shows that organized crime is a bigger problem in countries where the rule of law is not firmly established, most notably in countries lacking an independent judiciary.[82] These measures were strongly linked when compared in an international study on the interrelations between organized crime and the rule of law. Fifty-six countries were compared, and a strong correlation was found (r = 84; p<. 000; n = 56). The "cost of crime" was compared with the "rule of law" defined in more or less the same way as already established in this chapter. The analysis clearly indicated that the threat of organized crime is substantially reduced if the rule of law is properly applied. It was further found that the mutual combination of organized crime and official corruption greatly affected national income and growth. The rule of law is equally strongly related to national income per capita ($r = .83$; $p<.000$; $n = 55$), meaning that legal reforms should also be seen as an incentive for economic reform. It is further concluded that economic liberalization and sheer market mechanisms represent no guarantee for social stability and a healthy economic development in a country.[83] It is important to note, however, that an independent judiciary does not appear to prevent traditional crime. The judiciary also does not represent any guarantee against corruption, as the judiciary itself may become corrupt. Even in countries with an independent judiciary and a high rule of law score, there are serious incidents of high-level corruption. The United States recently experienced large-scale corruption cases like the Enron and WorldCom scandals, and the legal system has been directly involved in corrupt activities.[84] There is a global statistical indication, however, that an independent judiciary is a crucial factor in the reduction of corruption and organized crime. It introduces checks and balances of a systemic nature and aids considerably in guarding the guardians. Independence, however, does not function properly without the additional control of transparency in government.

Corruption is able to considerably damage an economy. On a global scale it is estimated to reduce the expected growth of a society by about 30 percent.[85] In

Table 3.3.   The Development of Inequality in China (Based on GINI-Coefficients)[a]

Year	Urban	Rural	Whole country
1978	0.15	0.212	0.180
1988	0.23	0.34	0.382
1994	0.37	0.41	0.434
1996	0.4003	0.4323	0.458[b]
2001	n.a.	n.a.	0.50

[a]Based on World Bank Report and PRC National Taxation Bureau data quoted from Liqun Cao and Yisheng Dao, "Inequality and Crime in China," and Guoan Ma, "Population Migration and Crime in Beijing, China," both in *Crime and Social Control in a Changing China*, ed. Jianhong Liu, Lening Zhang, and Steven F. Messner (Westport, Conn.: Greenwood Press, 2001), 69, 79; and X. L. Ding, "From Big Social Problems to Explosive Political Troubles? The Challenges of Managing a Huge Society under Rapid Transformation at a Politically Difficult Time," in *China's Post-Jiang Leadership: Challenges and Adaptation*, ed. John Wong and Yong-nian Zheng (Singapor: Singapore University Press, 2002), 192–93. Data from 2001 given by *China Center for Economic Research*, Beijing University in invitation document for the international symposium "Equity and Social Justice in Transitional China," Beijing (11–12 July, 2002).
[b]That figure was used by the National Taxation Bureau (NTB) in 1999, based on a sociological analysis from 1996 which pointed out that official statistics seemed to under-estimate the seriousness of the problem by using "formal income" only. The NTB corrected their previous figures of 0.295 in the urban areas, and 0.336 for the rural areas, making a nationwide GINI-coefficient of of 0.397.

addition it significantly enhances economic inequality, fundamentally affecting the social stability of a nation. One of the main achievements of comparative research methodology is that it has rekindled the mainstream criminology argument that poverty and inequality remain major factors of crime. Social development is thus seen to be the most important form of crime prevention, and international research indicates that such prevention does work. It has also been established that the prevalence of both property crime and violent crime are related to problems of economic deprivation in all regions of the world.[86]

The Chinese correctly emphasize crime prevention, but it is important that they also investigate social reform at the macro level. Inequality between social groups and classes as well as between urban and rural areas increased explosively in China during the last decade. Depending on the source of income data, the GINI-coefficient in China ranges from 0.4 to 0.5. This gives China one of the world's most unequal income distributions. According to some analyses, China now has a wider income gap than the United States (0.4) and has an equal or greater gap than Russia (0.48). Although there is insufficient data and different methods of arriving at GINI-coefficients, and it is sometimes confusing to look at different accounts of such rates, there is little doubt that income inequality has spiraled in China since the start of the reform period in 1978.[87] It should be added that the subjective element of visibility and the conspicuous consumption of the rich probably enhances the problem as people are faced with affluence and inequality in a direct way never before experienced in the People's Republic. The mere speed of this process adds a psychological element to the GINI.

Although crime levels in China are still comparatively low, the most alarming trends of the Chinese crime scene are pointing towards a scenario of increased organized crime.[88] The independence of the judiciary seems to be too radical a reform for the Party to accept at the present stage, potentially threatening its power. The paradox here is the argument of stability frequently used to justify the power monopoly of the Party. Instead of stability, limiting reforms to strengthen the judiciary will probably lead to increased corruption and mounting social unrest, eventually destabilizing the country. It might prove a dangerous strategy to attempt to stop corruption by mere policing.[89] The very rationale that is meant to stabilize China could instead lead to increased disorder, and the reluctance to reform the judiciary might well hamper the development of other reforms. China does not have to be unduly alarmed by their generally low rates of traditional crime but should be on the alert against the interlinked phenomena of corruption and organized crime. When an overloaded, undeveloped, and underresourced justice system is confronted by organized crime, the latter is guaranteed impunity. Corruption can further diminish the ability of law enforcement to accomplish its mission and hinder the efficient and fair functioning of a society. The answer for China does not rest on increased numbers of policemen or stricter punishment. These are factors more or less unrelated to crime. The problem of crime is mainly found on the macro level of society.

NOTES

1. See Adolphe Quetelet, *Research for the Propensity for Crime at Different Ages*, translated by Sawyer F. Sylvester (Cincinatti: Ohio, Anderson, (1831) 1984).

2. For a general discussion of such phenomena in criminology and criminal statistics, see Mike Maguire, "Crime Statistics, Patterns and Trends: Changing Perceptions and Their Implications," in *The Oxford Handbook of Criminology*, ed. Mike Maguire, Rod Morgan, Robert Reiner (Oxford: Clarendon Press 1994), 233–91.

3. For a discussion of such matters, see Graeme Newman, ed., *United Nations Global Report on Crime and Justice*, United Nations Office for Drug Control and Crime Prevention. Centre for International Crime Prevention, (Oxford: Oxford University Press, 1999), 1–25.

4. Børge Bakken, "Crime, Juvenile Delinquency and Deterrence Policy in China," *The Australian Journal of Chinese Affairs*, no. 30 (July 1993): 29–58; and Børge Bakken, *The Exemplary Society: Human Improvement, Social Control, and the Dangers of Modernity in China* (Oxford: Oxford University Press, 2000), 377–407.

5. Gordon Barclay, Cynthia Tavares, and Arsalaan Siddique, "International Comparisons of Criminal Justice Statistics, 1999," in *Home Office Statistical Bulletin*, no. 6 (May 2001): 10.

6. Russia is also well known for their soaring prison rates, and after the United States have the highest number of prison inmates in the world counted in terms of inmates per 100,000 population. The numbers are close to 700. See European Committee on Crime Problems, *European Sourcebook of Crime and Criminal Justice Statistics*, PC-S-ST (99) 8 DEF, (Strasbourg: 12 October 1999), and Barclay et al., "International Comparisons," 3.

7. In 1984 and particularly in 1991, the definitions of theft were changed; in 1984 the level of theft in order to constitute a crime was raised from 25 to 80 yuan in the cities and from 15 to 40 yuan in the rural areas. In 1991, the amount was raised from 300 to 500, in more developed places even to 600 yuan. The effects are shown in the statistics from 1992. See Kang Shuhua and Zhang Xiangjun, eds., *Xingshi fanzuixue* (Penal criminology) (Beijing: Qunzhong chubanshe, 2000), 58. Certain forms of petty theft, like the frequent crime of bicycle theft, was also taken out of the statistics, dramatically reducing the number of overall crimes. In 1992, the reporting practices were also changed; see *Zhongguo falü nianjian*, 1993 940. For the "crime boom" in the late 1990s, see *Qingshaonian fanzui wenti*, no. 4 (2002): 7; and Fan Zaiqin and Wang Hui, "2001 nian de shehui zhi'an" (Social and public order in 2001), in *2000 nian: Zhongguo shehui xingshi*

fenxi yu yuce (2001 Analysis and forecasts of the state of the social situation in China), ed. Ru Xin, Lu Xueyi, Li Peilin (Beijing: Shehui kexue wenxian chubanshe, 2002), 221; and data from *Gongan yanjiu*, no. 7 (2001), 95–96, and no. 6 (2002): 95–96, compared with estimated population.

8. *Zhongguo falü nianjian 1991* (Law Yearbook of China, 1991), estimated from 942, 952; *Zhongguo falii nianjian*, 1029, 1034.

9. Barclay et al., "International Comparisons," 5, 10. For U.S. data see also: http://www.aic .gov.au/stats/other/usa.html

10. Qin Liqiang, ed. 2004. *Shehui wending de anquanfa: Zhongguo fanzui yujing yu shehui zhi'an pingjia* (The safety valve of social stability: A forecast of Chinese crime and the evaluation of social and public order), Beijing: Zhongguo renmin gong'an daxue chubanshe.

11. The ICVS has countered several assumptions about the link between crime and development of the kind presented in modernization studies, like for instance Louise I. Shelley, *Crime and Modernization: The Impact of Industrialization and Urbanization on Crime*, (Carbondale: Southern Illinois University Press, 1982).

12. *UN Global Report 1999*, 103.

13. *UN Global Report 1999*, xiv.

14. *UN Global Report 1999*, 26, 42.

15. Zhu Hongde, former deputy director of the Institute for Crime Prevention and Criminal Reform at the People's Republic of China Ministry of Justice served as survey project director. See Ugljesa Zvekic and Anna Alvazzi Del Frate, eds., *Criminal Victimization in the Developing World*, publication no. 55 (Rome: United Nations Interregional Crime and Justice Research Institute, 1995).

16. See Li Zhang, *Strangers in the City: Refigurations of Space, Power, and Social Networks within China's Floating Population* (Stanford, Cal.: Stanford University Press, 2001). Zhao Shukai, "Criminality and the Policing of Migrant Workers," translated by Andrew Kipnis, *The China Journal*, no. 43 (January 2000): 101–10. Ma Guoan, *Zhongguo de liudong renkou yu fanzui* (Crime and China's floating population) (Beijing: Zhongguo fangzhi chubanshe, 2000).

17. In 1987, the ratio between floating population and permanent population was 22.03 percent in Beijing, 26.18 percent in Shanghai, and 33.21 percent in Guangzhou. See Cheng Li, "Surplus Rural Labourers and Internal Migration in China," in *Migration in China*, ed. Børge Bakken (Copenhagen: NIAS Publishing, 1998), 48.

18. See John van Kesteren, Pat Mayhew, Paul Nieuwbeerta, *Criminal Victimisation in Seventeen Industrialised Countries: Key findings from the 2000 International Crime Victims Survey* (The Hague: NSCR, Wetenschappelijk Onderzoek—en Documentatiecentrum, 2000).

19. Zvekic and Del Frate, *Criminal Victimisation in the Developing World*, 79.

20. Barclay et al., "International Comparisons," 17.

21. For discussions on sexual incidents in the ICVS report on China, see Zvekic and del Frate, eds., *Criminal Victimization in the Developing World*, 19, 41, 73.

22. Josine Junger-Tas, Gert-Jan Terlouw, and Malcolm Klein, eds., *Delinquent Behavior of Young People in the Western World: First Report of the International Self-Report Delinquency Study* (Amsterdam: Kugler Publications, 1994).

23. Wu Qingxiang, "Riben, Meiguo, he wo guo Shanghai diqu qingshaonian cuicuo yuanyin de bijiao fenxi" (Comparative analysis of the origins of criminal mistakes among youth in Japan, the United States, and the Shanghai area in China), in *Zhongguo qingshaonian fanzui yanjiu nianjian 1987* (Beijing: Chunqiu chubanshe, 1988), 540–44.

24. *UN Global Report 1999*, 16.

25. Zhigang Wei, *A Comparative Study of Juvenile Delinquency and Juvenile Justice in Shanghai, China and Brisbane, Australia* (Ph.D. dissertation, Griffith University, Brisbane, March 2002): 117. In this survey, theft was divided into different categories. Shanghai youth reported somewhat higher participation rates in illegal activities than in the 1987 survey, but the rates were still extremely low on an international comparative scale. In terms of theft, 0.7 percent had "stolen parts from a car," 0.5 percent had "stolen a bicycle or parts," 0.7 percent had "stolen an amount less than 10 yuan (about U.S.$1.25)," 1.9 percent had "stolen 10 yuan or more," and 0.5 percent had "stolen from machine."

26. Fan Zaiqin and Wang Hui, "2001 nian de shehui zhi'an" (Social and public order in 2001), in *2002 nian: Zhongguo shehui xingshi fenxin yu yuce* (2002: Analyses and forecasts of the social situation in China), ed. Ru Xin, Lu Xueyi, Li Peilin (Beijing: Shehui kexue wenxuan chubanshe, 2002), 221.

27. See Mike Maguire, "Crime Statistics, Patterns and Trends: Changing Perceptions and their Implications," in *The Oxford Handbook of Criminology*, ed. Mike Maguire, Rod Morgan, Robert Reiner, 233–91 (Oxford: Clarendon Press, 1994).

28. See Roger Hood and Richard Sparks, *Key Issues in Criminology* (London: Weidenfeld and Nicolson, 1970), 15–18

29. Mark Findlay, *The Globalization of Crime*, 144.

30. On the Xiao Li case, see *Zhongguo Funübao*, which had several entries on the case over a two-month period during November and December 2001. See in particular the Thursday column *Funü quanyi* (Women's rights). I am indebted to Tamara Jacka for leading me to this source.

31. Quoted by Michael Dutton, "Reflections on the Reform Years." XXX

32. Dai Yisheng, *Zhian celun* (On public security strategy), (Chongqing: Chongqing chubanshe, 1994), 5.

33. Here the degree of accuracy was listed at 48 percent. This information is based on Zhigang Wei's interview with Dai Yisheng; see Wei, *A Comparative Study of Juvenile Delinquency*, 21.

34. 2001 nian quan guo gong'an jiguan li'an de xingshi anjian fenlei jingji bao (Classified statistical index on overall numbers of criminal cases in China registered by the public security organs in 2001), *Gongan yanjiu,* no. 6 (June 2002): 95.

35. Jon Vagg, "Policing Hong Kong," *Policing and Society,* no. 3 (1991): 235–47.

36. See Dane Archer and Rosemary Gartner, *Violence and Crime in Cross-National Perspective* (New Haven, Conn.: Yale University Press, 1984).

37. Eric A. Johnson and Eric H. Monkkonen, *The Civilization of Crime* (Urbana: University of Illinois Press, 1996).

38. The aspect of transition is important here. More stable, cohesive *Gemeinschaft*-type societies based on tighter norms and informal social and normative control might have less crime than modern *Gesellschaft*-type societies although they have a less developed legal structure. Violence levels, however, are not proven to be lower in more traditional or "tight" societies. On the contrary, overall they seem to be higher in traditional settings. See Nils Christie, *Hvor tett et samfunn?* (How tight a society?), vols. 1 and 2 (Copenhagen: Christian Ejler's Forlag, Universitetsforlaget, 1975), (in Norwegian). See also Johnson and Monkkonen, *The Civilization of Crime.*

39. Jan J. M. van Dijk, "Does Crime Pay? On the Relationships between Crime, Rule of Law and Economic Growth," *Forum on Crime and Society* 1, no. 1, (February 2000).

40. In thirteen of the sixteen countries where the survey was conducted, less than 0.5 percent had experienced incidents of corruption over the preceding year. See van Kesteren, Mayhew, Nieuwbeerta, 2000, 37.

41. Zvekic, Del Frate, *Criminal Victimization in the Developing World,* 19.

42. He Zengke, ed., *Fubai xin lu* (New path to combat corruption), (Beijing; Zhongying bianji chubanshe, 2002), 52–53.

43. The Committee to Protect Journalists made Jiang Weiping one of the winners of the 2001 International Press Freedom Awards and the *Index on Censorship* magazine declared him "Whistleblower of the Year 2002." See Transparency International: Global Corruption Report 2003, 138, www.Cpj.org/awards01/Jiang.html: and www.indexonline.org.news/20020328_awards .shtml (18 June 2003).

44. For a more extensive discussion on the problems of defining "corruption," see John Gardiner, "Defining Corruption," in *Coping with Corruption in a Borderless World: Proceedings of the Fifth International Anti-Corruption Conference,* ed. Maurice Punch et al., 21–38 (Deventer: Kluwer Law and Taxation Publishers, 1993).

45. The annual Corruption Perception Index (CPI) is a composite index and the best international measurement we have to facilitate research into the causes and consequences of corruption. The CPI aggregates the perceptions of well-informed people and organizations with the regard of the extent of corruption, defined as the misuse of public power for private benefit. The extent of corruption reflects the frequency of corrupt payments, the value of bribes payed, and the resulting obstacle imposed on businesses. The strength of the CPI lies in the combination of

multiple data sources in a single index. Altogether fifteen data sources were used in the 2002 CPI, from nine different institutions: The World Economic Forum, the World Business Environment Survey of the World Bank, the Institute of Management Development in Lausanne, Pricewaterhouse Coopers, the Political and Economic Risk Consultancy in Hong Kong, the Economist Intelligence Unit, Columbia University, Gallup International on behalf of Transparency International, and Freedom House's *Nations in Transit*. The Bribe Payers Index (BPI) rates the likelihood that companies will pay bribes when they do business abroad. While the CPI concentrates on corruption in the public sphere, the BPI is the only major survey to track corrupt practices among international businesses. The BPI, however, is still in its infancy and, like all measures of corruption, should be used with caution. See Johann Graf Lambsdorff, "2002 Corruption Perception Index," in *Global Corruption Report 2003*, 262–65, and Frederik Galtung, "2002 Bribe Payers Index," in *Global Corruption Report 2003*, 266–67.

46. Transparency International, *Global Corruption Report 2003*, 264–65. The Corruption Perception Index (CPI) aggregates the perceptions of well-informed people with regard to corruption, defined as the misuse of public power for private benefit. See explanations of methodology, 262–63. www.globalcorruptionreport.com

47. Transparency International, *Global Corruption Report 2001*, Regional Report on East Asia and the Pacific, 11.

48. Hu Angang, "Fubai: Zhongguo zui da de shehui wuran" (Corruption: China's largest social polluter), in *Zhongguo: Tiaozhan fubai* (China: Fighting against Corruption), ed. Hu Angang, (Hangzhou: Zhejiang renmin chubanshe, 2001), 34, 61.

49. van Dijk, "Does Crime Pay?" 2–3.

50. *Xinhua News Agency* (28 April 2000), in *SWB-FE*/3486 (1 May 2000): G/4.

51. Sixth United Nations survey of crime trends and operations of criminal justice systems covering the period 1995–1997, Table 1.01 1–2. See also Kam C.Wong, "Policing in the People's Republic of China: The Road to Reform in the 1990s," *British Journal of Criminology*, 42, no. 2 (Spring 2002): 282.

52. In most developed countries we have numbers for "security personnel" working outside the police force. In China, however, we do not find such descriptions for people working on security in the work units. They are simply listed as administrative personnel without further specification.

53. See "Zhi'an guanli gongzuo" (Public security management work), in *Zhongguo Falü Nianjian 1996*, (Beijing: Zhongguo falü nianjian she, 1997), 167–68. Michael Dutton quotes the 1998 number from interviews with the head of the Beijing Private Security Company, August 1998. See Michael Dutton, *Policing the Chinese "Political": A History of Socialist Policing in China*, (Durham, N.C.: Duke University Press, forthcoming).

54. *BBC Summary of World Broadcast* (11 Dec. 2000), *SWB-FE*/4020, G/6–7.

55. See *UN Global Report 1999*, xvi, 121–51.

56. Wilbur Miller, "Police Authority in London and New York City, 1830–1870," *Journal of Social History* (1975): 81–101.

57. Zhao Bingzhi, Tian Hongjie, "Chuancheng yu chaoyue: Xiandaihua shiye zhong de Zhongguo xingfa chuqantong kaohe" (Inheriting and transcending: Examining the Chinese criminal law tradition from the viewpoint of modernization), in *Jujiao faxue redian* (Focusing on the hot topics of law) ed. Zhao Xianglin, (Beijing: Beijing falü chubanshe, 2001), 369–83 (374).

58. Jiang Zemin, speech at the meeting celebrating the 80th anniversary of the founding of CPC (Zai qingzhu Zhongguo gongchandang chengli bashi tongnian dahui shang de jianghua), (1 July 2001), in English and Chinese, *Beijing Review* no. 28, (Documents, part one), (12 July 2001), xiii–xiv.

59. *The Criminal Law and the Criminal Procedure Law of China* (*Zhongguo renmin gongheguo xingfa, Zhongguo renmin gongheguo xingshi susong fa*), (Beijing: Foreign Languages Press, 1983), 32 (English) and 86 (Chinese).

60. Wang Dawei, "Cong Ganshiqiao moshi dao shijie jingwu gaigede da qushi" (From the Ganshiqiao model to the trends of world policing reform), *Gong'an daxue xuebao*, no. 2, (2000), 1–15 (2).

61. H. L. Fu and D. W. Choy, "Policing for Profit: Fiscal Crisis and Institutionalized Corruption of Chinese Police," in *Corruption, Policing, Security and Democracy*, ed. S. Einstein and M. Amir (Huntsville, Tex: Office of International Criminal Justice (OICJ), 2003).

62. *BBC Monitoring Asia Pacific— Political* (20 June, 2002). "Top Security Official Calls for Tighter Discipline by the Police," *Zhongguo Xinwen She News Agency*, Beijing (19 June 2002).

63. On the situation of official campaigns to "purify" the police force, see Fan and Wang, "2001 nian de shehui zhi'an," 226.

64. The number of lawyers is not developing at the pace one should expect. In 1985, officials talked of training two million lawyers, a million judges, and a million defense lawyers, but the numbers were instead cut down to 150,000 lawyers by the end of the century. It was still no more than 100,000 in 2000. See Laszlo Ladany, *Law and Legality in China: The Testament of a China-Watcher* (London: Hurst, 1992), 102; and Jasper Becker, *The Chinese* (New York: The Free Press, 2000), 329.

65. Susan Trevaskes, *The Culture of Criminal Court Work in China: A Study of Grassroots Justice in Baotou, Inner Mongolia*, (Ph.D. dissertation, School of Asian and International Studies, Griffith University, Brisbane, 2001), 216–17.

66. Kanishka Jayasurya, "Corporatism and Judicial Independence within Statist Legal Institutions in East Asia," in *Law, Capitalism and Power in East Asia: The Rule of Law and Legal Institutions*, ed. Kanishka Jayasurya (London: Routledge, 1999), 196–97.

67. See the chilling interview with a former Beijing lawyer thrown in jail and stripped of his position in Jasper Becker, *The Chinese* (New York: The Free Press, 2000), 314–17.

68. Yin Chunli, "shenpan weiyuanhui gaige de shexiang" (Considering reform of the adjudication committee), *Zhongguo Lüshi*, no. 8 (1998): 55.

69. Meng Qingguo, Xiang Yong, "Lun Zhongguo sifa gaige" (On Chinese legal reforms), *Xiandai faxue*, no. 6 (2000): 11–15, 12. Even in Western societies the full independence of the judiciary might be an ideal situation rather than a fact of life. There are, after all, democratic political restraints on the judiciary. See Jonas Grimheden, "Strategies of Reform of the Judiciary in China: One Concept, Two Descriptions," *Newsletter der Deutsch-Chinesischen Juristenvereinigung* 9, no. 3/4 (2002): 114–29.

70. Chen Xingliang, "Xingshi sifa zhidu gaige de lilun sikao" (Theoretical reflections on the reform of the criminal justice system), *Fazhi Ribao* (28 October 1999): 7.

71. Some Chinese scholars challenge the view that Article 12 of the Criminal Procedure Law really represents the principle of the presumption of innocence (*wuzui tuiding*). It is rather talk of a "guilt by court decision" (*zui cong panding*) according to one legal scholar, advocating a change of the Criminal Procedure Law to include a proper representation of the presumption of innocence. See Zhou Guojun, "Yanjin xingxun bigong ruogan wenti tantao" (Inquiry into several issues concerning the prohibition of extorting confessions by torture"), in *Jujiao faxue redian* (Focusing on the hot topics of law), ed. Zhao Xianglin, 426.

72. Chen Xingliang, *Dangdai Zhongguo xingfa xin jingyu* (The new horizon of contemporary criminal law in China), (Beijing: Zhongguo zhengfa daxue chubanshe, 2002), 1–3.

73. *Xinhua News Agency* (5 August 1999), in *SWB-FE/*3607 (7 August 1999): G/7.

74. Just one among many reports states that "the provincial authorities (in Hebei) punished a number of . . . legal cadres and policemen, who tailored the law to suit their selfish ends and abused power for personal gain." *Hebei ribao* (13 June 2002): 2 in *Beijing Monitoring Asia Pacific— Political* (6 July 2002).

75. For an account of American entrepreneurialism and crime see Daniel Bell, "Crime as an American Way of Life," chapter 7 in *The End of Ideology* (Glencoe: The Free Press, 1962), 115–36.

76. Even in the Netherlands, a country of generally low-level violence, the homicide rate has risen steeply after the country has become a center for organized drug and prostitution syndicates.

77. *The Criminal Law of the People's Republic of China, Zhongguo renmin gongheguo xingfa*), (Beijing: Zhongguo fazhi chubanshe, 2000), 250–51.

78. *South China Morning Post* (25 April 2002): 9.

79. Xiaowei Zhang, "The Emergence of Black Societies Crime in China," *Forum of Crime and Society* 1, no.2 (December 2001): 53.

80. Professor Kang Shuhua is president of the Chinese Criminological Society, while Professor Jiang Lihua is vice president of the China State Academy of Procurators. See: *BBC Monitoring Asia Pacific—Political,* (8 April 2002). "Chinese Criminology Society President Warns on Criminal Underworld," Zhongguo Xinwen She broadcasting, in Chinese (5 April 2002).

81. In the heat of a campaign, however, it is always tempting and easy to overinterpret the level of organized criminal activity. Despite increased stress on the "accuracy" of the campaign's legal

procedures, there is every reason to believe that the very structure of campaign-style policing works against this ideal. A good sign in this regard is the emphasis the president of the Supreme People's Court, Xiao Yang, gives to "accuracy" when dealing with the campaign. Accuracy, Xiao claims, should be the top priority of all the people's courts in the "strike hard" campaign. This requires accurate assessment of evidence, strict observance of legal procedures, and adequate adjudication of all cases. See: *BBC monitoring Asia Pacific—Political*, (4 April 2001). "China to intensify enforcement of Jiang Zemin's anti-crime "strike hard decree."

82. van Dijk, "Does Crime Pay?" 10.

83. van Dijk, "Does Crime Pay?" 9–14. Post-socialist Russia is caught in this trap between market economy and a legal structure in transition, followed by increasing corruption and tendencies towards organized and violent crime.

84. For instance, the United States experienced through "Operation Graylord" that there were close connections between organized crime and the judicial system which was heavily involved in corrupt activities and crime. Here investigation successfully prosecuted and put in jail more Illinois sitting judges than any other state in U.S. history, including a corrupt Chief Judge.

85. van Dijk, "Does Crime Pay?" 1–11.

86. *UN Global Report 1999*, xvii, 191–221.

87. See the discussion by Chris Bramall, "The Quality of China's Household Income Surveys," *The China Quarterly* 167 (September 2000): 689–705. For an even more detailed account of the measurements of inequality in China, see Carl Riskin, Zhao Renwei and Li She, eds., *China's Retreat from Equality, Income Distribution and Economic Transition*, (Armonk, N.Y.: M. E. Sharpe, 2001).

88. According to incomplete statistics from the Ministry of Public Security on serious crimes solved in September 2000, organized criminal groups were involved in 22 percent of serious robberies and abduction cases, 16 percent of the serious thefts, 9 percent of the rapes, and 6 percent of the homicide and bombing cases in China. See *Chinese Law Network, Cases October 2000*, quoted from Zhang, "The Emergence of Black Societies Crime in China," 64. In addition comes the rapidly rising numbers of drug crimes.

89. More police obviously would not stop corruption. In the ICVS it was found that government officials and the police were the most corrupt groups dealt with by the public. See van Kesteren et al., *Criminal Victimisation in Seventeen Industrialised Countries*, 37.

PRISON AND PUNISHMENT IN TRANSITION

A Question of Difference: The Theory and Practice of the Chinese Prison

MICHAEL DUTTON AND XU ZHANGRUN

To tell the story of the Chinese reform-through-labor prison system, one must constantly read between the lines. Until recently, those lines seemed clear enough. On the one hand, dissident critics of the reform-through-labor or *laogai* system, such as Hongda Harry Wu, compared the Chinese penal sector to the Soviet Gulag or to the Nazi concentration camps. It differed from these two precursors only insofar as it added another level of humiliation upon the hapless criminal. Where the Soviet and Nazi systems meted out brutality, the Chinese system married that brutality to economy. "The products of the prisoners' labor are sold in domestic as well as foreign markets and have become an indispensable component of the national economy" claimed Wu.[1] Mainland academics and advocates would, of course, deny the brutality. As for the links between punishment and economic production, however, they would not only plead guilty to the charge but would regard the linkage as the system's saving grace. For the intellectual doyen of the reform-through-labor system, Li Kangtai, it is the prisoners' engagement in the labor process that enables their reform. "Dialectical materialists," Li informs us, "consider productive labor to be the most basic social practice .... thought transformation, therefore, is inseparable from productive labor."[2] Ultimately, Wu and Li represent the either/or positions of a political two-line struggle. Their black and white contrasts are, however, increasingly being rendered gray by a new body of scholarship that attempts to challenge their claims empirically.

The most influential work in this regard is by James Seymour and Richard Anderson.[3] They puncture the starkness of these two accounts by empirically detailing the nature of the reform-through-labor sector. Their empirical work suggests that neither Wu nor Li's account is entirely accurate when one looks on the ground. In contrast to Wu, they argue that penal labor in China is far from profitable, suggesting instead that it is a net drain upon rather than a benefit to the national economy.[4] While their work offers a devastating critique of Wu, it offers little comfort to scholars such as Li Kangtai. Indeed, in pointing to the rising recidivism rates in the era of economic reform,[5] their work casts doubt on the whole ethos underpinning reform through labor. Labor reform, it seems, is increasingly unable to reform the criminal.

It is not the intention of this chapter to adjudicate on the debate between Wu and his jailers nor to follow Seymour and Anderson and claim that we can offer a more "objective" formulation of the nature of *laogai* by looking at what is happening on the ground. Instead, we want to interrogate the continued discursive power of labor reform in the penal sector in China. We want to come to some understanding as to why thought and labor reform in China remains the guiding ethos of the system: why it can and has been read either as a crime against humanity (Wu) or as humanity's savior (Li).

To appreciate the Janus-faced quality of labor reform, we begin by establishing a clear theoretical link between contemporary Chinese penal labor and thought-reform strategies and early Western reformist penal agendas. This link is vital both for an understanding of the positive claims made about reform through labor and for an appreciation of the regime's ontological claims about it. Nevertheless, there is another, unconscious, indigenous tradition that we argue undercuts these positive evaluations and leads back to a revanchist view of penal labor.

In contrast to Li Kangtai's reading, then, we would suggest that the Chinese prison system is much less a "socialist new thing" than he imagines. It is, in fact, an amalgam of traditional methods and values wed to a Marxist theoretical framework. In reference to Harry Wu's work, we would suggest that the Chinese system is much more closely tied to Western penal endeavors than he would care to admit. We propose that the contemporary Chinese penal system has drawn on a legacy that is both indigenous and imported. While Dutton has dealt with the influence of Western penology and Soviet theory on the Chinese prison system in great detail,[6] far less has been written in English on the traditional indigenous technologies, methodologies, and values that have helped frame Chinese penal discourse. For that reason, we lay greater stress on elucidating this component of our argument. Having discussed some of the influences that have helped frame the labor- and thought-reform programs within the prison, we will then move on to examine the problems these programs have encountered in the period of economic reform.

The labor- and thought-reform programs were crucial in framing the success of the Chinese penal system in the early period of the People's Republic, but they have proven less resilient in the period after 1978 when free-market economic reforms robbed them of much of their moral resilience. Moreover, these economic reforms also radically reformulated the social landscape, producing a very different life-world to that which supported the reform-through-labor programs in the earlier era. Modernization and economic liberalization ripped into the traditional social fabric and induced the classic symptoms of social dislocation, namely high labor mobility, rising unemployment, rapid inflation, rising rates of crime, rising recidivism rates, and so forth.

This changed social landscape produced what Chinese police have long described as the most serious crime wave in China's contemporary history.[7] This not only resulted in a crisis in policing but also precipitated a flow-on effect in relation to penal strategies. Despite these huge social changes, the policing and penal strategies still cling to some of the key values and aspirations of prereform China.[8] Reforming the policing and prison system to cope with the new postreform conditions has therefore been very much on top of policing and penal agendas in recent years. This crisis, combined with a desire to outflank Western human rights groups and combat the claim that China's reform-through-labor prison system was simply "slave labor," culminated in a new law in December 1994 which replaced reform-through-labor laws with a new prison law. From this time onward China had a prison system, not a reform-through-labor system.

What we would like to suggest, however, is that the most significant reform to the penal system in recent years has not been in its change of name nor even the internal reforms this change encouraged. Rather, the reform of the penal sector ushered in during the Deng and post-Deng era, we believe, is significant not so much within the prison system itself, but in the "carceral spread" one notes around it. In an attempt to remedy many of the newer problems facing law enforcement agencies, new institutions are emerging or older carceral ones are redefined or reestablished. What we discover then, is an institutional "widening of the net." To understand the social dynamics that have resulted in these changing penal practices requires knowing more than the history of, and influences upon, the prison system itself. It requires knowing a little about recent social history and social change within which penal practices are framed. It is in the last part of the chapter that we will examine the social conditions that have led to prisons being "augmented" by other forms of detention.

This chapter begins by tracing the various theoretical traditions that have fed into contemporary Chinese penal discourse. It then explores the social crisis that has forced a series of reforms to the system. What we conclude is that contemporary economic reform penal strategies are neither the complete and systematic "brainwashing" machine that Wu would have us believe nor the perfected and advanced transforming mechanism of Li Kangtai's vision. Instead, we present a picture of an institution that is being buffeted by the winds of change and has adopted a series of ad hoc measures in order to cope. No longer part of an overall social enterprise, the Chinese penal sector now sits uneasily, and far less successfully, among a panoply of strategies designed to combat crime.[9]

The various attempts to reform inmates through labor are increasingly rendered impotent. The various methods designed to imbue a selfless socialist work ethic among prisoners seem strangely arcane in a period when the dominant social ethos presents material accumulation as glorious. While the penal regime has attempted to reform its education programs, it cannot shake off its attachment to a Marxist-inspired frame of reference. As the penal and policing regimes reform their past punitive strategies, they institute reforms that look strangely reminiscent of past solutions and bygone eras. Chinese penal strategies show a poverty of imagination that is perhaps best explained in the words of Marx himself, and it is therefore to Marx that we will turn in order to begin this genealogy of Chinese prison theory.

CHINESE PENAL DISCOURSE: LABOR REFORM

"The beginner who has learned a new language," says Marx, "always retranslates it into his mother tongue."[10] In China, the language of economic reform introduced in 1978 is the "new language," while the language of Marxism, which has been spoken since 1949, is the "mother tongue"—albeit one spoken with a strong Chinese accent! These are the two "languages games" within which most of the changes in this sector have taken place. Every reform undertaken within the penal sector in recent years seems to be transcribed into the mother tongue of Marxism and, through this, into the paradigm of reform through labor.[11] The strength and resilience of this paradigm should not be underestimated, but neither should it be simply thought of as the power of Marxism in China.

Clearly, this idea of reforming a subject through labor has Soviet and Marxist roots, but it also has a much older pedigree. The "magical power" attributed to productive activity upon the mind of the worker was not simply a product of Marxist theory or Soviet practice. Such thinking had its roots in the nineteenth-century wedding of positivism and utilitarianism that gained its clearest expression, in fact, in the early Western reformist schemes of punishment. Such schemes targeted the criminals' souls through a disciplining of their bodies. Bentham, more than any other, summed it up in the expression, "grind the rogues honest." Yet as has been argued elsewhere, such Benthamite "dreams of criminal conversion," while largely abandoned in Europe, were reborn in the unlikely setting of socialist China under the Marxist-inspired banner of reform through labor.[12] In China, then, this idea of labor as educative was a Western epistemological import. Significantly, it was an import that arrived on Chinese shores long before the revolution and certainly prior to any Soviet influence.

In the dying days of the nineteenth century, the last dynasty of China, in a desperate bid to modernize and "appear civilized," imported a whole range of new technologies and methods from Western countries.[13] One such idea was that of reforming criminals through labor. While the Nationalist Party that subsequently ruled China until 1949 picked up on the idea of reforming the criminal mind, it was only with the communists that "thought reform" and "labor reform" (as opposed to penal labor) were wed.[14]

Contemporary mainland Chinese texts on economic activity within the penal sector make clear the high valuation Chinese Marxism places on the concept of labor as transformative. Indeed, in contemporary Chinese analysis, labor is said to have a twofold effect involving both a transformation of raw inanimate materials and a cognitive transformation of the labor force.[15] In theory, at least, reform through labor should have little to do with the recruitment of a slave labor force as Harry Wu suggests. Rather, it is in theory based upon the proposition that productive labor has a positive cognitive value upon laboring subjects. Organized engagement in large-scale productive labor offers the prisoner the same organizational conditions that produced the proletarian subject. Seen in this light, one could read the inclusion of the products of prison labor in the state economic plan after 1956 very differently to the way Wu has done. Rather than being yet another device to further exploit the hapless criminal, it was, in theory at least, predicated upon a belief that the move would help transform the nature of prison labor. With prison production being incorporated into the central plan, the predominantly handicraft-based production of the prisons could give way to large-scale manufacturing or farming, and it was these latter forms of production, it was thought, that would ontologically transform the prisoner-worker into a proletarian.[16]

The only problem with this theoretical argument, however, is that it flies in the face of a large body of empirical evidence that suggests labor is indeed used as punishment within the Chinese penal sector. This has prompted most Western commentators to discount the worth of reform through labor as an ideology within the penal sector. For Seymour and Anderson, for example, the ethos of reform through labor, if it was ever effective, has long since disappeared under the pragmatic pressures of the economic reform era. We have reached the "end of ideology" as increasing demands for higher production within the penal sector wipe out any vestiges of a reformative ethos. Harry Wu is even less forgiving. For him, the fact that labor operates within the Chinese penal sector as a form of punishment does not signal the end of ideology as much as it reveals the communists' true ideological nature. For him, labor as punishment is the denouement of the publicly stated lie that is labor reform. Reform through labor is communist "doublespeak" for revanchism. Ideology is not dead; it is merely disguised.

Like Wu but contrary to Seymour and Anderson, we do not believe ideology is dead. Nevertheless, we would acknowledge that it is increasingly compromised as the era of economic reform develops. Contrary to Wu, we do not believe that labor reform is merely a "smoke screen" disguising the true "revanchist" ideology of the Chinese prison. Rather, we would suggest that no matter how one reads penal labor, it is always underpinned ideologically. That is to say, while Marxist ideology largely informs the publicly articulated view of labor as reformative, long-dormant tendencies from within Chinese tradition reify the contrary idea of labor as punishment. While this traditional ideology of labor as punishment is never articulated publicly, it still operates at an unconscious level to habituate certain patterns of thought and these then influence action. Such congealed, unconscious traditional values, we would argue, have radically undercut the high Marxist valuation of labor. They have the power to do this, we would suggest, because as Sun Xiaoli notes, one of the things that separates Chinese Marxism from its non-Chinese erstwhile forms is the vibrancy and strength within it of traditional Chinese culturalist values. Read as one moment in the "sinification of Marxism," this particular "tradition," when coupled with tendencies within Marxism to transform all issues into questions of "class struggle," leads away from that definition of labor offered in Chinese Marxist texts.

Shadowing the idea of labor as transformational is a far more arcane indigenous idea that penal labor is lowly and humiliating. It is at this point one discovers that Wu's idea of labor as punishment, while never adequately theorized in his work, is nevertheless not totally without foundation. It is in the ambivalent way in which prison labor is understood—consciously as transformational, unconsciously as punishment—that we can begin to understand the gap that separates Wu from Li. It also enables us to understand the resilience of this particular revanchist discourse. Reform through labor satisfies both revanchist and reformist constituencies. It operates like a bad penny with both sides reinforcing its value. Within China itself, however, this idea of labor as punishment is the side of the coin that always remains face down. Once again, to even see its presence, let alone understand its significance, we must read between the lines. We must return to the question of language and focus on those aspects of the word that its translation into the English word "labor" leaves out.

"When we learn to speak, we learn to translate" writes Octavio Paz: "The child who asks his mother the meaning of a word is really asking her to translate the unfamiliar term into simple words he knows already."[17] In explaining the task of a translator, Octavio Paz likens the process to child rearing. We are forced, he says, back to a "simple language." But as Paz goes on to note, even "simple words" are inadequate when it comes to cross-cultural understandings. Crossing cultures, he observes, still leaves an "inexorable foreignness" to the text, even in the best translation.[18] At least part of the reason for this, we would suggest, is because a translation cannot carry the etymological vapor trail that informs the meaning of the original word.

Translation obliterates the shadowy etymology that links words to their past meanings. This would be no more than an esoteric academic point but for the fact that such past meanings are all often still active in unconsciously framing the reception of words in their contemporary. The etymology of Chinese words like "labor reform" are quite different to English usages, and to fully appreciate the degree of difference and the power this gives to the other meaning of labor reform, let us return to the word.

There is a long (principally Confucian) tradition in China that separates mental and manual labor and this was largely signaled by class difference. This difference is summed up in the traditional Chinese saying that "those who work with their heads rule while those who work with their hands are ruled." Liang Shuming was insistent, however, that while this traditional Confucian philosophic distinction was always made, it was pragmatic and carried no moral valuation. It was, he insisted, simply the way things were. Indeed, he went on to suggest, in a manner similar to contemporary Chinese readings of Marx, that Confucius held the laboring people in high esteem and people should be solicitous of them and recognize them as the creators of all wealth.[19] While Liang's argument may well be true philosophically, it does little to alter the vernacular association that has traditionally linked physical labor to punishment. Physical labor, in China, has traditionally been regarded as a form of enslavement and disgrace, and this perspective is graphically illustrated in the penal vocabulary that operated in traditional times and which, interestingly enough, is still in use today. By returning to the traditional uses of contemporary words, we are able to see the etymological trail that, we would suggest, still stalks contemporary usage.

The word for imprisonment in contemporary Chinese is *tuxing*. This is a compound made up of two separate characters, *tu* and *xing*. In ancient Chinese, the character *tu* when combined with *xing* had a different meaning, and the character *tu* was often substituted for the character *nu* which had a similar pronunciation but a slightly different meaning. The character *nu* meant "to engage in physical labor." Hence, the compound *tuxing* when read as *nuxing*, translated literally, and continues unconsciously to be read in this way in popular Chinese imaginings, as forced labor undertaken through penal servitude. This association between forced labor and penal servitude was further reinforced by similar associations made in the popular rhyming dictionary of traditional times, the *Yun*. In this text, *tu* was explained as being in correspondence with the character *nu*, that meant enslavement. Such was the power of this form of coupling that it even found its way into the classical legal codes. In the highly authoritative *Tang Dynasty Code and Its Explanation*, the character *tu* was again described as having the character and meaning of *nu*.[20]

Through this association with *nu*, the text asserts, the full implications of imprisonment become apparent: "keeping criminals in conditions of enslavement and disgrace." Because China is a country where the past is revered, these understandings were not confined to the Tang Dynasty but were read into the legal codes of all subsequent dynasties. In this way, these values became part of the legal assumptions of each subsequent regime and part of the assumed cultural coordinates of the entire nation. They became part of that knowledge that, in another context, Paul Veyne once described as "the large zone of the unexpressed" which guides action but that is so deeply assumed it is never articulated or even consciously thought.[21] Penal labor as punishment, therefore, became an unconscious yet widely accepted notion long after the linguistic association between *tu* and *nu* died away. Moreover, it had become such an ingrained association that it was scarred onto the national mind-set and no subsequent reformist agenda was able to fully erase it.

The history of post-1949 penal discourse stands as a testimony to this struggle for erasure. It is a history of a struggle over this word, yet the vapor trails of the past, despite the very best of Marxist intentions, have never cleared enough to allow the "transformationist" agenda to be free of its ugly twin. The history of reform through labor reads like a constant battle between these two meanings. From the early accounts of prisons needing to produce goods in order to survive, to more recent cases of labor being exploited for personal gain, the history of the prison in contemporary China reads like a "two-line struggle" over this single word and its deeper meaning.

More generally, the battle line seems drawn not only between mainland accounts and their rivals, but also within mainland China itself. While the government has always presented the laboring masses as heroic and worthy of emulation, the popular response was always stalking this high evaluation with the tactic of derision and this found expression in both verse and rhyme. The popular expression, "Why must I do this? I am not a prisoner," aptly sums up this popular traditional sentiment that only prisoners should be forced to undertake the most arduous and dirty work, for it is only they who should be subjected to penal labor and servitude. A similar etymological search through China's past reveals that the idea of thought reform is also not really a "socialist new thing."

CHINESE PENAL DISCOURSE: THOUGHT REFORM.[22]

Long before the communists took power in China, the idea of thought reform was present in the moral discourses and "self-cultivating" practices of traditional discourse. Confucian pedagogy, for example, in developing codes for the correct comportment of the "gentleman-sage" (*junzi*) was resplendent with principles and techniques that were designed to bring forth ethical improvement. These principles and practices were largely based on the Confucian principle of benevolence (*ren*) as well as the idea of feeling, sentiment, or emotion (*eqing*). One discovers these ideas reappearing in prison vocabulary in the form of notions such as *ganhua*.[23] This term has no direct English language equivalent but could be roughly translated as "helping people to change through (moral) persuasion" or "setting an example by which to transform people and help them to change." *Ganhua* is a word made up of two parts and it is the different meanings of these two parts that is explored in the classical Chinese text of Character Explanations. In this volume, the term *gan* is said to mean the production of feeling that is powerful enough to move the heart, whereas the term *hua* is rendered as an action or actions on the part of a subject that brings forth change. Hence the term *ganhua* combines the emotional state of bringing forth change with the practical action of a person actually inducing it.

In classical times, it was the gentlemen-sages of Confucian discourse who combined these two attributes. In the practices of self-cultivation they improved themselves, yet in undertaking such a course of self-improvement, they stood as a model for others to emulate. In the contemporary period and within the prison, it is the cadre who occupies this particular role.[24] The prison cadre acts as moral guide and the inmate looks towards the cadre as a model for his or her own transformation. Through *ganhua*, correctional officers utilize the ethical and emotional ties they build up with the prisoner to bring forth a change in the inmate's life perspective.

Hence the idea of reform within the prison operates on a twin register. *Ganhua* and the assumptions upon which it operates are quite separate from those that underpin the Chinese conception of labor. This Chinese concept of labor emanates from the wedding of a strongly authoritarian Chinese "legalist" tradition with a more reformist, but no less authoritarian, Marxian one. The result is a highly ambivalent and often quite unstable notion that can swing from being a concept designed to transform to one being used solely to exploit and punish. For its part, thought reform is much less ambiguous. Based upon traditionally inspired technologies and unconscious cultural assumptions of the officials and inmates, this concept of *ganhua* actually builds on and into the cosmology of everyday life and simply works for its reconfiguration. This point is well summed up in the explanation of thought reform offered by the leading Chinese penal scholars Xu Juefei, Shu Hongkang, Shao Mingzheng, and Yu Qisheng. They explain the process of thought reform as one of "replacement" and they explain it, in part, as being the transformation of criminal forms of brotherhood (*yiqi*) with socialist ones. They illustrate this in the following manner:

> Youthful offenders who have taken the wrong road often do so because they have failed to pay attention to the communist morality of self-cultivation . . . we must begin from the criminals' own situation, inspire and lead them to recognize that their own criminality emanates from their inability to learn communist morality and the morality of the public and that this, in turn, is directly related to the allure of the morality of the exploiting classes and produces the same sense of revulsion. Later, we can gradually lead them to distinguish between civilization and barbarism, between criminal brotherhoods (*jianghu yiqi*) and comradely friendship, between desperadoes and heroes and between the morality of the exploiting classes and that of communism.[25]

What is important to recognize about this prison thought-reform process is how well it is in tune with the everyday cultural assumptions of daily life in China. Mayfair Yang, in her detailed study of social relations in China, believes that this idea of *ganhua*, along with the idea of *qing* or *renqing*—the emotional ties of affect and obligation—and brotherhood or *yiqi* form the basis of most daily social interaction in China and are the pillars upon which contemporary ideas of networking (or *guanxi*), "face" (or *mianzi*), and community are built.[26] It is these types of social emotions that have established the basis for a Maussian type of "gift-like

regime" of networks, friendships, communal ties, and face framing virtually all social and daily activity in China.[27] It is in this form of "group consciousness" that the
idea of *ganhua* can have great play. It can be effective, however, only because of a
radically different form of subjectivity that is operative in China and which, by and
large, is almost wholly absent from contemporary Western society.

While individuality has a high valuation in Western culture and law, it is the
group that constitutes the crucial social unit in China. Indeed the pictograph of
the character for benevolence (*ren*) upon which notions such as *ganhua, renqing*,
and *yiqi* rest, is itself split into two parts that combine to depict both the character for "a person" and the character for the number two (*er*).[28] In other words,
benevolence begins pictographically and often unconsciously from the care, concern, and importance of oneself in relation to others, and it is this that more or
less frames all the technologies for the construction of an ethical self in China.
Confucian patriarchal theory marks out the space where this concern for others
is both produced and perfected and that "space" was, in traditional China, the
family relation "from whence," it was claimed, "all other virtues spring."[29]

Socialist China may rely on other forms of "collectivity" to establish its own
form of social and ethical discourse—and we can see this in the way that the idea
of labor under Marxist influence has indeed traveled—but the continuing reliance
upon the collective nevertheless produces a need/desire to continue the reliance
upon modified forms of traditional social technology. Hence, despite, or possibly
because of, its Confucian nature, the concept of *ganhua* still has considerable purchase within contemporary Chinese socialism. In the contemporary prison where
the ideas of *ganhua* are said to be used to instill proletarian values, it is the prison
cadre and not the gentleman-sage or father who acts as the model of emulation.
The cadres' "proletarian character" and high moral values are said to "act" upon the
inmates to reconfigure their "distorted" sense of social collectivity.

The underlying idea of producing a form of socialist mutuality through collective bonding is then pressed into the service of forcing a reevaluation of the
criminals' life experiences. They are forced to confront their pasts and, through
this, begin to empathize with their victims. Evoking shame is said to be the first
act leading to rehabilitation and to the possibility of recovering a social sense of
face.[30] These techniques are still very much at the heart of the theory of thought
reform in China and, as the above should demonstrate, it is too simplistic to dismiss such processes as brainwashing.

At the same time, one begins to understand that such processes can only operate within a very specific cultural milieu. Yet this process whereby criminals in

China begin to empathize with their victims and through this develop a sense of remorse has, in recent years in the West, attracted a name and that name is reintegrative shaming."[31] The problem is, of course, that such reintegrative shaming strategies are, as the above argument makes clear, culturally specific and cannot be applied easily to societies without the collective customs and traditions that inform them. Moreover, these reintegrative strategies are wholly dependent upon the fact that the values they imbue and the technologies they deploy within the prison have a much wider social resonance. That these social resonances are now being called into question as a result of the 1978 Chinese economic reform program demonstrates that the problem of implementation is restricted to the prison itself.

SOCIAL CHANGE AND PENAL REFORM

In China, economic reform has brought forth a cultural sea change that has led to a questioning of certain aspects of the reform-through-labor ideal. Reform through labor is no longer being reinforced by popular social practices but is, in many cases, running almost in opposite directions to them. As a result of economic reform, there has been a break-up of the collective vision of society. This break-up of the collective vision is not just the growing disbelief in Marxism but has a structural and social expression.[32] The structural and social manifestations of the break-up of the collectivist vision are side effects of the economic forces unleashed by the process of reform. Prereform China had a highly regimented and policed sense of community with strict prohibitions on internal migration reinforcing a traditional, highly sedentary, and stable sense of community. Centralized planning, a high level of state ownership of industry, and an economy organized on the basis of a state plan rather than a market reinforced this and also offered a space for prison rehabilitative programs to stretch beyond the prison and into the community. Local industries were not only ordered to make products for the plan, but they were also forced to take the employees they were allocated by the planners. This included taking back former employees who had committed crimes and had completed their prison terms. The inmates therefore returned to their (social, moral and economic) community, and through reintegrative shaming and a highly coercive program of monitoring and surveillance, they were checked, monitored, and finally reintegrated.[33] The rehabilitative potential of *ganhua* and *renqing*, therefore, went beyond the prison gate and had a central place in post-penal transformational regimes of the work unit and the community. Post-reform China has robbed the prisons of these conditions.

First, there has been a massive growth in non-state-sector employment and that is, by definition, exempt from these sorts of commitments. After 1956, virtually all private-sector enterprises were nationalized and campaigns in the 1970s against "bourgeois tails" mopped up those that were not. Economic reform set about to undo all this, and by 1990 it had succeeded in reducing state ownership of industry to little over half (54.6 percent to be exact) of all enterprises, with this sector's production accounting for only 39.3 percent of all goods produced.[34] This new private sector was free to produce what it liked and hire whom it wanted. The result was that the buried forms of social discrimination suffered by ex-inmates surfaced overtly and they were once again discriminated against when it came to employment.[35]

Second, even state-sector enterprises have been buffeted by the cold, hard economic winds of change. Economically this was reflected in the reorganization of enterprises away from planned goods produced through a state quota system and toward goods made for the market. Between 1979 and 1990, the state radically cut the number of industrial products produced under quota from 120 to just 60. It also cut the amount of state-designated materials and finances from 256 items to just 27. At the same time, the Ministry of Commerce cut the number of products from 188 to just 24.[36] This cutting of quotas was a way of cutting enterprises loose. If an enterprise no longer produced goods for the plan, then its survival was not guaranteed by the planners but depended upon its own profitability. Profitability, in turn, demanded an examination of how things were produced, not simply what was produced. So began a series of other reforms that ended up giving these enterprises more managerial freedom and, most importantly, maximizing the conditions for profitability. Once these were experimented with successfully in non-plan-producing state enterprises, even the enterprises producing for the plan were reorganized in this way. This liberalization process culminated in the passing of the enterprise law by the State Council in July 1992. This law gave the enterprise managers the right to hire and fire wage labor as they saw fit. In giving managers this power, the state effectively offered managers in this sector the same "rights to manage" as existed in the private sector. Thus state-sector industry, concerned with profit and efficiency and fearful of trouble or loss, now had the power to refuse prison requests for reemployment of ex-inmates.[37]

The passing of this law was but the final nail in the coffin of the old, post-penal rehabilitative strategy. Prisons no longer had the collective capacity to place criminals back into their own communities. Yet the dreams of an imagined rehabilitative community structure still haunted penal authorities. Thus while prison officials speak of "reform" and in "the language of the new era," their dreams are of the past and how to recover it. Under this banner of reform, the search for a post-plan rehabilitative strategy began. It took the form of a disparate set of experiments that shared little in common other than a new language of professionalism and an old dream of rehabilitation and transformation. Part of the problem of reform for the prison was that it required a move beyond Marxist and Chinese traditions, yet the language and conceptual framework to enable this leap did not exist. The result, then, has been the production of a range of ad hoc reform solutions and experiments that are still very much written in the mother tongue of Marxism or China's past, and cannot adequately cater to the new situation China faces.

One example of this poverty of reconceptualization is found in one reform strategy being experimented with which attempts to establish a localized and privatized version of the employment conditions that had once existed in the era of the central plan. In a number of important experiments, prison management started setting up their own local enterprises to employ ex-inmates and thereby give them an opportunity to reintegrate.[38] Such enterprises are only operating on a very limited scale and it is doubtful whether they will become a feature of the "post-reform-through-labor" scenario. The problem for them, of course, is that they must compete economically in the marketplace and there are some crucial factors that militate against their success. First, the quality of their ex-prisoner labor force is well below that of an ordinary workplace,[39] yet in times of economic reform they must still compete on an open market. Second, these enterprises are "halfway houses" in so far as they train the ex-offenders and then encourage them to find employment elsewhere. Thus even if the quality of the labor force were to improve, the very nature of these enterprises militates against maintaining a stable and well-trained labor force. Lastly, there is the ongoing problem of stigmatization, which is regarded as one of the crucial issues blocking rehabilitation.[40] It was this stigmatization that forced the establishment of these enterprises, but that only delayed rather than solved the problem. Ex-inmates can find limited employment and training opportunities in such workshops and factories, but they must eventually leave and find employment elsewhere. Given that potential local employers generally know that these firms are centers for retraining ex-convicts, the problems of stigmatization appear once again, but this time in relation to ex-employees of these particular enterprises.

The high financial costs involved in setting up these enterprises, coupled with the difficulty prison authorities have in placing ex-convicts in ordinary enterprises, have led the Ministry of Justice to experiment with other post-release rehabilitative employment strategies. One such alternative strategy is to subsidize the ex-inmates' re-entry into society by sponsoring them as "individual traders." Indeed, the level of stigmatization suffered by ex-convicts in this shaming society can be gauged, to some extent, by the fact that "the vast majority of all recently released prisoners are going into business" for themselves.[41] Yet the high rates of bankruptcy in this sector, coupled with the fact that prison rehabilitative ideology suggests that it is the individual entrepreneurial ethos that has led to the decentering of socialist ethics and the rise in crime, make this rehabilitative strategy no less problematic than the setting up of enterprises. Free traders are also highly mobile and this, in turn, undermines the ability of policing agencies to survey and monitor ex-convicts. Given that the reintegrative strategies turn, in part, on heavy surveillance, the necessary mobility of the ex-prisoner turned free trader is also a problem that this strategy faces.

In prereform China, an extremely low recidivism rate was achieved, in part, by the tight demographic policing of the population. In post-reform China, the conditions for this generalized tight demographic policing have evaporated.[42] Traders need to go to their supply sources and to markets, labor is needed in city construction, and business people require fluidity and mobility. All these factors militate against the past practice of tight demographic policing. The state, therefore, needed to relax the tight demographic policing arrangements to allow the economy to develop. They did this but attempted to exempt certain types of people they were suspicious of or those whom they wished to continue to monitor and control. This group, known within policing parlance as the "focal population" (*zhongdian renkou*), was the focus of special police attention and continued restriction. This focal population consisted of a range of different "suspicious characters," but one group definitely included in their number was "those who had been released from reform-through-labor units, reform-through-education institutions, and criminal detention centers."[43] For those within this focal population, special case files were opened and tight controls over movement from one jurisdiction to another put in place. Beginning in May 1982, the Ministry of Public Security placed great weight on the policing of this group of people yet left the process of checking to individual police stations to determine. At the same time, however, they insisted that the handling of the focal population should be one key determinant in assessing the local police stations' overall performance.[44] The result was highly contradictory.

The police stations' performance assessment was based on the successful policing of this population, yet resources were scarce and stations understaffed. Moreover, conditions had so changed and police powers and abilities in this area so declined that the force was simply no longer able to institute tight demographic control over even this small fraction of the population.[45] The results were therefore mixed. Irrespective of the rate of success, one thing was clear: this attempt at tight demographic policing of the focal population ran in the face of the Ministry of Justice's new rehabilitative strategies, which either sent the ex-criminal on the road as a small-scale entrepreneur, or sent him on the road in search of work.

The economic reform program has, therefore, eroded the structural bonds that tied communities together which, in turn, produced the space for *ganhua* to operate beyond the prison wall. Essentially, it meant that the traditional reintegrative space that was once occupied by the ex-convict was no longer available. At the same time, economic reform brought forth such large-scale cultural change that even the internal operation of the prison's own rehabilitative program ran into problems. Economic reform introduced the idea of individual profit, and this not only made many of the models and ideals propounded in the prison education program redundant, but it also led to an erosion of the high moral standing of the cadre. This has occurred, in part, because corruption within the penal sector has become, as one Chinese commentator recently noted, quite "commonplace."[46] This fall from grace of the prison cadre seriously threatens the entire internal rehabilitative program for, as noted above, this program rests on the idea of *ganhua* that, in turn, necessitates a positive cadre-model to emulate. It is for this reason that the whole issue of raising the quality of cadres in the prison sector has become such an important issue in recent years.[47]

In addition to the emergence of corruption within cadre ranks, economic reform has also introduced the profit motive within penal enterprises, and this gives new life and an economic motivation to the old, traditional revanchist view of labor.[48] As noted earlier in relation to public enterprises, economic reform has led to greater enterprise autonomy and corporate responsibility over profit and loss. Prison enterprises have not been exempted from this trend. They, too, have come under similar sorts of pressures to make themselves more economically viable. To promote economic efficiencies, reform of penal enterprises and industry has been undertaken. There is now much greater managerial autonomy within the prison enterprises and a more generous remuneration of profit. These two factors reinforce a prevalent view that penal labor is the repayment of a social debt and not a mechanism of reform. Moreover, it increases the pressure to drive workers harder and, while this has been offset by the greater respect for prisoner rights that have emerged in post-reform China, this tendency is nevertheless all too apparent.[49] These new pressures emerge directly out of the economic rationalist logic that has been imposed on the prison sector. In the post-economic-reform period, the prison sector receives only part of its running costs from the central government. The rest must be made up out of its own productive activity. This has proven to be quite difficult for both the prison factories and farms.[50]

In relation to prison factories, the difficulties are fourfold: First, the state no longer provides the raw materials for production and these must, therefore, be bought on the open market at market prices. Second, the number of prisoners far exceeds the demand for labor within the prison enterprises, leading to underemployment and hidden subsidies.[51] Third, because the prisoners' skill base is low and equipment antiquated, the quality of goods produced is not good and it is difficult to find markets for prison-made products outside the state sector. Fourth, the prison units are not ordinary productive units and incur a range of additional costs for things such as inmate supervision, training, and so forth that other factories do not have to face, and these must be factored into the cost of their operations.

The problems are even greater if one turns to the prison farms. Since the early 1950s, about half of all prisoners have been located in this sector. Because they have always operated under the principle of avoiding competition with local people, prison farms were, from their inception, established in areas that are very backward, poor, remote, or difficult to farm. This meant that most farms were established in remote, backward, and thinly populated provinces or autonomous regions. Indeed, the vast majority of prison farms are located in the western part of the country in provinces such as Qinghai, or in the autonomous regions such as Xinjiang and Inner Mongolia. This makes economically viable cultivation almost impossible. Quite apart from the quality of the land, there are few people in these regions, even fewer markets, and high transportation costs.[52] Prison farms have therefore contributed greatly to the hardship of the entire penal economy. As economic reform develops, the declining profitability of this sector becomes more and more acute. Since 1990 in particular, the profit from prison production has turned to loss and this has induced what one report described as a period of "extreme economic hardship" within the prison sector as a whole. In 1980, eighteen provincial and city prison authorities reported profits in excess of ten million *yuan*, and only five provinces and areas reported losses. By 1990, there were only three provinces and cities recording profits in excess of ten million, and twenty-three provinces, cities, and areas recorded losses. Moreover, over half of these loss-making authorities recorded losses in the "tens of millions." The result has been a reversal of the order of the slogan, "reform first, production second," as prison enterprises desperately try to make themselves profitable once again.[53]

In essence, the problem the prisons currently face is that the cold winds of economic reform have begun to steer the collectivist thought-reform strategies aground while simultaneously reinforcing certain aspects of the traditional revanchist notion of penal labor. While this takes place behind prison walls, outside the prison the post-release rehabilitation programs have also run into problems and they have attempted to recover by a process of piecemeal experimental reforms.

All these problems within the prison take place at a time of massive changes in the nature of crime, the "culture of crime," and the profile of the criminal.[54] The rising recidivism rate not only illustrates the problems facing the prisons but, given the very close correlation between recidivism and crime rates in China, the problem of crime more generally.[55] The case statistics collected by the Ministry of Public Security tell a tale of rapidly rising crime with an average rise in cases of 32 percent between the years 1985 and 1991 and a 40 percent increase in violent criminal cases over the same period.[56] By the early "nineties the age of criminals had also begun to drop significantly with somewhere between seventy and eighty percent of all those arrested being between the ages of 14–25."[57] These new criminals are also far more mobile than they were in the past. Indeed, one discernable trend over recent years has been the enormous growth in mobile crime. These criminals are attracted to the richer population centers and along the developed eastern coastal regions, and they now feature prominently in criminal statistics.[58] Furthermore, all criminal activities are tending to be far more serious than in the past, and this is said to be a good indicator of a high likelihood of reoffence.[59]

While these problems are still far from serious by Western standards, the changing cultural and economic landscape, coupled with the inability of prison and policing authorities to halt this growth of crime, has the authorities worried. They look with concern as they see the revival in many of the crimes and misdemeanors that were stamped out after the revolution and suggest that what is currently being experienced is but a foretaste of things to come. As one highly influential text notes,

> In the fifties, our country eliminated such evil things as prostitution, the illegal drug industry, gambling, and the kidnapping and sale of women and children. In recent years, however, such crimes have come back from the dead and could even be said to be flourishing. Hence, we have undertaken to severely crack down on such things, to continuously attack them but even so, we have been unable to bring them to a halt. Part of the explanation for their resilience lies with the influence of foreign things, the allure of organized crime, and the spread of illegal trading,

smuggling and corruption. Another factor is the harmful influences the "trading consciousness" has had among certain people. It has washed away their morality, made them spiritually empty and vulnerable and, in their search for the good things of life, led them to carry out degrading activities. This is an extremely serious social problem, for if a society has these sorts of evil influences, then it will inevitably be from these seeds that crime and illegality will grow.[60]

The inability of the police and prisons to check this growth or turn it around has led to calls for the reform of these two sectors. Yet the reforms that have been instituted on both sides of the prison wall are not only piecemeal but also predicated on the logic and mind-set of the prereform Maoist era. Again, it is language that betrays this.

Innovative policing strategies in the reform era reflect their Maoist past. One key new strategy of policing has been the revival of the Maoist "campaign," but this time to use the technology against target crimes. Another reform has been to call for a strengthening of the mass-line approach to policing.[61] Detention strategies, too, display a similar romance with the stable Maoist past of the 1950s, and this is reflected in the resurrection of a range of institutions that have, in effect, seen a spreading of the carceral net. Like the police, the "penal remembrance" of the Mao era is not a clear, articulated, and unified vision of how society should be (although it is unconsciously built on recognition of this). Rather, it is an ad hoc and targeted series of responses to a number of problem crimes and misdemeanors. Just as police have targeted key areas (the eastern coastal regions and the cities) and suspect groups (the so-called focal population),[62] detention has "spread" to aid police work. Here one finds that, along with the prison sector, a shadow economy of detention has developed to deal with some of these more troublesome problems now encountered in a country undergoing economic reform. The detention sector is neither as well regulated nor as well funded as the more developed and formal penal sector. In many respects, it is like the police response to targeted crimes: a "severe strike" that is ad hoc in nature and punitive in character. Moreover, it is built upon and reflects the thinking of a bygone era. Such practices emerge, in part, from the experiences of the immediate post-liberation period when vagrancy, prostitution, and drug taking were a problem the communists inherited from the old regime and, in part, from the institutions set up to deal with political offenders in the 1950s. From these two strands has developed a somewhat ramshackle collection of institutions, some under the Ministry of Justice, others under the Ministry of Public Security, that are concerned less with thought or labor reform than with controlling and punishing the felon. These institutions have emerged, not because of the omnipotence or despotism of the Chinese state, but rather because of the state's inability to effectively control things. This has led to something of a governmental panic and this is reflected in the series of ad hoc institutions that have emerged to deal with specific types of crime. It is to this carceral spread that we will now turn for it is, to our mind, this sector that constitutes one of the most important and yet rarely discussed effects of economic reform on the penal sector.

CARCERAL SPREAD

Incarceration in China is divided into two forms: the detention sector and the prison sector. Unlike the prison sector, detention falls within the purview of the Ministry of Public Security. Unlike Western lockups and watch-houses, Chinese detention centers can hold more than just suspects; they can also hold convicts. Three types of detention centers exist. These are the *juyisuo* which are like local jails, the *jiuliusuo* which are like city versions of the *jiyisuo*, and the *kanshousuo* which are like a watch-house or lockup. There is a huge overlap in their responsibilities and all three tend to be used both as lockups and jails. Indeed, convicted criminals on minor offences that are sentenced to two years or less of incarceration can actually end up doing their time in the *jiuyisuo* rather than the prison. Generally, however, such centers are used to detain those who have been charged but not yet convicted. Detention in the *jiuyisuo* runs from fifteen days to half a year. In the *juliusuo*, suspects are generally held for no more than fifteen days, while in the *kanshousuo* they can be held for up to ten days prior to charges being laid, and then three months if charged.[63] Apart from this form of short-term detention, there are also other forms of incarceration that lie outside the prison sector proper. These are for people who have committed no breach of the criminal code but whose actions or attitudes are in breach of certain administrative regulations. There is, then, a distinction between administrative and criminal detention.

In Chinese law, there are two types of detention: one is administrative detention, where the detainee receives labor education in a reform-through-education institution, while the other is criminal, and the prisoner undergoes labor reform within the prison sector proper. Since 1983, both the prison and the reform-through-education institutions have operated under the Ministry of Justice. The differences between the prison and reform through education are, in theory at least, quite significant. Actions that warrant detention for labor education are those which are regarded as insufficient to warrant a criminal charge being laid but serious enough to require "transformation."

Criminals have penalties imposed by the courts on the basis of the criminal code and sentences can range from between one year to life imprisonment. Generally, within the prison sector, those incarcerated for ten years or more or those regarded as "sensitive prisoners" go to prison, while light offenders go to prison camps.[64] In contrast, labor education is a noncriminal administrative sanction imposed by a reform-through-education management committee, and while it leads to punishment, it does not result in a criminal record. The administrative regulations allow sentences of up to three years, with a possible fourth year extension. Sentences are imposed by a reform-through-education management committee that is made up of people from the local Party and government, the procurate, and the police. The history of reeducation through labor is different from reform through labor insofar as it emerged from a different set of needs and at a different time than the prison sector.

Basically, education through labor emerged as a device of the Maoist political campaign.[65] First muted in 1955 by the Party Central Committee in its "Instructions on Completely Wiping Out Hidden Counter-Revolutionaries," reform through education formally came into existence in August 1957 with a State Council "Decision" on problems in reform through education.[66] The main source of inspiration for this system came from Mao Zedong, who wanted a way to transform the ideological outlook of political opponents.[67] It is therefore not surprising that the first uses to which reform through education was put were in relation to the rightists rounded up in the anti-rightist campaign of the late 1950s. In the anti-rightist campaign of the late 1950s, large numbers of people, particularly intellectuals, were found to have "incorrect thoughts" that required attention. While they were political "deviants," their errors were regarded as being insufficient to warrant a charge of "counter-revolutionary criminal" being laid against them. The idea behind the reform-through-education system was to introduce a form of political reeducation that would offer a nonstigmatizing space different from, but with the same aims as, the more draconian reform-through-labor system. So began reform through education.

Until 1983, reform through education was administered under the reform-through-labor system. Both of these were then transferred from the Ministry of Public Security to the Ministry of Justice and, after that, they slowly separated. From 1985 onwards, official sources insist they were completely separate, although other sources raise some doubts about this.[68] This separation allowed for different financial arrangements to be made between labor education and reform through labor. From this time onwards, internal conditions within reform through education began to improve. Unlike the prison sector, that must provide for some of its own costs, reform through education has its facilities fully provided by local authorities and the rest of its needs fully financed by the central government.[69] Nevertheless, the reform-through-education units are a cause of concern, given the less stringent demands over evidence required for one to be interned. Hence reform through education has proven an increasingly useful device in the targeted, "flexible" campaign style of policing that has been the hallmark of the Chinese police since 1978.

With post-reform legal developments hardly keeping pace with the changing face of crime, administrative detention, including the reform-through-education system, has proven to be a convenient mechanism. The committees that have the power to sentence people to periods of detention are not independent of the police. Hence incarceration in a reform-through-education institution can offer the police an "easy option" when dealing with many of the newer, more minor problems they face. While police "colonized" the Maoist political technology of the campaign and transformed it to cater to the new post-economic-reform demands, penal authorities "colonized" reform through education and transformed it so that it, too, was better suited to the needs of the police. A system that began life dealing with minor political offenders shifted its target in post-economic-reform China to petty criminals. Inmates were no longer political deviants with "bad thoughts" but targeted "bad characters" caught in the sweep of the police campaign.

Administrative incarceration also offered the regime another advantage. Along with a range of other noncriminal forms of incarceration, reform through education has until quite recently drawn much less Western attention than the significantly larger and better-known reform-through-labor prison system. Incarceration of minor offenders in a reform-through-education institution, therefore, allows at least some of the negative consequences of economic reform, which are highly embarrassing to the regime, to remain less visible. Why are the negative consequences of economic reform so embarrassing? To understand this requires some understanding of traditional Chinese notions of face and law as well as an understanding of Chinese socialism.

Face, in China, as mentioned earlier, not only operates at an interpersonal level, but also plays a crucial role in framing all political discourse. Face always requires that the subject be regarded as dignified. Dignity rests with the appearance of being in control. A lack of control is, by definition, a loss of face. This conceptualization of governmental face is reinforced by the Chinese legalist tradition. This traditional legalist theory suggests that good government is strong government. Legalist theories of government posit the idea of a strong, strict state and suggest that the strength and endurance of good rule lies in its ability to force compliance. This traditional discourse feeds directly into contemporary socialist notions of the "people's dictatorship" and Party rule. Face, in this context, becomes the ability of the state to ensure not only adherence to its rules and laws, but also to its dreams and imaginings. Crime not only disrupts the rules and laws of the state, but threatens its dreams also. This is because until very recently, Chinese socialist theory posited the belief that socialism cannot spawn crime and must lead to its eventual eradication. The development of socialism should signal a declining rate of crime. The current rising crime rates gravely embarrass the Party and rob it of its socialist face.

Framing the problem in terms of socialist face helps to account for the rationale behind the crisis mentality that has enveloped government as police and prison strategies fail to halt the growth of crime and recidivism. It also helps us understand the way a form of political "utopianism," to use the words of Huang Jingping, Li Tianfu, and Wang Zhimin, can reassert itself in this most pragmatic of spaces. Yet it is this form of "utopian pragmatism," we would argue, captured historically in the low crime rates of the 1950s—and one should remember that in the very year that China declared itself socialist (1956), it had its lowest ever crime rate—and replicated in the belief that socialism eliminates the conditions that spawn crime, that has fuelled the popular political demand for harsher, quicker, and more effective measures against crime.[70] It is against this benchmark that both police and penal authorities have been judged and found wanting. It is also because crime in China is thought of in such politically sensitive terms that it has become such an embarrassment to the regime and is dealt with behind closed doors as quickly and expeditiously as possible. Crime in China is never "common crime" for it always has something of the stigmata of class marking it out. Note, for example, the language used to describe new post-economic-reform crimes by the former Deputy Minister of Public Security, Yu Lei. He talked of crimes in China "increasingly displaying the characteristics of the Western advanced countries."[71] Police campaigns against crime, then, are closer to the political campaigns of old than we might at first imagine. They are still political because as crime increasingly appears Western, it is increasingly characterized as emanating from bourgeois Western thought. Moreover, this way of registering crime not only enables the crime to be read politically, but the action taken against it to be registered politically also. It introduces a kind of utopianism that warrants harshness of punishment in the name of class struggle.

Such utopian pragmatism, we would argue, not only fuels the extensive desire to keep all materials related to this process of policing "classified" and out of the public (and particularly foreign) domain, but it also encourages abuses through the desire to deal with crime in one sharp, harsh blow. It is into this discursive space that reform through education, with its lower levels of evidentiary requirements and procedures and which allows for "fast-track" incarceration, proves a useful adjunct to a police force committed to campaigns designed to "speedily and harshly" stamp out crime.[72] Indeed, the whole of the noncriminal administrative detention sector has become something of an incarcerating adjunct to the flexible police campaign style of targeting particular types of crime and criminals.

It was used in the 1983 "severe strike campaign" against street crime despite the fact that the criminal code had been modified to allow for easier arrests, prosecutions, and incarcerations of targeted offenders. In the three and a half years (August 1983 to January 1987) that this campaign was run, some 1,647,000 counterrevolutionary and criminal cases were mounted, 1,772,000 criminals detained, and 322,000 people sent off for reform through education while 15,000 juveniles sent off to juvenile detention centers.[73] Reform through education was used even more extensively in the early days of the 1989 campaign against the "six evils" of prostitution; producing, selling and disseminating pornography; kidnapping of women and children; planting, gathering and trafficking in drugs; gambling; and defrauding people by superstitious means. By 1990, over 213,000 cases had been opened and 770,000 people charged. Of these, 6,129 were given criminal sentences, 5,650 were sentenced to reform through education, and the remaining 536,000 were punished under the public security regulations of the administrative law.[74]

The flexibility of the campaign style of policing seems tied to a new way of using this more "flexible" penal space. Yet while both policing and administrative detention are fuelled by a utopian desire to eliminate crime, their methods have actually resulted in dystopic abuse. One must be concerned by a penal regime that offers flexibility to the police that is based primarily upon a lack of strict legal regulations covering its operation. Yet this is precisely the advantage detention centers operating under the administrative regulations have. When particularly troublesome forms of offence do emerge—for example the newly targeted areas of illegality such as prostitution or transient crime—they are dealt with by detention in centers operating under the administrative and not the criminal code. As a result, quite apart from the reform-through-education institutions, there are at least two other forms of detention that have been established or reestablished in recent years which appear to be governed by no legislation other than the public security regulations within the administrative code. These two institutions are the shelter and investigation centers and the "forced educational measures" taken against prostitutes.

SHELTER AND INVESTIGATION CENTERS AND THE "FORCED EDUCATIONAL MEASURES" TAKEN AGAINST PROSTITUTES

The shelter and investigation centers began life in the early 1960s after the famine pushed large numbers of peasants into the cities despite the tight internal migration laws. These institutions were used specifically to offer short-term shelter and repatriation of peasants who had illegally entered the cities in breach of the internal immigration rules. They were set up on the basis of a 1961 internal document entitled "Forced Labor and Investigative Detention." In the period of economic reform, with greater internal mobility, this basic document has been augmented with further, more elaborate sets of rules and regulations. On 1 November 1978, a document entitled "The Public Security Ministry Notice Concerning the Rectification and Strengthening of Investigative Detention Work in Relation to Fleeing Criminal Elements" was put into effect. Later, further clarification and detail came from a National People's Congress directive of 2 February 1980 entitled "A Notice from the NPC Concerning Two Measures United into One to Strengthen Labor and Investigative Detention in Labor Education."

The reasons for such legislative action in relation to shelter and investigation detention centers was because, for the police, these centers were proving particularly useful in the period of economic reform. First, as detention centers they were under police and not Ministry of Justice control. This meant the police had far more power and flexibility over their internal operation than they would have with reform through education. Second, their flexibility was guaranteed by the fact that they were not organized and run through formal laws but through police and ministry regulations.[75] Lastly, because of their history, they were particularly well suited to dealing with one of the key target groups of the post-economic-reform period, the transient criminal. After 1986, the severe strike campaign shifted its focus of attention to transient criminal activity and criminals on the run, and the shelter and investigation center took on a new augmented role: housing suspect transient criminals.[76]

The problem for the police in dealing with transients was obvious to all. The tight demographic policing of the past had given way to much freer movement under the impetus of economic reform. The tight internal migration laws had become something of a dead letter by the 1980s, leading to huge numbers of peasants going into the cities in search of higher-paid work. According to public security sources, there are currently about fifty to sixty million people per day on the road in China and the figure doubles if one includes intraprovincial movement.[77]

Even the most conservative accounts put the figure at forty million with at least half heading into the cities and accounting for around 15 percent of the total cities' permanent population.[78] But even on these conservative figures the perilous nature of the situation for the police is all too obvious. In Beijing, for example, there are over 1,000,000 transients, yet there are only 50,000 beds in hotels and specially designated accommodations. Transients are therefore forced to accommodate themselves either on the streets or illegally, thus increasing the difficulty of policing and reinforcing a social panic that has increasingly seen transients represented as an illiterate, semicriminal population. This popular rendition of the transient is reinforced by police-supported research which not only highlights the connection drawn between transience and crime but goes on to argue that a substantial proportion of city crime is now committed by transients.[79] This research both justifies the harsh ad hoc policing and detention measures taken and ensures popular support for such action.

Because of the large numbers detained in shelter and investigation and because of their lack of a stable financial base for these institutions, they were reputed to be the worst form of detention in China, even by the Ministry of Public Security that ran them.[80] But if conditions within the centers were a cause of concern, so too were the flexible rules under which they operated. A suspect was supposed to be detained for no more than three months, and after this period, was supposed to be released or the authorities were to ask for an extension. But the period of calculation of that three months only began after the verification of the name and address of the detainee.[81] One 1989 study from Hunan reported that approximately 30 percent of the detainees had been held for longer than the stipulated three-month period. Indeed, the study indicated that some detainees had been held for two-, three- and even five-year periods during which time nothing had been done to solve their cases.[82] What it discovered was that these centers were being used as an ad hoc and flexible form of prison for a new type of crime. Indeed, as one examines the targets of police campaigns, one invariably finds that where there is a target group, there is a harsh response built in part on this form of ad hoc detention. Prostitution, for example, is another target crime that has come to the attention of officials in recent years.

With the launching of the six evils campaign in 1989, prostitution fell into this category of a target population. The situation had become increasingly serious over the period of economic reform, especially in the larger eastern coastal cities. Indeed, it was suggested by one source that there were tens of thousands of prostitutes in the province of Guangdong alone.[83] Police response was quick and harsh. In 1981, police were advised to fully utilize the discretionary powers made available to them under the public security management punishment regulations and warn, fine, or even administratively detain offenders.[84] In addition, police could even impose forced reparation on recalcitrants and demand that they undergo medical checks and treatment.[85]

Building on these regulations was a 1983 document (number 23) issued by the Ministry of Public Security, the Party central, and the Women's Federation. This was entitled a "Report Concerning the Resolute Outlawing of Prostitution."[86] In this document police were given regulatory cover for a series of calibrated punishments to be utilized in places where prostitution was rampant. By 1985, documents were already discussing the existence of a new form of detention known as "female education and fostering centers," which, it was claimed, were "designed specifically to educate and raise females who are prostitutes or who have engaged in hoodlumism."[87] By 1987, many of these detention measures were of national significance. In that year, a notice was issued supplementing the reform-through-education implementation methods, and this enabled the police to be more flexible in their response to reoffence. For prostitutes whose activities were regarded as insufficient to warrant criminal charges being laid, but who nevertheless continued to work after police warnings and punishment, detention for education was now the order of the day.[88] These harsher measures involved reviving institutions of detention and education that were once used to reeducate prostitutes soon after liberation. These institutions triumphantly ceased operation in 1956 when China proclaimed itself socialist and simultaneously proclaimed the elimination of prostitution.[89]

The reemergence of prostitution in the post-1978 period of economic reform was yet another "crime" that could be said to have caused Chinese socialism an immense loss of face by depriving it of some of its key moral claims. At the same time, the reemergence of prostitution also offered older revolutionaries, suspicious of the new economic reforms, the chance to claim that the politics of the reform era had eroded the hard-won successes of earlier periods of "true" socialism. This politically charged and highly unfavorable comparison they drew with past "socialist" successes has fuelled the current movement for the revival of early reformative strategies.[90] Hence one finds a return of the post-liberation "women's reform-through-education" centers in everything but name.

Question: Why has it proven necessary to force prostitutes and streetwalkers to undertake concentrated education?

Answer: Among the prostitutes and streetwalkers there are some who cause deep social harm and quite a few of them have sexually transmitted diseases. To get them to abandon their harmful life-style, quite a number of areas have had impressive results by adopting measures to force them to undergo educational transformation. On the basis of experience and [police] regulations, the police, in conjunction with related departments, can get them together and force them to undergo legal and moral education and productive labor and in this way make them turn over a new leaf. Prostitutes can be held in such places for six months to two years and this is a type of forcible administrative education measure. While undergoing education they can also have medical checks conducted and any sexually transmitted diseases cured.[91]

In 1949, the revolution glowed brightly. China had "turned red." In a perverse sort of way, this offered the policing authorities more leeway in dealing with prostitution for no one could doubt their determination to deal it "a final blow." A two-tier system of brothel closure was put into effect at that time. In places of political significance or where conditions allowed, brothels were immediately closed. The women, depending upon the extent of their culpability, were "rehoused and retrained" in women's production education and fostering institutes (*Funü shengchan jiaoyangyuan*) or prostitute retraining centers. In places (Tianjin, Wuhan, Shanghai, etc.) where the material conditions did not permit this, the brothels remained open under a policy known as "first control and then prohibit." This policy continued to be implemented until 1954 when the last brothel was closed and the remaining women sent for reeducation.[92]

In the contemporary period, all brothels are underground and all police suspect. Stories of police corruption are legendary and older Party cadres' criticism vehement. Police no longer have a residue of mass popular faith in their incorruptibility, nor do they have mass political support to help them "control" the problem. Nevertheless, the Party, conscious of its own slipping halo, demands of the police the impossible: bring prostitution to a halt and revive socialist spiritual civilization. While internal corruption and the sheer scale of prostitution make the total eradication of the problem inconceivable, it has nevertheless forced police to take harsh measures and be seen to be acting. Pressed to act, the police have opened detention education centers nationwide.[93] Unlike the immediate years after liberation, however, the police could not afford to wait until they had the physical resources to make them work effectively. Consequently, these centers were opened without the necessary financial support to make them viable. Particularly in the south, where prostitution is quite severe, accommodation is found for the interned in old, worn-out buildings desperately in need of repair.[94] Moreover, because these centers were run "without any clear legal basis,"[95] they were not subject to the same checks as the prisons or the reform-through-education centers. Police, pressed for resources, interned a woman on the basis of little other than a letter from the woman's work unit or from her neighborhood committee, and a woman could be sent to these centers simply because she had contracted a venereal disease.[96]

Pragmatism, pressure, and a fond remembrance of things past have fuelled the carceral spread in post-reform China. Nevertheless, as this spread envelops the society, its failure to halt the drift away from socialist "spiritual civilization" becomes increasingly obvious. As various measures visibly fail to recapture the "glory days" when "over eleven million criminals were successfully reformed, including the successful transformation of Japanese war criminals, Nationalist war criminals, and all sorts of counterrevolutionary and common criminals,"[97] the authorities move from the warm embrace of persuasion and *ganhua* to the cold, steely revanchist solutions offered within the tradition of classical legalism. Legalism dreams the dreams of socialism. It too posits a centralized and strongly obedient society, yet it believes that only by following the rules of the prince can this state be achieved. It is these rules that now turn upon those who are socially marginal. Caught in this ever-expanding but ever-degenerating legalist web are the subalterns: the gypsies, thieves, prostitutes, and pimps that economic reform has enabled, if not encouraged. This, then, is the carceral spread and it is this that constitutes, to our mind, the key element in penal discourse in the post-reform era.

CONCLUSION

There is a character in traditional Chinese philosophy that can mean both reciprocity and yet, in another context, it can mean revenge. In both cases, it is a form of repayment of a debt. In many respects, the Chinese idea of face is similarly constituted. Face is something one is given through reciprocity and something one seeks revenge for if it is not given. Face makes the Chinese reintegrative strategy of *ganhua* possible, but face will also demand its revenge should this method falter. This is because what is at stake with reintegrative *ganhua* is not just the criminal's face, but also the face of the cadre, the police, and the Party.

In the past, in those halcyon days of Chinese socialism, it was through work-ing to reestablish a criminal's social face that the reformative strategies worked so effectively. Guards, police, Party, and felon shared in this process of "giving and receiving face." For the felon face came with social reintegration, while for the cadre, police, and Party, face came in the form of an incontestable slogan: Only socialism can save your soul.

As the economic reform process erodes the conditions that enabled prisoner rehabilitation in the past, the bold claims of socialism's past seem ever more dis-tant.[98] The higher crime and recidivism rates indicate a declining ability to re-store the felon's social face and this, in turn, leads to a loss of face for the prison authorities and, ultimately, the Party. It is because of this that we can understand why, despite what are, by Western standards, very low crime and recidivism rates, the Party feels the urge to hide this new "ugly face" of Chinese socialism by mak-ing much of the information about crime and the penal sector "for their eyes only." Moreover, it is because of the loss of face that this "ugly face" induces and the lack of response of those felons offered face and who do not respond appro-priately, that one finds the reciprocity of past notions of *ganhua* being replaced with more draconian legalist notions of revanchism.

There is a character in Chinese that aptly expresses the Janus-faced message of this gift of face. This is the character *bao*. Under certain circumstances, this char-acter can mean a gift offered in appreciation, while at other times it could mean to extract revenge. This linguistic slip stands as a sign of a much deeper concep-tual slippage that an incorrect response to the gift can bring. If the gift of face, of love, benevolence, and support is spurned, then the face of the giver is lost and revenge sought. *Ganhua, renqing,* or *yiqi* can therefore turn the giver of love and support into the deliverer of retribution.

Here, then, is the secret of face-giving. Without this concept of (social) face, reintegrative strategies could not operate, yet with this concept, the surfaces of consideration extend beyond the inmate and envelop the guard, the police, and most importantly, the Party. Reintegrative strategies that restored the criminal's face also enhanced the Party's. Tied into this weblike relation, prisoner and Party shared the enhancement to face that success would bring, but released a much more destructive impulse when the relation began to fail. It is for this reason that penal discourse in post-liberation China was never simply about *ganhua, renqing,* or *yiqi* but has always been stalked by its authoritarian partner, namely classical legalism. Hence one sees in the current climate a degeneration of the process to the point whereby legalism is considered the only really viable option. Transients, prostitutes, and other subalterns cannot be immediately reformed but must firstly be immobilized and controlled. The carceral spread attempts to still their movement, but in so doing threatens the movement essential for economic reform. This carceral spread, like the idea of face, is caught in the horns of a dilemma. It cannot conceive of success in its strategic field without inducing a massive defeat for the economic reform process. To do this, however, would bring on the ultimate loss of face for the Party and as such, is inconceivable.

NOTES

We would like to express our thanks to the Australia Research Council for help in funding this research. We would also like to thank Li Tianfu who helped research this chapter and Shaorong Baggio, Kaz Ross, and David Martin for help in preparing it for publication.

1. Hongda Harry Wu, *Laogai: The Chinese Gulag* (Boulder, Colo.: Westview Press, 1992), 5.

2. Li Kangtai, ed., *Gaizao jiaoyuxue* (The study of reform through labor education) (Beijing: Qunzhong chubanshe, 1985), 47.

3. James D. Seymour and Richard Anderson, *New Ghosts, Old Ghosts: Prisons and Labor Reform Camps in China* (Armonk, N.Y.: M. E. Sharpe, 1998). Published in Chinese as *Xin gui, jiu gui: Zhongguo laogai ying ji shi* (Hong Kong: Mirror Books, 1999).

4. Seymour and Anderson, *New Ghosts, Old Ghosts*, 210.

5. Seymour and Anderson, *New Ghosts, Old Ghosts*, 199–201.

6. Michael Dutton, *Policing and Punishment in China—From Patriarchy to "The People"* (Melbourne: Cambridge University Press, 1992).

7. Dai Wendian, "Dui Woguo xianjieduan fanzui wenti yanjiu de yixie sikao," (Some reflections on research into current problems of crime in China) in *Zhongguo xianjieduan fanzui wenti yanjiu di yi juan* (Research into the problem of crime in China in the contemporary period, vol. 1), ed. Yu Lei (Beijing: Zhongguo renmin gong"an daxun chubanshe, 1989), 4.

8. To this end, it is interesting to note that some in the Chinese police might still regard the contemporary post-economic-reform crime rate as "abnormal." There have, in the not too distant past, been suggestions that the low crime rates of the early 1950s—a period when the glow of revolution was still fresh and the economy was centrally planned—are the norm and that the police should be working toward a return of these low rates. For more details see Michael Dutton, "Dreaming of Better Times: 'Repetition with a Difference' and Community Policing," *Positions 3*, no. 2 (Fall 1996): 415–44.

9. The number of prisoners in the reform-through-labor (or, as it is now called, the prison) sector is hotly disputed. Harry Wu suggests there are three to four million prisoners in the labor camps alone; see Wu, *Laogai*, 11. These figures are substantially greater than the official figures. The 1992

Australian Human Rights Delegation to China was told there were 1.2 million inmates in prisons and camps and 150 thousand people in administrative detention; see *Report of the Second Australian Human Rights Delegation to China* (Canberra: Australian Government Publishing Service, 1992), 21. Official sources interviewed by us also suggested similar figures to those given to the Australian delegation. The prison population was said to be 1.3 million with a further 170,000 inmates in the noncriminal reform-through-education sector (Interview with leading cadre at the Ministry of Justice, Crime Prevention and Reform-through-Labor Research Institute, Beijing, 17/10/93). For more details on the reform-through-education sector, see below.

10. Karl Marx, "The Eighteenth Brumaire of Louis Bonaparte," in *Surveys from Exile*, ed. David Fernbach (Middlesex: Penguin Books, 1973), 143–249.

11. The "prison law" of 1994 is a case in point. As noted earlier, this was the first time since the revolution that the term "reform through labor" was dropped and replaced by the more Westernized expression "the prison system." Nevertheless, despite the abandonment of the expression "reform through labor" as the overall name for the system, this expression is constantly used throughout the new law and remains the guiding principle of the new prison system.

12. Dutton, *Policing and Punishment in China*, 291.

13. It is interesting to read this early adoption of the idea of reforming through labor alongside the recently introduced reformist "prison law." This law, which was passed in 1994 by the National People's Congress, suggests that significant changes are underway within the system. Yet Chinese specialists in the area have insisted to us that while the expression "reform through labor" is no longer used to designate the system, its influence is still great. Moreover, one of the main reasons for changing the name is because of Western misunderstandings about the system (Yang Shiguang; Shao Mingzheng; Sun Xiaoli, Interviews)

14. The nationalist government called their prisons *Ganhuayuan*, or institutes of persuasion. The early penal practices of the CCP in the revolutionary base areas also used this expression. The first communist penal camps were set up in the revolutionary base areas from February 1932 on the recommendation of Liang Botai. These institutions were called institutions of labor persuasion or *laodong ganhua yuan*. See "The Institutes of Labor Persuasion," *Gong'an shi ziliao* 2 (Public Security Historical Materials), no. 6 (1990): 30–32.

15. Wang Tai, "Shilun laodong gaizao de jiben lilun yiju,"(A brief outline of the theoretical base upon which labor reform is founded) in *Laodong gaizao faxun gailun caikaoziliao* (Research materials outlining reform through labor legal studies), ed. Zhao Mingdong, Xu Zhangrun, and Zhu Ye (Beijing: Zhongyang guangbo dianshi daxun chubanshe, 1987), 243–59. Also see *Laigai jingji guanli* (Reform through labor economic management) (Beijing: Quanzhong chubanshe, 1989).

16. Michael Dutton has dealt with this at length elsewhere and tied it back to certain strands in Soviet Marxism. See Dutton, *Policing and Punishment in China*.

17. Octavio Paz, "Translation: Literature and Letters," in *Theories of Translation*, ed. Rainer Schulte and John Biguenet (Chicago: Chicago University Press, 1992), 152.

18. Paz, "Translation: Literature and Letters," 153.

19. Liang Shuming, *Dongfang xueshu gaiguan* (An outline of Chinese arts) (Sichuan: Bashu chubanshe, 1986), 99–103.

20. *Tanglu shuyi* (Tang dynasty code and its explanation) (Beijing: China Publications, 1983).

21. Paul Veyne, "The Inventory of Difference," *Economy and Society* 11, no. 2 (May 1982): 191.

22. This section extends arguments dealt with by Xu Zhangrun in his book, Xu Zhangrun, *Jianyuxue* (Penology) (Beijing: Zhongguo gong'an daxun chubanshe, 1991), 238–65, and also in work he has undertaken with Guo Xiang; see Guo Xiang and Xu Zhangrun, "The Theory and Practice of Criminal Re-education, Training, and Employment in China," in *International Forum on Education in Penal Systems, Conference Proceedings*, ed. Sandy Cook and Bob Semmens, trans. Michael Dutton (Melbourne: IFEPS,1994), 38–48.

23. Indeed, it is worth mentioning that the State Council's "White Book" on *Criminal Reform in China* devotes an entire chapter to the issue of *ganhua* (chapter 5); see State Council, *Criminal Reform in China* (Beijing: Law Press, 1992), 16–18. (Henceforth referred to as the "White Book").

24. The term "cadre" was first used only in relation to active Party workers but has subsequently been expanded to include virtually all government workers. Virtually anyone within the government who is not a manual worker is a cadre of some sort.

25. Xu Juefei, Shu Hongkang, Shao Mingzheng, Yu Qisheng, *Laodong gaizaoxun* (Reform-through-labor study) (Beijing: Qunzhong chubanshe, 1983), 135.

26. Mayfair Mei-hui Yang, *Gifts, Favors and Banquets: The Art of Social Relationships in China* (Ithaca: Cornell University Press, 1994), 119–23.

27. The term "gift" is used here in the Maussian sense. See Marcel Mauss, *The Gift: The Form and Reason for Exchange in Archaic Societies*, trans. W. D. Halls (London: Routledge, 1990). To understand the relevance of this concept in relation to Chinese culture, see Yang, *Gifts, Favors and Banquets*.

28. Xu Zhangrun, *Jianyuxue*.

29. "*Xiaojing*," (The classic of filial piety) in *Shisanjing zhushu* (The interpretation of the thirteen classics) (Beijing: China Publishing House, 1980), 2545.

30. There is little time or space here to go into the intricate nature or importance of face in China. For more details see Andrew Kipnis, "'Face': An Adaptable Discourse of Social Surfaces," *Positions* 3, no. 1 (Spring 1995): 119–48.

31. John Braithwaite, *Crime, Shame and Reintegration* (Melbourne: Cambridge University Press, 1989).

32. On the growing disbelief in socialism and communism and how this affects crime, see Li Junren, ed., *Zhongguo chongxin fanzui yanjiu* (Research into recidivism in China) (Beijing: Falu chubanshe, 1992), 153–54.

33. In post-economic-reform China such practices were continued under the term "controlling the special population," see Yu Lei, ed., *Zhi"an xingzheng guanlixue* (The study of public security administrative management) (Beijing: Zhongguo gong"an daxue chubanshe, 1987).

34. Li, *Zhongguo chongxin fanzui yanjiu*, 145–46.

35. Li, *Zhongguo chongxin fanzui yanjiu*, 134; Wang Wenyuan et al., "Yibu juyou zhongguo tese de chongxin fanzui yanjiu de lilun zhuanzhu," (A specialist theoretical discussion researching the special character of recidivism) in *Fanzui yu gaizao yanjiu* (Research into crime and reform through labor), no. 2 (1993): 6–16.

36. Li, *Zhongguo chongxin fanzui yanjiu*, 144.

37. Guo and Xu, "Criminal Reeducation," 44.

38. Liu Chenggen, "Promote Community Developments, Control Serious Cases of Repeat Offence" (Unpublished paper presented at the International Conference on Education, Training and Rehabilitation of Prisoners in Correctional Institutions, Chengdu, October 1985).

39. Xu, Shu, Shao, and Yu, *Laodong gaizaoxun*.

40. Wang et al., "Yibu juyou zhongguo tese," 7

41. Guo and Xu, "Criminal Reeducation," 45.

42. Along with this have gone the lower recidivism rates. Recidivism is defined as criminal re-offence within a three-year period of release. In an internal document put out to explain to cadres the publicly released State Council "White Book" on the Chinese reform-through-labor system and crime, Wang Mingdi reveals the extent of this rise. While the "White Book" concentrates on the low recidivism rate of China in comparison to the West, Wang charts the rise in the rate in recent years (State Council, *Criminal Reform in China*, 2). Prior to the Cultural Revolution, recidivism rates were around 2–3 percent. During the Cultural Revolution (1966–1976) these rates rose to 8–10 percent and currently stand between 6–8 percent; see Wang Mingdi, "*Zhongguo gaizao zuifan de zhuangkuang" yewu peixun jiaocai*," (Educational materials for professional training on "*The White Book on Criminal Reform*") (Beijing: Falü Chubanshe, 1993), 75. For more details see footnote 22.

43. Yu, *Zhi' an xingzheng guanlixue*.

44. Deng Zhaoren, Yang Weixin, Zhao Fengcan, eds., *Chengxiang Paichusuo yewu zhishi wenda* (Questions and answers to help understand the professional work of rural and urban police stations) (Beijing: Qunzhong chubanshe, 1987), 3.

45. This interview was undertaken with a leading member of the Ministry of Public Security research unit in January 1994.

46. Zhang Peitian, "The Corruption of Chinese Prison Staff and Its Effects on Criminal Re-Education" (Unpublished paper presented at the International Conference on Education, Training and Rehabilitation of Prisoners in Correctional Institutions, Tasmania, November 1995).

47. Zhu Hongde, "Banhao kanwu shi tigao ganjing suzhi de xuyao," (Developing this publication is necessary to raise the standards of the cadre) in *Fanzui yu gaizao yanjiu* (Research into Crime and reform), no. 1 (1993): 1.

48. This emphasis on production at the expense of transformation within the prison system is identified by a number of scholars as a problem leading to a failure of the reform-through-labor program according to Cao Zidan, see Cao Zidan; *Zhongguo fanzui yuanyin yanjiu zongshu* (A summary of research on the causes of crime in China) (Beijing: Zhongguo zhengfa daxun chubanshe, 1993), 365.

49. It should be added here, however, that there are countervailing trends. The introduction of the 1994 prison law, with its deemphasis on labor reform, would suggest that labor is no longer the focus of rehabilitative attention and is increasingly seen as offering technical training for prisoners rather than spiritual and cognitive reformation. The increasingly Western view of law as a mechanism to ensure rights and responsibilities are recognized is also beginning to find a place in Chinese discourse, largely as an effect of the reform program.

50. Unless otherwise stated, the following points regarding prison factories and farms came from an interview with Li Zenghui and Lu Jialun of the Ministry of Justice, Crime Prevention and Reform-through-Labor Research Institute, 1 November 1993.

51. "*Mao Zedong sixiang guanyu laodong gaizao zuifan lilun de jicheng yu fazhan*," (Mao Zedong thought on carrying out and developing the theory of criminal reform through labor) *Fanzui yu gaizao yanjiu* (Research into crime and reform), no. 1 (1994): 9.

52. "*Mao Zedong sixiang*," 9–10.

53. "*Mao Zedong sixiang*," 8.

54. Crime, according to official statistical accounts and commentaries, has changed dramatically in recent years. In the past, most criminal cases were said to be counterrevolutionary in nature and committed by people from "bad" (former ruling class) backgrounds. In the post-reform era, most cases are motivated by potential economic gain and are committed by young, working class, or peasant males. While one should be wary of relying too heavily on such distinctions, for they are in part an effect of the different taxonomies deployed and different policing strategies adopted, neither should one dismiss the distinction totally. These changes are, in part, a reflection of the changing value systems that have accompanied the economic reform process. As Cao Zidan notes, there has indeed been an attitudinal sea change in recent years that is illustrated rather dramatically in the popular expression, "Being honest is for losers." See Cao, *Zhongguo fanzui yuanyin*, 363. Clearly this is a long way from the socialist ethics the prison sector tries to imbue in inmates.

55. Li, *Zhongguo chongxin fanzui yanjiu*, 130. Nevertheless, one should not exaggerate this problem which, by Western standards, is minuscule. On the basis of a five-year survey covering eight provinces, cities, and autonomous regions (Shanghai, Tianjin, Shandong, Zhejiang, Guangdong, Hubei, Shanxi, Xinjiang) that was conducted between the years 1982 to 1986, the average recidivism rate was found to be 7 percent. A more detailed survey of adult recidivism rates

covering twenty-seven provinces, cities, and autonomous regions puts the rate at 5.19 percent but when added to this "recidivism" in the noncriminal reform-through-education sector, this rises to 6.59 percent. See Li, *Zhongguo chongxin fanzui yanjiu*, 4. While this is remarkably low by Western standards, it masks the sharpness of the rise in recent years. As Wang Mingdi noted, comparing 1990 recidivism rates to those of 1987 reveals a rise of over 61 percent in such cases. See Wang, *Zhongguo gaizao zuifan*, 9. Moreover, an equally worrying trend is the rate of youth recidivism which accounts for 20.54 percent of cases according to Yu Shutong, (Quoted in "Yibu juyou zhongguo tese," 9) and 30 percent and above according to Xu Hanmin, *Renmin zhi'an 40nian* (Forty years of people's policing) (Beijing: Jingguan jiaoyu chubanshe, 1992), 77.

56. Yu Lei, ed., *Zhongguo xian jieduan fanzui wenti yanjiu zong juan* (Research into the problem of crime in China in the contemporary period, summary volume) (Beijing: Zhongguo gong"an daxue chubanshe, 1993), 45. Before 1978 the number of violent crime cases ranged from a low of 180,000 cases in 1956 to 540,000 cases in 1977. On average, the figure hovered between 200 and 400,000 cases. This figure rose rapidly after economic reform was introduced in 1978. In 1979, there were 636,000 cases, while in 1989 there were over one 1,900,000 cases. The 1990s have seen this trend continuing. In 1990 there were 2,216,997 cases while in 1991 nearly 2,400,000 cases; see Yu Lei, ed., *Dangdai Zhongguo gong'an gongzuo* (Contemporary Chinese police work) (Beijing: Dangdai zhongguo chubanshe, 1992), 45, 324.

57. Yu, *Zhongguo xian jieduan fanzui wenti yanjiu zong juan*, 45.

58. Yu, *Zhongguo xian jieduan fanzui wenti yanjiu zong juan*, 342–43.

59. *Zhongguo laodong gaizao* (Research into reform through labor in China) (Beijing: Zhongguo kexue wenxian chubanshe, 1992), 439–40.

60. Li, *Zhongguo chongxin fanzui yanjiu*, 154.

61. Dutton, "Dreaming of Better Times," 415–47.

62. Michael Dutton and Li Tianfu, "Missing the Target? Policing Strategies in the Period of Economic Reform," *Crime and Delinquency* 39, no. 3 (July 1993): 316–36.

63. Interviews, 1992, 1993.

64. Shao Mingzheng, Wang Mingdi, Nui Qingshan, eds., *Zhongguo laogai faxue baike chishu* (Encyclopedia of Chinese law on reform through labor) (Beijing: Zhongguo renmin gong'an chubanshe, 1993), 347.

65. Most of the information given here, unless otherwise stated, comes from an interview with Li Zenghui and Lu Jialun of the Ministry of Justice, Crime Prevention and Reform-through-Labor Research Institute, 1 November 1993.

66. *Report of the Australian Human Rights Delegation to China* (Draft Copy) (Canberra: Australian Government Publishing Service, 1991), 33.

67. Laslo Ladany, *Law and Legality in China: The Testament of a China-Watcher* (London: Hurst and Company, 1992), 115.

68. The separation of the reform-through-labor and reform-through-education programs is debatable, see Ladany, *Law and Legality in China* and Wu, *Laogai.*

69. Interview Li Zenghui and Lu Jialun, 1993.

70. Huang Jingping, Li Tianfu, and Wang Zhimin, "Gong'an guanli xianzhuang," (The situation with regard to public security management) *Gong'an yanjiu* (Public Security Studies), no. 4 (1988): 6.

71. Yu, *Zhongguo xian jieduan fanzui wenti yanjiu zong juan,* 337.

72. This was one of the key slogans of the 1983 "severe strike" campaign.

73. Yu, *Dangdai Zhongguo gong'an gongzuo,* 37.

74. Dai Yisheng and Jiang Bo, "Dongyuan he zuzhi shehui gejie shehui liliang jiaqiang shehui zhi'an," (Mobilize and organize all possible social forces to strengthen public order) *Renmin gong'an* (People's Police), no. 4 (1990): 4–9.

75. *Yushen kanshou gongzuo shouce 3* (Handbook on preparatory investigations and watch-house work, vol. 3) (Beijing: Qunzhong chubanshe, 1988), 234–35.

76. Largely as a result of Western pressure, the system of shelter and investigation was abolished in early 1996. Despite this, the problem of transient crime remains and the abolition was also accompanied by legislation extending police powers of detention. Thus, while the centers have gone, the problem has not, and the likelihood is that the police will simply use other detention centers under their control to house suspected transient criminals.

77. Interview with Zhang Qingwu, 1994. Professor Zhang is the director of the Population Research Institute, China's Public Security University, Beijing. In the interview, Zhang added that these figures could easily be doubled if the definition of transient included interprovincial movement.

78. Xu, *Renmin zhi'an 40 nian,* 136.

79. Yang Wenzhong, Wang Gongfan, "Liudong renkou dui shehui zhi'an de yingxiang,"(The influence of the floating population upon social order) *Gong'an yanjiu* (Public security studies), no. 2 (1989): 52–53. Xu Miaofa, "Cong renkou liudong kan huji guangli tizhi gaige qushi," (Examining the reform tendencies within the household registration system from the perspective of the transient population) *Shehui kexue (Shanghai)* (Social Science), (February 1989): 37–40.

80. *Yushen kanshou gongzuo shouce 2* (Handbook on preparatory investigations and watch-house work, vol. 2) (Beijing: Qunzhong chubanshe, 1985), 188–89.

81. *Yushen kanshou gongzuo shouce 3,* 229–31.

82. Li, *Gaizao jiaoyuxue.*

83. Interview, 17 October 1993.

84. Zhang Sihan, ed., *Liuhai anjian falu shiwu* (Legal materials on cases from the six evils) (Beijing: Zhengfa daxun chubanshe, 1993), 420.

85. *Shehui zhi'an zonghe zhili zhengce fagui huibian* (A collection of rules, regulations, and policies on the comprehensive handling of social order) (Beijing: Qunzhong chubanshe, 1992), 163–65.

86. Zhang, *Liuhai anjian falu shiwu,* 414.

87. *Shehui zhi'an zonghe zhili zhence fagui huibian* (A collection of rules, regulations, and policies on the comprehensive handling of social order) (Beijing: Qunzhong chubanshe, 1992), 119.

88. Zhang, *Liuhai anjian falu shiwu,* 424–25.

89. The Ministry of Public Security, Public Security Historical Materials Collection Research Leadership Small Group Office, ed., *Gong'anshi zhishi wenda* (Questions and answers on knowledge of public security history) (Beijing: Qunzhong chubanshe, 1994), 80. From the time of the communist takeover in October 1949 to the announcement of socialism in 1956, China was said to be in the new democratic stage. While prostitution was said to be eliminated, it was not until 1964 that it was claimed that sexually transmitted diseases had been more or less eliminated in China. See "State Council Notice" (9 January 1986) in Zhang, *Liuhai anjian falü shiwu,* 418.

90. Indeed, some of the notices even begin with a preamble to this effect. See the Ministry of Public Security (10 March 1981) in Zhang, *Liuhai an'jian falu shiwu,* 419.

91. Zhang, *Liuhai anjian falu shiwu,* 413.

92. *Gong'anshi zhishi wenda,* 80; Ma Weigang, ed., *Jinchang Jindu* (The prohibition on prostitution and drugs) (Beijing: Jingguan jiaoyu chubanshe, 1993), 11.

93. *Shehui zhi'an zonghe zhili zhengce fagui huibian,* 142.

94. Interview, 1993.

95. *Shehui zhi'an zonghe zhili zhengce fagui huibian,* 142.

96. Interview, 1993.

97. Zhang Jinsang, "Renquan yu zhongguo tese de laogai gongzuo," (Human rights and the special character of China's reform-through-education work) in Wang, *Zhongguo gaizao zuifan,* 67–90.

98. It is noteworthy, in this regard, how old examples that are no longer relevant still feature prominently in government propaganda. In the State Council's "White Book" on penal reform, the opening remarks feature the example of the successful reform of Japanese war criminals, former Nationalist officers, and counterrevolutionaries; see State Council, *Criminal Reform in China,* 2, but the rehabilitative "community" the prisons have faced since the early 1980s are predominantly young people from "families of the laboring classes" who have committed common, not political, crimes; see "Mao Zedong sixiang," 5.

Sizing Up China's Prisons

JAMES D. SEYMOUR

Popular conceptions of China's system of incarceration have tended to be rooted in the experience of past decades, especially the Mao Zedong era when vast numbers of citizens were rounded up and herded off to prison farms. This has given rise to high-profile allegations that even in recent years China's prison system has held many millions (up to twenty million) prisoners[1] (as well as minimalist estimates of a mere one million). This chapter examines the changes that have taken place in China's prison system in recent decades, and in particular the knotty problem of determining the size of the prisoner population. Resolving this confusion should lead to an improved understanding of Chinese society.

There are a variety of ways that China punishes people convicted of serious crimes. Usually this involves some form of imprisonment. The main prison regime is traditionally known as "labor reform" (*laodong gaizao*, or "*laogai*" for short) and is now officially called simply imprisonment. The word "prison" (*jianyu*) has actually had various and evolving meanings in the Chinese context. It can refer to any unit where sentenced prisoners are kept, most of which were until recently known as labor reform institutions. In the more rural provinces, most prisoners are in prison farms. The term "prison" can, of course, be used in a more limited sense to mean a prison in the usual English sense of the word—a building or building complex. On the other hand, most of the prison farms located in the northwest are not of this sort. Sometimes they do not even rely on surrounding walls; the desert or vast expanses of grassland are barrier enough. Later we shall examine the alternative form of incarceration, "labor reeducation."

How to manage the whole complex system has always been a challenge for the leadership. Long before they came to power, the communists briefly maintained a Soviet-style centralized state security and judicial system in areas under their control. However, they quickly became aware of the potentials for abuse in such a system and how in the long run it was politically counterproductive. Following the demise of the Jiangxi Soviet in 1934, the existing security organ—the State Political Security Bureau—came to be seen as too independent of Party control. Indeed, it had actually infiltrated both Party and Red Army units (in the same manner that Stalin's security apparatus did). Dissatisfied with this situation, the communists allowed the Security Bureau simply to die out. The bureau's cadres served as the "rear guard" for the CCP forces as they fled on the famous "Long March." After arrival in Yen'an, the remnants of the former organization were assigned to other institutions.

Around 1939 the bureau was succeeded by a Social Affairs Department positioned directly under the Party committee at each level. In many areas, with the prison-guard bureaus and security bureaus, it was a case of "same office, two signs." To the extent that these guards and security bureaus were the ones that were actually in charge of the prisons, the result appears to have been a quite decentralized prison system.[2] It remains such to this day. As a result, when it comes to the administration of justice, China must be seen as a collection of largely self-administering provinces, with general guidelines laid down from the center.

In Mao's time, the purposes of imprisonment were as much as anything else political—to safeguard the political power of the leadership. There was much effort to affect inmates' ideology and turn them into loyal citizens. In the 1980s, however, Maoist concepts of thought reform went out of favor, and the authorities began to rethink the *laogai* with its heavy social and financial costs. Now prisons and labor reeducation camps were removed from the jurisdiction of the Ministry of Public Security and transferred to the Ministry of Justice and the provincial justice departments. This reflected an effort to professionalize and "legalize" the system. The new official mind-set was first reflected in changing terminology. Beginning in the first half of the 1980s, some provinces began to use the hitherto little-used term "prison" (*jianyu*). This change did not become widespread until the mid-1990s, when, for example, even *laogai* institutions in the remote northwest were for the first time officially called "prisons" (though the older terminology tended to linger in popular parlance).

CALCULATING THE SIZE OF THE PRISONER POPULATION

China has one of the world's largest prison systems, but that is not surprising given that it is the country with the largest population. To be sure, in the 1950s by world standards the rate of imprisonment was also extremely high. But the prisoner population, which peaked in the 1950s,[3] has since declined, while the overall population of the country has more than doubled.

In the book which was published in 1998,[4] it was estimated that for China as a whole there were about 1,250 prison units (including both *laogai* and labor reeducation) or fewer than half the number that existed in the late 1950s. It now appears that in a sense even the 1,250 figure may have been too high, and that in 1996 the number of units was about 987: 704 prisons (a figure that has remained fairly stable[5]) and 283 labor reeducation camps. In addition, there were 2,004 jails[6] of various sizes, some of which hold sentenced prisoners for perhaps a year.[7] The total number of institutions in which sentenced prisoners could be kept (i.e. prisons and jails) was about three thousand.

Determining how many inmates are in these institutions, however, is still an inexact science.[8] The number of prisoners held between 1949 and 1995 has been officially put at an improbably low "ten million."[9] The total number of prisoners who entered the Chinese prison/labor reform system between 1979 and 1998, inclusive, is officially reported to be 5.92 million.[10] The number imprisoned between 1983 and 1995 is said to have been 3.84 million.[11] But even if we were to give any credence to such figures, how are they to be translated into point-of-time figures? There are various data and methodologies to use in making an estimate. The book emphasized a bottom-up approach, but also looked at the big picture.

Internal sources indicated that the system's overall ratio of custodial personnel[12] to prisoners is no more than one for every five prisoners,[13] and it would appear that there were about 300,000 such personnel in the country.[14] (The government now officially asserts that there are 280,000 "prison policemen,"[15] and the real number is probably not much more than that.) This would suggest an overall population in China's prisons (narrowly defined) of 1.5 million.[16] This is consistent with a figure in an official (internal) document giving the total number of prisoners (including those undergoing labor reeducation) in January 1995 as 1,464,325. Although this is not the whole story, the figure is not altogether without credibility. It is consistent with the earlier conclusion that the total number of prisoners of all types that year was close to two million.[17] In the mid- and late 1990s the prison population (including people in jails, military labor reeducation, national security cases, etc.) seemed to stabilize around this level.

But absolute numbers are less significant than the rate of imprisonment relative to the total population. Of course, some places have had fairly high rates of imprisonment—525 in the Xinjiang Uyghur Autonomous Region (1995 figure). By comparison, the rate for the country was found to have been 166.[18]

The reasons for Xinjiang's traditionally high rate of imprisonment are not hard to find. Although most Chinese convicts are imprisoned in their home province, in the past the more crowded eastern cities and provinces have shipped large numbers of prisoners to China's northwest and northeast. In the case of Xinjiang, most of these transplanted prisoners went into the Xinjiang Production and Construction Corps (or "*Bingtuan*"), a quasi-military, quasi-private economic conglomerate,[19] whose prison system has operated largely autonomously. Another important recipient province has been Qinghai—primarily during the 1950s and early 1960s. But whereas in 1995 this province had 23,000 prisoners, by the turn of the century there were probably no more than 14,500, of which fewer than a thousand were imports from other provinces.[20] Despite its reputation, the size of Qinghai's prison system is now "appropriate" compared to the country as a whole.

This is despite the fact that the prisoner population of the country has also declined. Although reliable nationwide figures on this question are not available, table 5.1[21] illustrates how, at least in some provinces, prisoner populations have declined since the first decade of the PRC. It is assumed that the figures on the left side of the chart represent the approximate all-time highs. The highs were hit in the 1950s everywhere except Tibet, over which the Chinese did not gain full control until 1959. These provinces should not be taken as typical of the country as a whole. In Qinghai and Xinjiang in particular, the percentage drops are extreme due to the past importation of large numbers of prisoners. Still, it can be safely said that since the 1960s there has been a general decline in the prisoner population nationwide, even if it has not occurred uniformly.

What about today? Some areas still have relatively high rates of imprisonment. Aside from Xinjiang,[22] with its imported prisoners, it is likely that Guangdong's rate of imprisonment is far above the national average. Although precise imprisonment figures are not available for the province, Guangdong sentences more than twice as many convicts as do other provinces of similar size. The explana-

Table 5.1.   Prisoner Numbers and Rates of Selected Provinces (per 100,000 population)

Province	Year	Number	Rate	Year	Number	Rate (change)
Heilongjiang	1958	230,000	760			
Ningxia	1965	30,000	2,100	2000	11,500	210 (−90%)
Qinghai	1959	190,000	7,300	2000	15,000	290 (−96%)
Tibet	1961	28,000	2,500	2000	4,500	180 (−92%)
Xinjiang	1956	130,000	2,400	2000	75,000	420 (−98%)
Yunnan	1952	130,000	760	2000	75,000	180 (−76%)

tion lies in the many people who have "floated" into Guangdong from other provinces (so, in a sense, these are also "imported prisoners").

But elsewhere the situation is different, with prisoner populations stabilizing or even declining. The huge province of Sichuan is a case in point. Sichuan "exports" millions of young workers to other areas of China, which results in fewer crimes committed in Sichuan and therefore a lower rate of imprisonment. Thus rates of imprisonment are moving targets, and the picture is very different from one province to another and one year to the next.

So overall the prison population stabilized in the 1990s—despite an increasing crime rate and expanded definitions of what constituted "crime." For various reasons, there simply has been no surge in prisoner numbers. Shorter sentences are being meted out; only those deemed to be the most egregious criminals are now sentenced to long terms. True, the number of prisoners sentenced to more than five years does not appear to have changed much. But an increasing portion of arrests are of drug offenders, who usually do not get long sentences.[23] In general, formal arrests (as distinct from unwarranted detentions) seem to have a stronger legal basis than in past decades. Indeed, in 1998 at least, the procuracy often denied police requests to formalize the arrest of suspects. According to Procurator-General Han Zhubin, this happened in 93,218 instances, where the individual's deeds were deemed noncriminal or trivial. In the cases of another 11,225 people who were arrested, it was decided not to prosecute.[24] The procuracy also "stated its views" concerning the excessively long detention of 70,992 inmates. All of this is tending to keep the number of prisoners down somewhat.

Reducing previously imposed sentences is also increasingly common. People are often released early for "good behavior." Early-release regulations apparently were first codified around 1990.[25] At first the new leniency was only in effect in a few provinces (like Hunan), and on average in 1991 only 1.6 percent of all Chinese prisoners enjoyed early release. But since then commutations have become much more common. This practice is now supposed to benefit a fifth to a quarter of the prison population (which would mean that this many are either released or promised shortened terms), though in 1995 only about half that number (approximately 13 percent) actually enjoyed reduced sentences. The way it has worked is that prisoners accumulate points based in part on the hazards and difficulties of work performed. For example, heavy labor in a dusty cement factory would yield more points than work in a greenhouse. The early release program now seems to be in effect in all provinces (even Tibet[26]), and over the course of the 1990s had an ever-greater effect on the size of the prison population.[27]

In fact, by the year 2002, proponents of law and order seemed to have con-cluded that the trend of reducing the prisoner population had gone too far. Chief Procurator Han Zhubin complained to the National People's Congress that the ef-forts to reduce crime were becoming half-hearted, reflected in local authorities "refusing to place cases on file for investigation and prosecution, fining criminals instead of imprisoning them, and penalizing serious crimes with too light sen-tences." He also noted that there had been 8,548 "illegal" commutations (which the procuracy reversed).[28] Of course, official malfeasance can tend to both increase and reduce the number of people in the prison system. Again, Han Zhubin stated,

> The procuratorial organs . . . have been working hard to investigate and punish po-sition-related judicial injustice, strictly handling, in accordance with the law, judi-cial personnel found abusing power, seeking or taking bribes, prosecuting or sentencing innocent people in violation of the law, releasing detainees without of-ficial approval, commuting sentences for, paroling, or allowing friends or relatives [of prison administrators] to serve sentences outside the prison in violation of the law. In 2001 the procuratorial organs at all levels placed on file for investigation and prosecution a total of 4,342 judicial personnel involved in the above cases.[29]

Clearly, these problems are serious, but since they can cut both ways, it is doubt-ful that they have a large impact on the size of the prisoner population.

One factor that tends to elevate the number of prisoners slightly is the declin-ing escape rate.[30] In 2001 China's top prison official, Du Zhongxing, claimed that the escape rate had dropped to a record low.[31] While Du himself offered no sta-tistics,[32] it had been said that in 1997 the national escape rate was 0.54 per thou-sand, down from 0.82 per thousand the year before.[33] The escape rate is probably higher in labor reeducation camps, which are less heavily guarded. On the other hand, Du Zhongxing also claimed a reduced recidivism rate, which would tend to reduce the prisoner population.

Over the course of the 1990s another development began to affect the number of detainees. This concerns the burgeoning phenomenon of internal migrants (usually peasants staying in cities), most of whom are technically illegal. Many of these people ended up in detention in so-called Custody and Repatriation Centers. Unlike prisons and labor reeducation camps, these were not administered by the Ministry of Justice, but rather by the Civil Affairs bureaus—until 2003 jointly with the Public Security bureaus. For a while, these detainees (whom the authorities did not count as "prisoners") tended to escape attention internationally. In 1989 such detentions numbered about one million. By the year 2000 the number had risen to

3.2 million.[34] This does not mean that the number of prisoners actually rose by this amount because the average length of detention would appear to be 8.3 days. If this is correct, this would suggest that there was an average prisoner count of roughly 70,000.[35] But then something remarkable happened. After "custody and repatriation" received much attention and negative publicity in China and abroad, in June 2003 the State Council put the Civil Affairs bureaus in sole charge, and the abuses which had been taking place (cited were extortion and forced labor) were ordered stopped. Indeed, illegal migrants are no longer supposed to be held against their will, and forcible repatriations are supposed to have stopped. Although at this writing (October 2003) it is too early to discern the actual situation on the ground, it appears that China no longer has this category of prisoner.

The upshot of all these countervailing tendencies is that the overall number of incarcerated Chinese has been fairly stable. The number of "prison" inmates (narrowly defined as those in what used to be the *laogai* system) has been reported in internal documents to be 1.4 million at the beginning of the year 2000,[36] while the labor reeducation system (discussed below) had 271,300. The figures for the beginning of 2001 were similar: 1,418,750 in prisons, 270,000 undergoing labor reeducation. These figures appear to be reasonably accurate, though to arrive at a realistic total number of prisoners it is necessary to add hundreds of thousands to account for various other types of prisoners, especially the detainees in jail (also discussed below). This leads to a total (in 2003) of about two million prisoners/jailees plus about two hundred thousand for quasi-medical detainees like drug addicts and fifty thousand in minor categories.

The rate of imprisonment, then, seems still to be in the general range of 160 per 100,000 population. Should we consider that low, or of gulag proportions? In Stalin's time, the population of the Soviet Gulag can very conservatively be put at around three million,[37] or 2,000 per 100,000 general population (and the rate was much higher at the time of Stalin's death). Two thousand was more than twelve times the current rate in China.[38] Various contemporary comparisons are shown in table 5.2. These figures reflect different years and inconsistent standards, so the table should be taken only as the roughest of guides. Still it demonstrates that in recent years China's prison population, relative to the overall population, has been higher than, but in the same general range as, the world average. It is interesting that the rate is actually lower than the other two ethnic-Chinese lands, Taiwan and Singapore. The China picture, however, is affected somewhat by the high rate of executions, which reduces the prisoner population by at least 5 percent.[39] On the other hand, China is more rural and thus has a relatively low crime rate.[40]

Table 5.2.   International Prisoner Populations (per 100,000 population)

India	25[a]
Japan	37[b]
Germany	65[c]
Norway, 1998	53[d]
Azerbaijan	80[e]
United Kingdom	80[f]
Netherlands	85
World average	105[g]
(China—official figure)	107[h]
China	160–165[i]
Taiwan	187[j]
Singapore	210[k]
South Africa	380[l]
United States	709[m]

[a]Inferred from the total prisoner figure of 231,000 given in Roy Walmsley, Research Findings, no. 88 (Home Office).

[b]*Time* (Asia Edition), October 28, 1995, 21.

[c]*The Economist*, June 8, 1996, 24.

[d]Nils Christie advises that the figure would be 55.95 if those outside ordinary prisons were included.

[e]Figure for 1993 (shortly after the dissolution of the Soviet Union). *The Human Rights Watch Global Report on Prisons* (New York, 1993), 225.

[f]Derived from *The Human Rights Watch Global Report on Prisons*, 241.

[g]Rough estimate for 1986. *The Human Rights Watch Global Report on Prisons*, 127.

[h]The official Chinese government figure for the 1994 prison population was 1,286,000, or "10.7 per 10,000 people." State Council, "Human Rights Progress in China," December 25, 1996, FBIS, June 10, 1996, 29.
     In 1993 China reported to the UN that there were "about 1 prisoner per 1,000 inhabitants," i.e., 100 per 100,000. It appears that 107 has been rounded downward, a common practice.

[i]In our book (Seymour and Anderson, 206 and passim) we put the figure at 166 for 1995. Because the population has increased and the prison population probably has not, I have here slightly lowered the estimate.

[j]Based on year-end 1995 figures, supplied to me by the Taipei Economic and Cultural Office (unofficial consulate), New York.

[k]*The Economist*, June 8, 1996, 24. *The Human Rights Watch Global Report on Prisons* (New York, 1993), 126, gives a figure of 144.

[l]*The Economist*, June 8, 1996, 24.

[m]According to U.S. Justice Department statistics, in June 1994 there were 100,000 prisoners in the United States federal prisons, one million in state prisons, and 500,000 in local jails. (*New York Times*, December 4, 1995, and July 7, 1996). The population of the U.S. at the time was 260,714,000. A more recent figure for the number of incarcerated Americans is 1.8 million for mid-1999. The number 709 is taken from Nils Christie, *Crime Control as Industry* (London: Routledge, 2000), 32.

Another reason why the prison population is levelling off is the changing structure of the Chinese population. With the one-child policy already in force for a generation now, the number of young adult males relative to the entire population is on the decline. Young males of any country are the most likely segment of the population to be imprisoned. China's population has grown by over 200 million during the past twenty years, but this is due largely to lengthening life-spans. This decline in the proportion of young males has reduced the crime rate and therefore the rate of imprisonment.

Although the proportion of female prisoners has risen, the absolute numbers are still not enough to have a substantial effect on the size of the total prison population. It was previously estimated that about 2 percent of all prisoners were female.[41] In recent years, the number of women sentenced for crimes by courts has been increasing—from 3.04 percent (16,734 women) in 1995 to 3.85 percent (20,580) in 1998. Of course, it is not easy to translate such figures into point-of-time prisoner numbers. If women serve about half a year in prison or jail, then the proportion could be as low as 2 percent, but it is probably more than that. In 2002 it was reported that "less than 5 percent" of prisoners were women, occupying twenty institutions.[42] (It might be noted that in the West, typically 2 to 3 percent of prisoners are female.) A major factor in the increase is prostitution (which is primarily, but not exclusively, female). Sex workers are becoming more common in China. In the past most of those convicted were simply sent to general labor reeducation camps. Only a few large cities had special facilities for convicted prostitutes. But with the problem becoming widespread, a national system of reeducation centers (*shourong jiaoyu suo*) have been set up. By 1996 there were 195 of these accommodating the 31,000 arrested women that year. But since most are detained for much less than a year (typically three months), the number of "reeducation" prisoners at any given time would be less than half that.[43]

Many of the female prisoners are drug offenders, a problem which of course also afflicts men. Facilities for males and females have been greatly expanded, and now there is a substantial network of detention centers for drug offenders. In 1995 the national system was comprised of 479 such centers.[44] The previous year a total of 80,000 people passed through the various drug-related detention systems (30,000 labor reeducation, and 50,000 in the others). Since then, these numbers have been increasing, sometimes at an annual rate of 50 percent. According to *Legal Daily*, the prosecution rate in 1997 was about 30 percent higher than that of the previous year, and the arrest/detention rate was up about 58 percent.

ADMINISTRATIVE DETENTION

These drug offenders are examples of people who usually are not tried and sent to "prisons," but instead are held "administratively." China has various forms of administrative detention[45] under which a wide variety of minor (and sometimes not so minor) offenders can be held.

One type of administrative detention is "reeducation through labor" (*laodong jiaoyang*, or *laojiao*), to which frequent allusion has been made. Reeducation through labor is intended for urbanites whose behavior is deemed to have fallen "between crime and error." The roots of this system can be traced to the early 1950s (when the institutions went by such names as "new life schools" and "loafers' camps"); it became formalized and widespread during the anti-rightist campaign of 1957–1958. In January 1958, the State Council issued a set of regulations concerning "rightists" in universities. Of the six categories of dissidents, the most errant of the rightists were to be subject to labor reeducation. Although there was then no formal law on the subject, in August of that year the State Council adopted a brief set of provisions by which petty offenders could be sent to labor reeducation sites.[46] Included in this category were those who did not engage in proper employment, minor "counterrevolutionaries," and "anti-socialist elements." This system survived the Mao era. In the 1980s there were calls for change, but with the 1989 crackdown such voices were muted, and the system persists to this day.

Labor reeducation sentences require little in the way of legal procedures. But whereas until 1979 one could be given labor reeducation sentences of unlimited duration, punishment is now shorter termed and more clearly defined. Compared to the regular prison regime, labor reeducation is supposed to be less onerous (more on this below). By 2001, 3.5 million offenders are said to have been "reeducated" over the years.[47] Between 1983 and 1991 the number sent to reeducation camps was officially put at about 100,000 annually,[48] but one cannot extrapolate from that figure the number of prisoners at any given point in time. Actually the number of reeducation prisoners has fluctuated widely. In 1980 there were about 400,000; after that an effort was made to keep the population smaller and more manageable, and the number has normally been closer to 200,000. At the beginning of 1998 there were officially reported to be 230,000 offenders accommodated in 280 labor reeducation camps (eighty-six of which were exclusively for drug offenders).[49] But because these days the courts are meting out fewer intermediate-length sentences and more shorter sentences, some people who would have been sentenced instead to regular prisons are sent to labor reeducation. Thus, unless the system is fundamentally changed, the labor reeducation population is unlikely to drop much (and if it increases, the above-stated factors will be the reason).

Each province decides for itself what numbers of detainees receive trials before imprisonment and what numbers are sent directly to administrative incarceration. This means that the size of the labor reeducation population is decided by the provincial departments of justice. If a province's labor reeducation system has a large capacity, it is likely that fewer detainees will have the benefit of a trial. Some provinces, such as Guangdong and Liaoning, have very large labor reeducation systems. The situation has been quite different in other areas, such as the province of Qinghai, which has had a vast prison (labor reform) capacity but only one labor reeducation facility.

Although labor reeducation sentences can be imposed by courts, in a great many cases such sentences are imposed directly by the police (*gong an*) without trial. The trial-less portion has varied greatly over time and from place to place, but it is often more than half. Sentences can also be meted by security departments at all levels, including those in the larger work units and provincial justice departments. A "mere" administrative determination can result in terms of labor reeducation of up to four years. Authority to impose these sentences, being widely dispersed, is often abused, sometimes being invoked as part of a personal vendetta on the part of the sentencer.

Like regular prisons, labor reeducation facilities are usually run by province-level departments of justice.[50] Conditions in reeducation camps vary greatly; they are often quite harsh and occasionally brutal.[51] The work is usually agricultural, which is hard on these urbanized prisoners. On the other hand, these prisoners occasionally receive mild treatment. Dissident Liu Xiaobo, on completion of his three-year term, described his labor reeducation near Dalian as quite benign. "The conditions there were pretty good. I could do physical exercise and they didn't make me do much labor. . . . I did a lot of reading, mainly politics and philosophy."[52] But this has hardly been the normal experience.

Labor reeducation is also applied in special situations, such as within the People's Liberation Armed Services (PLA). Labor reeducation institutions for errant soldiers are generally fairly small and are at the "group army" (*jituan*) level. They accommodate disciplinary cases, not serious criminals (who are sent to the regular prison system[53]). The PLA appears to have had fifty to eighty such labor reeducation installations, with the prisoner population not exceeding 5,000.[54]

Despite talk among certain circles of eliminating at least longer-term administrative detention, the national trend at the turn of the century appeared to be to establish more labor reeducation camps and make the system a permanent fixture within the Chinese penal system. The Party has apparently decided that labor reeducation is here to stay.

A more temporary and localized form of administrative detention has been "shelter and investigation" (*shourong shencha*), a practice which was first introduced in 1958. People are not supposed to be sheltered and investigated for more than three months. However, in the case of political prisoners[55] this time limit is often exceeded, and prisoners have been known to be so held for as long as five years. (Chinese law journals have criticized the illegal application of the shelter-investigation detentions.[56]) In the year 2000, 2.9 million people were sheltered and investigated, but because the average duration of such detention was probably a matter of a few months, the number of such prisoners at any given time was perhaps some fraction of a million. The total number of administratively detained people (all categories) probably fluctuates between a half million and a million—usually residing toward the lower end of this range.

POLITICAL AND RELIGIOUS PRISONERS

The vast majority of prisoners are presumed by the government to have committed a crime in the international sense of the word. However, some people are in prison for political or religious reasons. This was especially true in the early 1950s when most of China's inmates were people who had served the Kuomintang or were deemed "counterrevolutionaries" for other reasons. Relatively few people were imprisoned for committing crimes unrelated to politics. This began to change in 1957, and by 1958 there was already a large increase in the number of criminal inmates. Thus in one albeit unrepresentative sample, the proportion of political prisoners declined in the late 1950s to only one-third.[57] Although the portion of political prisoners probably rose during the Cultural Revolution, since then it has declined again. Today actual prisoners of conscience[58] represent a very low percentage of the overall prisoner population, though it is difficult to be very precise about this. While there are surely more political prisoners than the 2,679 imprisoned "counterrevolutionaries" which were officially admitted to in 1995,[59] this figure is probably closer to the truth than the perhaps 600,000 suggested (for the mid-1980s) by one critic.[60] The decline in political imprisonment and the concomitant increase in the working-class portion of prisoners have been accompanied by the near abandonment of the dreaded "class struggle" vehicle for prisoner reform, which itself translates into at least a modest improvement in conditions. At any rate, today politics (in the usual sense of the term) is not a factor in most convictions.

In 1996 the authorities began replacing the concept of "counterrevolution" with a new prohibition against "jeopardizing state security," but this terminological change was not accompanied by any real easing of restrictions on expression or association. Both terms are vague, and can denote nonviolent political critics as well as violent activists and real spies. Certainly the elimination of the crime of counterrevolution has not meant that the concept of political crime is dead. It appears that the semantic step has been taken in part to improve China's human rights image, but also to focus more meaningfully on China's rising crime rate. According to Wang Hanbin, a vice-chairman of the NPC's Standing Committee, "Revision of the crime of counterrevolution is made out of the consideration that China has left the era of revolution to enter the era of construction." Maintaining social order appeared to be a major concern. "Criminal groups have come into being and sometimes commit organized offences, running amok in neighbourhoods, lording it over the people in an area, perpetrating outrages and riding roughshod over and slaughtering people."[61]

In an attempt to gain a better understanding of political imprisonment in the 1990s, we have unearthed some internal statistics concerning counterrevolutionaries and "state security" offenders. It should be noted that the terms are not synonymous. Counterrevolution and counterrevolutionary propaganda used to be separate offences, but by 1996 both were included in the state security category. Furthermore, the figures for state security violators not only omit all other people (nonsecurity defendants) whom we could reasonably deem to be political prisoners, but the security cases generally include only those convicted in a normal court and sentenced to imprisonment for more than one year (in some cases more than two years). Not included are those sentenced by police to labor reeducation or to a term in a local jail. It would appear that, if included, these categories would add at least a third to the total number of people sentenced as security problems. It would increase the total number convicted for broadly defined political reasons in the country by at least 100 percent, and in sensitive places (for example, Xinjiang and Tibet) by 200 to 400 percent. And political detainees (except for a few who benefit from international scrutiny) have generally been less eligible than criminals for commutation or parole.[62]

The rate of political imprisonment among the non-Chinese (i.e., non-Han) peoples of the western half of the PRC is disproportionately high. Each year more than a third of all security cases involve Tibetans and Uyghurs. If Mongols are included, the ratio would be about 40 percent. As a result, it would appear that as many as two-fifths of all PRC political prisoners are Tibetan, Uyghur, or Mongol, even though altogether the three groups comprise only about 1 percent of the PRC's population.

In Tibet, political imprisonment peaked in the mid-1990s. Furthermore, table 5.3 shows that "cases"[63] in the Tibet Autonomous Region (TAR) between 1996

Table 5.3. "Security Cases" in Tibet Autonomous Region

Year	Sentenced Individuals	Sentenced Cases	Rate Per 100,000 Population	Rates (Cases), PRC:TAR
1996	84	38	173 cases	1:96
1997	64	25	114 cases	1:52
1998	44	26	103 cases	1:61

and 1998 were being sentenced on state security grounds at roughly fifty to one hundred times the rate in China proper.

Around the turn of the century the rate of political imprisonment in Tibet did decline.[64] However, prison conditions there continued to be excruciating, with the rate for death-from-abuse (including suicide) running at 1:22 for female political prisoners and 1:32 for males.[65] On the other hand, Tibetan political offenders are more likely to enjoy the "benefit" (if any) of formal judicial proceedings (labor reeducation for Tibetan dissidents having been low). By contrast, judging by the official figures, the rate of political imprisonment among Hans is small—only about one serious case for every eight million inhabitants. Of course, the official figures are misleadingly small but are instructive in terms of the relative rates of political imprisonment among ethnic groups.

Political imprisonment not only varies from province to province, but also, of course, from year to year. Using the data in table 5.4 as a rough approximate for political imprisonment,[66] it would appear that the number sentenced was fairly high in 1986 and 1987 (doubtless in part due to the communists' reaction to ethnic unrest), declined in 1988, then rose in the wake of the 1989 Beijing massacre. After 1991 such political arrests declined, in 1997 reaching half of the 1987 level. By the end of the decade, the crackdown on the China Democratic Party and especially the Falungong spiritual movement certainly resulted in a major increase in the number of prisoners of conscience, involving far more people than even the 1989 post-Tiananmen crackdown. (However, they do not show up on the table because most were not deemed state security cases.) The northeast was particularly hard hit

Table 5.4. PRC "Counterrevolutionaries" or "State Security Criminals"

Year	Cases Received	Cases Sentenced	Individuals Sentenced
1986	391	386	805
1987	372	295	575
1988	214	180	328
1989	572	488	739
1990	716	728	1127
1991	354	413	961
1992	231	253	580
1993	192	187	472
1994	180	180	368
1995	208	208	435
1996	229	221	497
1997	280	271	657
1998	213	208	616
1999	344	248	660

[a]It is unclear whether "counter-revolutionaries" in this instance includes persons found to have engaged in disseminating "counter-revolutionary propaganda."

with Falungong arrests. In the year 2000 in Liaoning province alone, approximately 4,000 were sentenced. This does not include those detained for a short time or only fined. In the country as a whole, the number of Falungong prisoners held between 1999 and 2002 is believed to have been in the tens of thousands.

Although it is difficult to arrive at a total number of political and religious prisoners (the term "political prisoner" defying definition), even the most expansive category would be a tiny percentage of all prisoners. Thus although any political imprisonment at all has a deleterious effect on the life of the nation (it is the linchpin of the communist political order), the phenomenon must be kept in perspective.

Contrary to what has been said by others, it turns out that China's overall labor reform regime is no longer integrally related to China's peculiar political system, but is only a small part of what the system is about. Though political arrests are essential to the communists' retaining their grip on power, this is not the main purpose of the prison system. The overwhelming majority of the inmates of the labor reform and labor reeducation camps are presumed by the authorities (whether correctly or otherwise) to have committed real (nonpolitical) crimes or misdemeanors; few are there under "pretexts."[67]

THE ECONOMICS OF THE SYSTEM[68]

Although not all prisoners in China work, inmates undergoing either *laogai*/ imprisonment or labor reeducation (which together comprise the vast majority of all prisoners) are almost always required to do so. Sometimes the sheltered and investigated also work. Of course, prisoners elsewhere in the world, including many incarcerated in various states in the United States, are required to work, but in China the conditions of work can be extremely harsh. Both defenders and critics of the prison system have often argued that the system has been highly profitable to the state. By official reckoning, between 1947 and 1965 the system earned a "profit" (*lisui*) of thirty billion *renminbi*, or *yuan*, derived from 871 agricultural and industrial units.

But extracting material wealth from prison labor is not as easy as it may sound. To be sure, the labor is virtually free. But there are qualitative and quantitative problems with the labor force. As was noted in a Chinese penological journal, "Convicts working in a labor reform factory are not masters of the enterprise; they are society's criminals, and there is a negative, antagonistic and disruptive side to them." As for quantity, after the Mao era the *laogai* officials had less human resources and material capital with which to work. By 1978 the amount of prison land under cultivation had actually declined by 60 percent compared to two decades earlier. After that, the downward trend in *laogai* output did slow (between the rise of Deng Xiaoping and the anti-crime crackdown which began in 1983, total output declined by only 3.3 percent), but in terms of financial profitability the picture was quite different. By 1983, "profit" had declined 86 percent in five years. After the conclusion of the 1983–1984 crackdown, productivity finally began to climb, but even increased productivity did not translate into high "profit margins," which never even recovered to claimed 1978 levels. Compared with that year, "profit" in 1987 was down 54 percent.

During the 1980s there was considerable experimentation, all in the context of China's new marketized economy. Although, as we noted above, the various provincial prison systems evolved somewhat differently from each other, this does not mean that the provincial administrators have ever been free to conduct business any way they have wanted. They have been under various constraints, and one of these is indeed central policy. At the time of the market reforms in the early 1980s, it was decided that "market principles" should be applied to the entire *laogai*. To facilitate this, prison administration was separated from the economic enterprises. This policy was variously called "separation between prison and enterprise" (*jian qi fenli*) or even "one prison, two systems" (*yi jian liang zhi*). The prison system was to retain "the power of enterprise ownership," while the administrators of the enterprises were to have "the power of management." The prisons would supply prisoners to its *laogai* enterprises on a contractual basis; typically, they would be engaged in basic manufacturing—as distinct from the more refined end-stage operations, which would usually be performed by civilians. These reforms, in the works for years, still appear to be ongoing as of late 2003.[69] In September 2003 they were set to be fully executed (with prisons being completely funded by the government and receiving no funding from the enterprises) in five areas on an experimental basis.[70]

According to national policy, prisoners' standard of living has been governed by various factors: a prisoner's behavior and productivity, his or her needs, and local conditions (prisoners not supposed to be better off than civilians living in the surrounding area). Although the general guidelines were laid down by the center, until the early 1990s any costs not covered by funds generated by prison enterprises had to be covered by local governments. Because the prisons almost always fell far short of being self-sustaining, this meant a heavy burden on local government. Chinese reports on the prison system have been quite revealing about this. A 1989 production report claimed a total agricultural and industrial prison production of over five billion *yuan*, and yet carried no claim of profitability. On the contrary, production was said to account for only a small part of the system's "input," which came increasingly from the government, especially (despite its wishes to the contrary) from the central government. Thus, it can be concluded that more prisoners may have equated with more output, but not profitability.

By the early 1990s the central authorities came more fully to understand that the *laogai* was uneconomical and that the "self-financing" policy had been a failure. Whereas there had once been some hope that the *laogai* system would be a financial asset to the country, it was now obvious that this was not the case and that the system could never be profitable. There was the growing realization that the old idea of a symbiotic relationship between labor and resocialization was an empty myth.

The first big change in official thinking was signalled at a high-level meeting on 30 November 1993, attended by Premier Li Peng, Vice-Premier Zhu Rongji, and various officials concerned with the nation's economy. On that occasion, a resolution on the *laogai* and smaller *laojiao* (labor reeducation) systems' economic problems was passed, calling for a substantial increase of government funding for the prison system. Wages for prison personnel, and funding of prisoner-livelihood costs, were thereafter to be funded by the center. The central government was to increase yearly subsidies for prison building and renovation by 75 percent. During the same period, matching funds (with local governments paying two-thirds of the cost of any capital construction, and the central government paying one-third) were to be increased sevenfold, with the center's share rising from ten million *yuan* to eighty million annually.[71] But of course it would take many years before the results would be manifested as substantial improvements in the living conditions of prisoners. In 2001 the annual per capita "allowance" for prisoners in the eastern part of the country was reported to be still under 2,400 *yuan*, and of course in the west it was even less. In a general way, however, the new policy on central financing of prisons would gradually have an impact.

The reason the subsidies are necessary has to do with the huge expense of running prisons, which is a continuing problem. On 4 August 1999, *People's Daily* published some information that sheds light on the amount the system had been costing. "The state has introduced a financial and investment safeguard system for prisons, laying a foundation for the prison becoming a state penal institution and better performing its function. By 1998 financial authorities at various levels were earmarking about 6.4 billion yuan (per year), accounting for 60 percent of prison expenditures." This suggests that production by prisoners accounts for only two-fifths of the total cost of running the prisons. The number of inmates may have stopped increasing, but the cost of imprisoning them is not coming down.

CONCLUSION

As table 5.2 revealed, when it comes to the size of its prisoner population, China is roughly in line with international norms. The country is also in line with a trend that can sometimes be seen elsewhere, in that its prison population is leveling off. In short, contrary to the old conventional wisdom, it is not the size of China's prison system that is outrageous. Rather, it is the "selection process,"[72] and what goes on within the many prisons which are substandard. The first of these problems owes to poorly trained judges, ineffective legal counsel for defendants, and the generally politicized nature of the judiciary. Punishment is supposed to "placate public outrage," which can mean satisfying the whim of the behind-the-scenes Party secretary who calls the shots—often literally. Indeed, crackdowns on crime have been largely politics driven. High-profile incidents, such as an airplane hijacking, or the murder of a journalist from the official media, can galvanize the Party into action.[73] At other times, much wrongdoing can go unprosecuted because the Party has looked the other way.

But this chapter has been primarily concerned with a different problem, the dubious state of China's prisons. Some are bad indeed. In particular, prisons holding Tibetans[74] and prison mines of Xinjiang are especially inhumane places. Until now, secrecy has prevented research on the subject of prison mines. Although Chinese mines in general are notorious for their poor working conditions and frequent accidents,[75] all indications are that prison mines are even worse then civilian ones. Aside from accidents, many miners suffer the aftereffects of this most unhealthy line of work. Only in 2003 did the authorities begin seriously addressing these issues.[76]

At the other extreme are the model, one could almost say Potempkin, institutions. In 1997 there were reportedly twenty such prisons (in places like Shandong and Beijing) and fifteen model labor reeducation centers.[77] This represented a sharp rise from the previous year, when there had only been five of each, so this can be taken as a slight improvement. Since 1997 such progress seems to have slowed. In 1999 the number of "modernized and civilized prisons" remained at twenty, or less than 3 percent of the total.

Neither of the extremes represented by the ideal or the most horrendous, of course, tell us much about the country's prisons in general. The fact that there are so few high-standard prisons suggests that problems are widespread. Studies by the Ministry of Justice and labor reform bureaus make it clear that the authorities are not satisfied with the prison system. The claimed low recidivism rate notwithstanding,[78] there just is not much *gai* (reform).[79] Prisoners are increasingly defiant; they resist any reform efforts and even engage in criminal activities while still in prisons. Meaningful "mutual surveillance" among prisoners appears to be a thing of the past, and self-criticism meetings are rarely held.[80] Clearly, things have changed since the 1950s.

But what of the future? It has been said that "the *laogai* will gain in strength because the government needs it to increase production and keep totalitarian control."[81] Whether or not the prison population increases, however, a modern national economy simply cannot be built on a foundation of forced labor. Furthermore, a limited number of political arrests, combined with other repressive measures, may be enough to enable the communists to retain control of the country. To paraphrase a Chinese aphorism, it is necessary to kill only a few chickens in order to scare most of the monkeys. If the communists cannot maintain control in this manner, a higher rate of political imprisonment will not help them.

What, then, is the real intention of the national prison administration regarding the future of the Chinese prison system? It is realized that the system needs to be reformed, and that in particular inmates' living conditions need improvement. If we examine, in the light of internal publications, what was accomplished in the years 1997–2000, we can conclude that the intention is to build a system similar to Western countries and of reasonable size. The prison systems of countries like Australia and Finland have been studied by the Chinese in detail, and the translated articles on this subject have been widely circulated. (On the other hand, materials on countries with large prison populations are not widely disseminated, and certainly the American and Russian systems are not held up as models to be emulated.) This seems to be pointing in the right direction.

So, too, have the Ministry of Justice demarches of more recent years. In October 2002 the Ministry of Justice held a "work meeting" concerned with upgrading the administration of both the prisons and the reeducation regime. It was admitted that "our efforts to build up a prison police force (*ganjing*) for the prisons and education-through-labor regimes have yet to completely meet the demand of the new situation and new tasks. The overall quality of the police force needs further improvement, and they need to constantly strengthen their law enforcement in a strict, fair, and civilized manner." An ambitious three-year program was announced to improve the situation.[82] But carrying out such a plan would not be easy, and one could detect a note of frustration in Justice Minister Zhang Fusen's call "to address the sharp struggle in reform and antireform as well as corruption and anticorruption."

Thus, improving this vast system is an awesome challenge, and not simply a matter of rewriting laws and regulations. With the important exception of the problem of administrative detention, laws and regulations are in place which in theory should provide China with a decent penal system. But progress so far has been spotty, with huge variations from province to province and prison to prison. Experience demonstrates that with sufficient determination and allocation of resources, prison conditions can be made satisfactory. The national administration is fully aware of which prisons are succeeding and which are not. If the authorities really want to raise standards, the far west would be a good place for them to begin—and the relatively enlightened prison regime in Shandong would be a good model to emulate. One hopes that there will be the political will to effect Zhang Fusen's program, or at least that the stated goal of bringing half of the country's prisons up to optimal standards by the year 2010 will be realized.

NOTES

1. Estimates have ranged all the way from one million to twenty million (with figures in the middle of that range tending to receive considerable credence). Harry Wu has made a conservative estimate that "at present [1992] 16–20 million are still confined in these camps." Harry Wu, *Laogai: The Chinese Gulag* (Boulder, Colo.: Westview, 1992), 15. The "twenty million" figure was also mentioned as a possibility by Wu to the *Sunday Times* (London), November 3, 1996, 2.

2. In a forthcoming monograph, Murray Scot Tanner examines this history in detail.

3. See James D. Seymour and Richard Anderson, *New Ghosts, Old Ghosts: Prisons and Labor Reform Camps in China* (Armonk, N.Y.: M. E. Sharpe, 1998). Published in Chinese as *Xin gui, jiu gui: Zhongguo laogai ying ji shi* (Hong Kong: Mirror Books, 1999), 203, n. A.

4. Seymour and Anderson, *New Ghosts, Old Ghosts* , 205 and passim.

5. The figure remained about the same in 2003. On September 10, Xinhua reported that there were "some 700 prisons" in the country. FBIS-CHI-2003-0910.

6. The most common official term for jail is *kanshousuo.* In underground argot, the term *"gong"*(palace) is popular.

7. In most provinces, the maximum sentence served in jail is one year, but there are exceptions, notably Sichuan, where the limit is two years.

8. One reason that it is difficult to gauge precisely the size of the prison population is that such figures are generally applicable as of the first of the year, and therefore probably understate the prison population because of the practice of releasing prisoners at year-end. Thus, the January 1 figures are not representative of the prisoner statistics over the course of the year. Although in the

case of prisons the distortion is in the range of 5–10 percent, it is greater (10–20 percent) when it comes to *laojiao.* Thus it is likely that in the early autumn the prisoner population is roughly 100,000 greater than is indicated by January 1 statistics. (The motivation underlying this bureaucratic device has to do with reducing the financial obligations to the state and also to comply with the state policy of reducing the official number of prisoners.)

9. Justice Minister Xiao Yang, quoted in Hong Kong *South China Morning Post* (hereafter: *SCMP)* February 15, 1995, and Reuters, January 27, 1995.

10. *People's Daily,* August 4, 1999, 11, Foreign Broadcast Information Service (hereafter; FBIS), August 26, 1999. (The source does not explicitly say that this is the figure for labor reform only, but it appears that non-labor-reform prisoners are excluded.)

11. Xiao Yang, *SCMP,* February 15, 1995.

12. The term "civilians" includes not only guards, but also administrators and workers (but not civilians who work in enterprises associated with prisons).

13. This includes both guards and administrators. The ratio of prisoners to guards inside the camps is seldom more than 1:10, and can be as low as 1:42. The "300,000" figure reported in Seymour and Anderson, 205, and since reiterated by Xinhua (New China News Agency, *South China Morning Post,* November 20, 2000) appears to have been quite stable.

14. Reuters, May 15, 1997, and otherwise confirmed.

15. *People's Daily,* August 4, 1999, 11, FBIS, August 26, 1999. (This probably slightly understates the total.)

16. Other observers' estimates are much higher. Jean-Luc Domenach hypothesizes 4 or 5.7 million for the mid-1980s (including people on *jiuye*). *Chine: l'archipel oublié.* [Fayard: N.p. (Paris?), 1992], 489. (Regarding *jiuye*, see Seymour and Anderson, chapter 6.) As noted above, Harry Wu has on occasion put the maximum estimate at twenty million, but on other occasions his minimum figure seems to have been four million. He seems to have settled on "eight million." *SCMP,* March 30, 1998. In 1996, in examining Wu's four–six million prisoner and eight–ten million *jiuye* figures, U.S. State Department analysts opined that Wu had been "working from . . . outdated data and unjustifiable assumptions." The once classified document is now available at www.hfni.gsehd.gwu.edu/~nsarchiv/NSAEBB/NSAEBB19/11-01.htm.

17. Seymour and Anderson, *New Ghosts, Old Ghosts,* 206.

18. Seymour and Anderson, *New Ghosts, Old Ghosts,* 206.

19. For general information on the Bingtuan, see Seymour, "Xinjiang's Production and Construction Corps, and the Sinification of Eastern Turkestan," *Inner Asia,* 2, 2000, 171–93. In 1996, 2500 eastern prisoners were accepted by the Bingtuan; it is not known how many, if any, have been sent since then.

20. These had mainly been brought from Beijing, Shanghai, and Zhejiang around 1984.

21. Most of the figures in this table are based on numbers of prison and *laojiao* inmates (which are known), plus estimates of other categories (such as prisoners in jail).

22. Although it is difficult to obtain precise information on the direction of Xinjiang's prisoner population, there is anecdotal information. For example, in 1997 it was announced that the Xinjiang Bingtuan had released the last of its Tianjianese and Hainanese prisoners. *Xinsheng bao,* May 2, 1997, 1. On the other hand, some of the *Bingtuan's* regiments continue to build prisons, suggesting that they expect to receive more prisoners from the east in the future.

23. Many drug offenders are not given trials at all, but instead are sent to labor reeducation camps, where they comprise between 30 and 40 percent of the prisoners.

24. These figures are slightly offset by the procuracy's taking the initiative in other arrests (6,957).

25. *China Daily,* May 25, 1994, 3, FBIS, May 25, 1994, 27.

26. The deputy head of the Tibet Prison Bureau, Losang Geleg, has said that 30 percent of Tibetan prisoners have their sentences reduced annually. Xinhua, May 27, 2002, FBIS-CHI-2002-0527.

27. Although it does not substantially affect the size of the prisoner population, it is noteworthy that in 1998 and 1999 there was a dramatic increase in the number of laogai prisoners allowed to return home for the Lunar New Year. Even remote regions like Ningxia have implemented this policy.

28. Xinhua, March 11, 2002, FBIS-CHI-2002-031. Also on the subject of correcting improper paroles and commutations, see Xinhua, May 29, 2001, FBIS-CHI-2001-0529—concerning "inspection and supervision" of prisons having turned up 4,355 illegal commutations between 1997 and 2000. But the problem did not go away, and in 2002 Ministry of Justice Head Zhang Fusen again called attention to it, declaring, "Under no circumstances shall prisons and reeducation-through-labor centers collect fees" from inmates and their relatives for reduction of sentences. Xinhua domestic service, August 23, 2002, FBIS-CHI-2002-0823.

29. *Renmin ribao* (Internet version), January 30, 2002, FBIS, February 6, 2002.

30. Escapes were discussed in Seymour and Anderson, 84–86. Since then, the government has released some statistics on the subject. It is said that in 1997 the national rate was 0.54 per thousand, down from 0.82 per thousand the year before: *China Daily,* February 6, 1998. The number of prisoners who managed to escape from the prison system in 1997 and 1998 has been put at 775 and 523, respectively. The escape rates appear to be the highest where prison conditions are the worst, such as in Tibet. Because Laojiao institutions are lightly guarded, the escape rates are higher there than in prisons. The Laojiao escape rate in 1998 was 0.24 percent compared with 0.036 percent for prisons.

31. Xinhua, August 26, 2001, FBIS-CHI-2001-0826.

32. Xinhua reported "More than 50,000 escaped criminal suspects and prison runaways have been rounded up" in the "run-up to next month's fiftieth PRC anniversary celebrations." The main

targets had been criminal suspects and offenders who had escaped from prison, reeducation centers, and labor camps. It is not clear how many were actually escaped convicts. *SCMP,* August 14, 1999 citing *China Daily.*

33. *China Daily,* February 6, 1998.

34. See *Institutionalized Exclusion,* i. Also available at: http://isohrichina.org/download.repository / HRIC%20Full%20Report%20Nov%202002.pdf

35. I am indebted to Nicolas Becquelin for this information (based upon the *Civil Affairs Statistical Yearbook—2001* (Beijing: Statistical Publishing House, 2001), Table C-80, 248–249). On the basis of the indicated 24,302, 402 people-days, and 2,926,526 detentions, the average length of detention would be 8.3. That being 2.27 percent of a year, this indicates a point-of-time population of 66,548. If one uses the 3.2 million figure, the point-of-time number would be 72,640.

36. This was the situation in the wake of the release of 218,200 from prisons and 80,180 from labor reeducation in 1999.

37. Between 1938 and 1953 it was probably more than double that. The prisoner population was probably about twelve million in 1953.

38. Alan Bullock, *Hitler and Stalin* (New York: Random House, 1993), 284. The disparity is even more stark if one were to compare death rates.

39. Between 1980 and 1999 China probably executed somewhere between 150,000 and 200,000 people. Had these people been given long sentences instead of being executed, the prison population would be 5 to 9 percent higher (allowing for some dying natural deaths).

40. In 1992 the crime rate was said to be "two per thousand per year." State Council, "Criminal Reform in China," *Beijing Review,* August 17, 1992, 11. Although beginning in the 1980s rural crime surged, one can still assume that the urban crime rate is higher than the rural crime rate. See Wei Pingxiong and Yu Debin, "An Analysis of China's Current Rural Crime Problem," *Zhengfa Luntan* (Politics and law tribune), No. 47, Oct. 1992, 29–36, U.S. Joint Publications Research Service, January 25, 1993, 50–56.

41. Seymour and Anderson, *New Ghosts, Old Ghosts,* 10.

42. Xinhua, August 23, 2002, FBIS-CHI-2002-0823. In Tibet, women are said to comprise 3 percent of the inmate population. Xinhua, May 27, 2002, FBIS-CHI-2002-0527.

43. For local historic information, see Kang Shu-hua et al., *Nü xing zuifan lun* (On female prisoners), (Lanzhou: Lanzhou University Press, 1988).

44. Included were 251 long-term drug addict detention centers *(changqi jiedu suo),* 153 short-term drug addict detention centers *(linshi chang suo),* and 75 labor reeducation addict detention centers *(laojiao jiedu chang suo).*

45. This term is somewhat confusing. The term "administrative detention" (especially in English) can be used to describe the various forms of administration described in this section, but within

this general category the term *xingzheng juliu* can also refer to a specific form of administration—up to fifteen days in jail for minor offences, usually violation of public order. This is pursuant to a 1957 law amended in 1986: the Security Administration Punishment Act.

46. English translation in *Chinese Law & Government*, September 1994, 61–62. The more detailed 1982 guidelines can be found on 68–83.

47. *China Daily*, May 2, 2001, www.chinadaily.com.cn/cndydb/2001/02/d1-law.205.html.

48. Human Rights in China, "Reeducation through Labor (RTL): A Summary of Regulatory Issues and Concerns" (New York, 2001) 1, citing *China Law Yearbook (1987–1997)*, China Law Yearbook Press, 1998. Also on labor reeducation and so on, see Amnesty International, *China: Punishment without Crime: Administrative Detention*, (London, 1991).

49. *China Daily*, February 6, 1998. This compares with 235 reeducation camps which we reported in the book for 1995. We estimated that the labor reeducation population had been generally under 200,000.

50. Typically, the organization of a department will reflect that of the national Ministry of Justice, with two sections: one responsible for prison administration (the former laogai) and one for labor reeducation.

51. A case of a prisoner being beaten to death by his fellow inmates is recounted in *Ming Bao* (Hong Kong), July 13, 2003, B6, FBIS-CHI-2003-0714.

52. Agence France Press, October 8, 1999.

53. Each year around one hundred soldiers are given heavy sentences (five years to execution), and several hundred are given lesser sentences (one to five years). Other than *laojiao*, the PLA itself has no prisons for convicts.

54. For the regulations concerning imprisoning errant noncommissioned officers, see articles 59–60 of "PLA Regulations for Managing Noncommissioned Officers"—promulgated on January 20, 2001, by the General Staff Department, General Political Department, General Logistics Department, and General Armament Department, Beijing *Jiefangjun bao* (Internet version), May 23, 2001, FBIS-CHI-2001-0523, November 2, 2001.

55. In this paper, the term "political prisoner" is used to indicate people imprisoned because of their identification with one or more issues of national importance, whether or not they have advocated or been involved in violence. The term is to be distinguished from "prisoner of conscience," which is someone who has neither advocated nor engaged in violence. People who have simply offended local cadres or officials are not included, though these people also have a good claim to the title.

56. See Seymour and Anderson, *New Ghosts, Old Ghosts*, 21 n. C.

57. Dikötter, 150. (One reason the sample is unrepresentative is that this was in a Beijing jail, not a *laogai* camp.)

58. See note 63.

59. Reuters, January 27, 1995, citing an anonymous Ministry of Justice official.

60. Wu, *Laogai—The Chinese Gulag* (Boulder, Colo.: Westview, 1992) 19. Wu quotes a 1985 "internal document" as follows: "Of those currently detained, counter-revolutionaries comprise almost 10 percent; those with a historical counter-revolutionary background comprise only 1.6 percent of the total inmates." Wu follows the quotation immediately with this sentence of his own: "This 400,000 figure [the first time we have seen this number] does not include those imprisoned under the auspices of RTL [reeducation through labor]; the number of RTL convicts is probably not much less than 400,000. RTL is very convenient for dealing with counter-revolutionaries and 'anti-socialist elements.' This seems to imply that Wu considers a substantial portion of labor reeducation inmates to be political cases, with an overall total of upwards of half a million political prisoners. The U.S. State Department (according to a recently declassified 1996 document) found "no evidence to substantiate" the claim that China had upwards of a million political prisoners. www.hfni.gsehd.gwu.edu/~nsarchiv/NSAEBB/ NSAEBB19/11-01.htm.

61. *New York Times,* March 6, 1997, 10.

62. See "Clemency for State Security Prisoners," *Dialogue: Newsletter of the Dui Hua Foundation,* no. 6 (Winter 2002).

63. A "case" can involve one or more individuals.

64. In May 2002 it was officially reported that the Tibet Autonomous Region had only one hundred security prisoners (out of a total of 2,300 inmates in the Autonomous Region's three prisons). Prisoners serving terms of ten years or more numbered 30 percent of the total. The proportion of women (3.3 percent) was about in line with the national average. Xinhua, May 19, 2001, FBIS-CHI-2001-0519 (via Internet).

65. Based largely on the experience of Drapchi prison, where a majority of Tibet's serious political offenders are held. Tibet Information Network, December 27, 1999.

66. However, this "proxy" application has its limitations. First, the pre- and post-1996 figures are not comparable, because the old term "counterrevolutionary" did not include "counterrevolutionary propaganda" offenders, whereas "state security" does include this. Second, the huge number of turn-of-the-century Falungong prisoners were not deemed state security cases.

67. It is implied to the contrary in Harry Wu's *Laogai Handbook* (1994), 1.

68. This section draws upon a manuscript which will appear in a volume edited by Philip Williams and Yenna Wu. Citations for quotations, etc., will appear therein.

69. See "Labor Reforms Offer Hope of Decent Prisons," *South China Morning Post,* August 13, 2003, a glowing account that treats the reforms as a novel approach newly underway.

70. Josephine Ma, "Penal Reform Removes Prisons' Profit Motive," *South China Morning Post,*
August 13, 2003. (The areas chosen for the "experiment" were Heilongjiang, Jiangxi, Hubei, and
Shaanxi provinces, and Shanghai and Chongqing municipalities. It was expected that all this
would cost the government an extra four billion *yuan* annually.)

71. "*Guowu yuan di 17 ci zongli bangong huiyi jiyao*" (Record of the seventeenth state council
premier's office meeting), *Jianyu gongzuo shouci 1993.4-1994.12* (Handbook on prison work, April
1993–December 1997), Falü Chubanshe, Beijing, June 1999, 124–25.

72. Although the problems associated with arrest and conviction lie beyond the scope of this
paper, it may worth noting that Justice Minister Zhang Fusen has called for a beefing up of
China's hitherto hopelessly inadequate legal aid system. *Renmin ribao,* January 30, 2002, FBIS-
CHI-2002-0130. On legal aid centers, see also Xinhua, January 26, 2002, FBIS-CHI-2002-0126.

73. Jean-Louis Rocca, *L'empire et son milieu: la criminalité en Chine populaire* (Paris: Plon, 1991),
101–4.

74. In 1999 Human Rights Watch released a report based largely on reports of exiled Tibetans,
three of whom had been held in Kham (western Sichuan) and two in Gannan (southern Gansu).
All had been treated brutally. "Profiles of Tibetan Exiles," New York, 1999, vol. 11, no. 5 (C), For a
much more upbeat account of Tibetan prisons, see Xinhua, May 27, 2002, FBIS-CHI-2002-0527.
Data on Tibetans in prison outside of the Tibet Autonomous Region is available on the CD-ROM
"Tibet outside the TAR," information about which is available at www.savetibet.org/background/
outside_tar.html.

75. For example, in 2001, nine prison miners were reported to have died in a single Sichuan
incident. http//www.dajiyuan.com/news/epochnews/big5/2001/12/18/157842.htm. The same year,
thirty-seven miners (probably mostly prisoners) were killed in a Shaanxi coal mine disaster.
Xinhua, May 9,2001, FBIS-CHI-2001-0509 (via Internet).

76. One official has been quoted as saying, "After the [planned] reform, inmates will no longer be
forced to undertake dangerous tasks. For example, factories involving contact with lethal material
or quarries will have to be shut." *South China Morning Post,* August 13, 2003.

77. *China Daily,* February 6, 1998. This was up from fifteen model prisons and ten model
reeducation centers reported in *China Daily,* December 22, 1997. For a model prison for women,
see Xinhua, August 23, 2002, FBIS-CHI-2002-0823. On some Beijing prisons where vocational
training is emphasized, see Xinhua, August 5, 2002, FBIS-CHI-2002-0805.

78. In 1997–1998 the recidivism rate was variously reported as "below 10 percent" for labor
reeducated, and "less than 8 percent" (apparently referring to the labor reformed). However, any
such statistics assume that the government knows how many former prisoners commit crimes. If
an ex-convict commits a crime and then the wrong person, or no one, is arrested, that would not
be reflected in the statistics. On the other hand, given the nature of trials in China, many
"recidivists" are doubtless innocent.

79. Some, but very little, attention is paid to psychological counseling; Professor Luo Dahua, who
specializes in this subject, has said, "We cannot make too much of psychological therapy, since it is

a part of the whole which includes education through labor, philosophy education and penology to reform criminals." *Xinhua*, January 7, 2002, FBIS-CHI-2002-1017.

80. The previous sentences in this paragraph are based upon information derived from Harold Tanner, "Policing, Punishment, and the Individual: Criminal Justice in China," *Law and Social Inquiry* 20, no. 1 (Winter 1995): 277–303.

81. Harry Wu, quoted in *Financial Times*, November 25, 1995, xxii.

82. Measures to include (1) A new system of screening and evaluating *ganjing* recruits, who henceforth are all supposed to be college-educated; (2) An annual evaluation system, with personnel failing to meet the requirements two years in a row to be dismissed; (3) An upgraded training system; (4) Prison officials to be rotated at least once a decade; (5) An improved supervision and inspection system, including legal training for the staff. Zhongguo Xinwen She, October 23, 2002, FBIS-CHI-2002-1023.

III

POLICING "MARKET SOCIALISM"

6

Campaign-Style Policing in China and Its Critics

MURRAY SCOT TANNER

One of the most controversial aspects of Chinese public security work has been the continued use of "campaign-style policing" to attack what police officials describe as the ever-increasing "high tides" of crime that have afflicted China since the mid-1970s. Campaign-style policing refers to concentrated, fixed-term, special targeting of particular categories of crime for arrest and severe punishment—hence their nickname "stern blows" ("*yanda*") campaigns. While the most famous of these campaigns have been nationwide (as in 1983–1987, 1990, and 1996), more localized campaigns are quite common. These campaigns are characterized by frenetic overtime police activity; large waves of arrests; swift trials with even weaker procedural protections than have historically characterized post-Mao Chinese criminal justice; severe punishments, in particular the use of execution on a tremendous numerical scale (according to some estimates, China's percentage share of total reported world executions during these campaigns dwarfs even China's one-fifth share of world population).[1] A key feature of these anti-crime struggles has been the use of Maoist techniques of mass campaigning. Deng Xiaoping, who had called for an end to such mass campaigns (*yundong*) in 1978, nevertheless argued in 1983 that without mass involvement, these struggles would not succeed. With hallmark bluntness, he accordingly labelled these "campaigns that we simply will not call campaigns."[2] Their organizational heart was strong mobilizational leadership by local Communist Party secretaries, coupled with heavy official publicity, intense efforts to involve large numbers of citizen security activists in capturing suspects (including, as Michael Dutton has pointed out, the increasingly widespread use of "contracts" to produce results), public parading and mass sentencing rallies for convicts just before they are executed, and afterwards, public displays of crime scenes and the executees' photos emblazoned with a trademark red check mark. One internal public security study claims that more than three million persons took part in the 1983–1987 campaign, at a time when total police forces nation-wide numbered only about 658,000.[3] While it remains highly questionable whether more recent campaigns have been able to maintain similar levels of mass involve-ment, the "mass-line" form remains a defining feature of these campaigns.

Elsewhere, I have argued that a major source of Chinese policing practices is the highly politicized process of debating the "institutional lessons" to be ab-sorbed from key crises in the history of policing and internal security.[4] Just such an internal debate was touched off by the massive 1983–1987 *yanda* campaign— by far the largest post-Mao anti-crime campaign, and almost certainly the blood-iest chapter in post-Mao politics. That debate smoldered throughout the early 1990s and was rekindled by the 1996 *yanda* campaign—a major nationwide cam-paign, but nevertheless smaller than the 1983–1987 offensive. This article at-tempts to extend that analysis by examining the long-running debate over the value of campaign-style policing and considering why this practice hangs on even in the face of considerable criticism among upper-level public security officials.

MOTIVATIONS FOR CAMPAIGN-STYLE POLICING

Western scholars have highlighted several factors that have motivated the use of *yanda* campaigns. Many have stressed their intended ideological and social educa-tion functions—what legal history scholar Harold Tanner terms an effort to pro-duce a morally and ideologically civilized society to compliment the materially advanced society being forged by economic reform.[5] Michael Dutton has argued that public security officials, faced with a major increase in crime, unconsciously reached back and "redeployed" the revered Maoist-era technique of mass cam-paigning with important "differences" to meet the new demands of a more mar-ket-oriented society, such as widespread use of contracts as a mobilizational adjunct to traditional ideological and political methods.[6] I have argued that these campaigns represent, in part, an organizational response to China's comparatively very low ratio of professional police officers to citizens. Low police/citizen ratios force police to rely heavily on the active cooperation of nonprofessional citizen se-curity activists and other average citizens to maintain social order. Chinese police officials fear that major increases in crime, especially high-profile violent crime, might cause citizen activists to reassess whether it was the state or the criminals who controlled the "balance of awe" in society. The police feared that if criminals came to be perceived as the more immediate and intimidating social presence, citizen activists could become so fearful of offending criminals that this vital social control monitoring system could become paralyzed.[7]

Another powerful force for the continued use of campaigns has been the official "institutional lessons" of public security history—that campaigns are effective in lowering crime, and that they embolden the law-abiding masses to cooperate with the state against criminals. The key organizers of the 1983–1987 campaign, such as then-Minister of Public Security Liu Fuzhi, continue to argue that the campaign contributed to a fundamental improvement in social order.[8] Many police analysts still point to this campaign as one of Deng Xiaoping's most valuable legacies in legal and security policy and a significant contribution to the theory of the "People's Democratic Dictatorship."[9] To the present day, official public security texts used at police colleges recite the familiar statistical mantra of how effective the campaign was in bringing down crime rates and restoring a sense of security among the masses.[10] For more than a decade, reformist police officials and campaign critics have had to struggle carefully to call this powerful official institutional lesson into question.

Finally, as Bakken and others have correctly pointed out, *yanda* campaigns are in large measure motivated by a "deterrent" theory of crime and social order management that is widely accepted not only by most Chinese security officials, but also by the general political leadership as well.[11] This analysis can be carried a step further. *Yanda* campaign advocates have always relied on a particular, implicitly "rational" theory of crime deterrence that holds, rather simplistically, that criminals and prospective criminals calculate their actions mostly in response to the *severity* of the punishment they might face if caught. Campaign supporters contend that sharp waves of severe, highly public punishments can result in what we might call "social learning"—that is, sustained, long-term decreases in crime. The rich, ancient metaphors trotted out by police campaigners are redolent with this implicit calculus of deterrence: "puncturing the puffed up arrogance of criminals," "slaughter the chicken and let the monkey see," and the classically rationalistic "kill one to warn a hundred."[12] In an analysis written at the height of the 1996 campaign, Shanghai Public Security Bureau Chief Zhu Daren stressed that the "severity" of punishment (*yanlixing*) is "the most fundamental special characteristic" of these campaigns. "In curing chaos, we must use heavy models, we must use severe measures. Otherwise we cannot shake down the arrogance of criminal elements. As Comrade Xiaoping said, 'Only by being severe can we cure crime *for good*" (emphasis added).[13] But amidst the obsession with making punishments severe, campaign supporters have tended either to ignore or assume away another key element of any rational calculus of deterrence—a prospective criminal's perceived *probability* of being caught and punished. Supporters have assumed that massive, Party-mobilized campaigns would automatically keep the perceived probability of capture high. But as will be shown, campaign critics have gradually exposed some of the ways in which *yanda* campaigns undermine police thoroughness, thus calling into question both the certainty of capture and punishment and the overall notion of deterrence.

CRITIQUES OF *YANDA* CAMPAIGNS AND EXCESSIVE PUNISHMENTS

Until recently, the massive use of the death penalty during these campaigns was almost exclusively a critique employed by Westerners. Despite repeated official declarations that the use of the death penalty during these campaigns is entirely justified, China has treated the issue with extreme sensitivity, attacking Amnesty International (AI) and other organizations for allegedly exaggerating these campaigns' brutality. Drawing overwhelmingly from official press sources, AI has totalled more than 6,100 death sentences, 4,367 actual executions, and 424 death sentences with a two-year reprieve during the 1996 *yanda* campaign. This total is greater than the sum of those monitored for the previous two years in China, and is more than the observed total for all of the other countries in the world combined for 1996.[14] But nearly fifteen years after the 1983–1987 campaign, official internal public security sources scrupulously omit any estimates of executions, and even senior police and legal scholars report they cannot get access to the data. Outside of China, numerous efforts were made at the time to estimate the number executed, but mostly during the campaign's most intense early months.[15]

Official statistics on arrests and punishments released years after the campaign by public security and court sources, plus other internal data uncovered by Dr. Harold Tanner, make it possible to generate rough estimates of death sentences and other punishments for the entire campaign. According to a Party document found by Tanner, between August and December 1983, about 861,000 criminals were sentenced nationwide, over 24,000 of whom were sentenced to death (a death sentence rate of 2.79 percent). This figure, it should be stressed, apparently includes not only actual executions, but also those persons sentenced to death with a two-year suspension of sentence—a large percentage of whom ultimately have their death sentences commuted to long prison terms.[16] Relatedly, an official Supreme People's Court history reports courts nationwide sentenced 1,721,000 persons between August 1983 and December 1986, of whom 0.7 percent were found not guilty, 59.65 percent (or 1,026,577 persons) were found guilty and given sentences lighter than five years imprisonment, and 39.65 percent (682,377 persons) were sentenced to five or more years imprisonment, life imprisonment, death with a two-year suspension, or death.[17] According to other court sources, the corresponding figures for the entire campaign (August 1983 to December 1987) are 2,047,839 total sentenced, 1,251,639 sentenced to lighter than five years imprisonment (61.12 percent), 781,865 persons to five years imprisonment or stiffer punishment (38.18 percent), and again, just 0.7 percent found not guilty.[18] If the death sentence rate for the entire three-and-a-half-year campaign never declined from the 2.79 percent rate Tanner found for the four-month "high tide," the maximum death sentence figure would be just over 57,000 persons (e.g. 2.047 million times 0.0279). But the fact that the percentage of convicts receiving the most severe sentences declined greatly as the campaign progressed strongly suggests that the 2.79 percent death sentence rate was almost certainly not sustained through December 1987.[19]

One method of estimating total death sentences (though not actual executions) for the whole 1983–1987 campaign would therefore involve estimating how sharply sentencing severity fell off between January 1984 and December 1987 (e.g. after the 2.79 percent period), and what the average death sentence rate was for the entire period. If the death penalty percentage of all sentencees fell off from 2.79 to an average of 2 percent for the entire period of the campaign, that would yield a total of 40,957 persons sentenced to death. An average 1983–1987 rate of 1.5 percent death sentences would yield a total estimate of 30,716 persons (only about 4,000 more than for the period covered by Tanner's documents). If we estimate that of the 1,186,000 persons sentenced after December 1983, the death sentence rate was just 1.0 percent (taking literally the ancient maxim, "kill one to warn a hundred"), that would add 11,860 death sentences to the 24,000 already cited by Tanner, for a campaign total of 35,860. Thus, based on official statistics, the Harold Tanner documentation, and what I would contend are reasonable numerical assumptions, we can reasonably estimate that the total number of persons sentenced to death (but not necessarily executed) during the anti-crime campaign may have been solidly in excess of thirty thousand persons. It is also significant to note that, according to a 1988 report by Supreme People's Court Chief Justice Zheng Tianxiang, of all those *actually executed* during the campaign, over 90 percent were executed for committing one of the seven categories of serious crime specified as campaign targets.[20] The tragic corollary of Zheng's claim, however, is that perhaps more than one or two thousand people might have been executed for crimes that were not even objectives of the campaign.

The release of these very partial official figures during the 1990s may indicate the beginning of an effort by legal officials to come to grips with the magnitude of death sentence use in anti-crime campaigns. Nevertheless, overt criticism of death penalty usage is only beginning to emerge within police and legal circles, and is usually indirect. Questions have focused, for example, on its unfair or improper application in specific cases, or on how the secrecy of death penalty statistics prevents even government criminologists from impartially assessing its deterrent capacity. Some officials have raised the possibility that the improper application of the death penalty could produce local resentment or a backlash against police campaigns. Some legal officials have also called for making executions more "humane" and "civilized," and since the 1996 campaign China has reportedly drafted regulations to end public parading and begin experimenting with lethal injection instead of the customary bullet in the back of the head.[21]

Still, there is no shortage of powerful defenders for the widespread use of such punishments. In a 1994 article, the Shandong Public Security Bureau director complained that the standards of evidence required by law enforcement departments were too high in some regions, and consequently not enough criminals were being punished severely.[22] During the 1996 campaign, for example, Shanghai Public Security Chief Zhu Daren pointedly endorsed the old weak legality of the 1983 campaign. He recalled approvingly the September 1983 NPC Standing Committee decision that placed a thin legal veneer over the widespread use of executions and other penalties that exceeded the standards in the 1979 criminal law for the seven targeted categories of crime. It is noteworthy that Zhu spoke at a time when China had already passed, and was just about to enact, new criminal and criminal procedure laws with more clearly defined sentences and tightened procedural protections for accused persons. Zhu stressed, however, that the 1983 decision "fully embodied the ideology of "being strict."[23] With undisguised contempt, a number of public security officials have attacked foreign and Chinese critics of such punishments for their misguided "humanitarianism," contending that the "true humanitarianism" lies in severely punishing criminals who prey on the people.

EMERGING CHINESE POLICE CRITIQUES OF *YANDA* CAMPAIGNS AND INCENTIVES FOR STATISTICAL FRAUD AND "EMPTY EXAGGERATION"

The critique of death penalty abuses in campaign-style policing that has dominated Western analyses has only recently begun to show signs of gaining a foothold in Chinese legal circles. Within the public security system, the criticisms that have shown the most political power have been more narrowly "professional" in orientation— that the effectiveness of campaigns has been exaggerated, that their effects are not sustainable, and that they undermine efforts to improve police professionalism. Some police officials and scholars have also begun to argue that campaign excesses are corroding police relations with citizens rather than strengthening them.

For more than a decade police sceptics of campaign-style policing have attacked the MPS's official claims about its effectiveness in reducing crime, charging that to a great degree these claims represented statistical "smoke and mirrors." Instead, they have pointed to innumerable ways in which the heavy-handed involvement of "generalist" local Communist Party leaders in police campaign work has created incentives to fabricate positive campaign reports. During *yanda* campaigns, when local Party officials are more closely graded by their superiors on their control of social order and their "administrative accomplishments" (*zhengji*), their police subordinates are pressed hard to show campaign successes. The local Party secretaries' capacity to elicit compliance with such statistical fraud is considerable, since police wages, budgets, personnel hiring, and promotion are all largely determined by local Party committees rather than superior-level public security departments. Amidst the high-publicity atmosphere of a campaign, interprovincial and interregional competition to report the most favorable statistics can emerge.

Official police sources demonstrate that in addition to simply falsifying statistical reports, local police have developed a vast array of "rational" tactics to manipulate these data.[24] For example, three of the key statistical goals during a campaign are lowering the overall number of criminal cases, increasing arrests, and increasing the percentage of officially opened case files that are solved (the famous "case-cracking rate") (*po'an lü*). To lower the overall number of criminal cases, some local Party leaders have simply issued maximum case quotas to local police, either simply forbidding them to officially open more cases than this during a year, or imposing substantial wage, bonus, and promotion penalties on departments that do not comply. In 1993, Li Maolin, the Public Security Chief of Inner Mongolia, levelled a detailed attack on this practice.

> The leaders in some places, in order to make their "political achievements" (*zhengji*) appear more outstanding, will send down quotas to the public security organs concerning the establishment of [security] cases which are completely divorced from reality; if the [police] exceed these [case quotas], then they are punished (*shoufa*), if

they don't exceed them, then they are given rewards (*youjiang*). This leads to cases which occur not being reported (*you'an bubao*), empty exaggerations (*nongxu*), and falsifications (*zuojia*). The current problem of attacking [crime] with insufficient force is directly related to this.[25]

Local police often artificially inflate arrest rates by rearresting and recharging past offenders for "newly discovered offences," or by focusing their attention on arresting easy-to-capture petty criminals while ignoring more hard-core, violent, or mobile criminals who are the intended targets of most campaigns.[26] A senior Anhui provincial criminal investigator has attacked one practice he calls "storing up water to raise fish" (*xushui yangyu*) in which local police during noncampaign periods deliberately refrain from arresting criminals that they should arrest, "saving them up" to arrest during the next campaign when superiors are watching.[27] Police often artificially raise their "case-cracking rates" by refusing to officially open a case file ("establish a case" or *li an*) unless they feel confident that they can solve it. Alternatively, in gang-related cases, police have been known to declare a case "cracked" if they seize one member of the gang, even if the main culprit remains at large.[28]

Reformist police officials and scholars have decried the corrosive effect these fraudulent campaign reporting practices have on police professionalism and the state's capacity to gather the accurate social order data it needs to make criminal policy. But once these statistical abuses have started, they become politically difficult to stop. One senior analyst has also noted that such inflated social order statistics are politically "sticky" because any current official who ignores the exaggeratedly good crime statistics of the past and begins reporting more "honest" current figures (which are usually more pessimistic) lays himself open to a charge that "social order has deteriorated" on his watch.[29]

ROUTINIZATION OF CAMPAIGN-STYLE POLICING

Classic theoretical discussions of political campaigns have long stressed their tendency toward routinization, which gradually undermines their value in mobilizing the public and raising its consciousness of the target problem. Police campaigns, with their attractive political symbolism of "declaring war on crime" are no less susceptible to this tendency. Numerous police officials have criticized the tendency for authorities in many regions to turn these "special struggles" into a routine, almost constant state of affairs. One provincial official described the routinization process this way:

As the slogan of "Stern Blows" is incessantly put forward, the Public Security organs are soon singing only "the song of four seasons." One campaign follows another, one dragnet is thrown out after another. . . . Soon many basic level police
come to see these serious campaigns as just another routine part of their work.[30]

An Anhui provincial police official noted the case of one unnamed province that
in 1994 alone organized five provincewide campaigns, the longest of which ran
to four months. He quoted basic-level police as complaining that "month after
month we have unified operations, day after day there are 'specialized struggles.'
There are 365 days in a year, and every one of them is supposedly the 'key link.'"[31]
Lest this claim of campaigning every day of the year sound like hyperbole, a Ministry of Public Security source notes that in the calendar year 1988 the Harbin
Public Security Bureau devoted a total of 340 days to various campaigns and
"specialized struggles."[32]

Even many officials who defend the effectiveness of the massive 1983–1987
campaign charge that the costs of constant campaigning are severe. Higher-
level political officials order such campaigns with little regard for their impact
on basic-level police work. Street-level officers become physically and mentally
exhausted by long, largely uncompensated overtime hours. Meanwhile other
badly needed long-term force development goals are sacrificed. The combination of fatigue and overtime means that additional training time devoted to
improving investigatory procedure, legal knowledge, and other police skills is
out of the question. Over the long run, constant campaigning undermines efforts to strengthen police professionalism, further eroding the system's "human
capital."[33]

Even more disturbing to these officials are the incentives that "routinized"
campaigns create in career criminals, many of whom have learned to recognize
the pattern of campaigns and avoid punishment. Senior officials have noted that
the "regular" times of the year when anti-crime crackdowns tend to be
launched—around the New Year, Lunar New Year, May Day, the June Fourth
Tiananmen Anniversary, and the October 1 National Day—are well known in society. The pattern of the campaign policy process is no less predictable: announcement of the policy, meetings to make organizational deployments, a burst
of propaganda to whip up public support, investigation and case cracking, and
then concentrated waves of arrests and quick trials. With experienced criminals
learning to lay low and avoid detection, public security officials often turn to arresting "more superficial" offenders just to meet expected targets.[34]

IMPACT ON PUBLIC OPINION

Both defenders and critics of campaign-style policing have battled over the impact these campaigns have on public opinion and relations between the police and citizens. Campaign advocates have long draped the campaigns in the language of "socialist democracy," claiming that the Party-state not only enjoyed widespread popular support for its attacks on crime, but indeed had little choice but to launch a campaign in order to maintain its popular legitimacy. This argument about the campaign's popularity has always rested to a considerable degree on an assumption that only the truly guilty get punished during campaigns, and that the masses, fearful of spiralling crime rates, would welcome dramatic action by the police. There is certainly a wealth of anecdotal evidence that before the 1983 *yanda* campaign was announced, average urban workers (especially women) and lower-level officials were anxious about crime and desirous of some official action. The need to maintain popular support was a key theme Deng Xiaoping voiced in his July 1983 speech launching the campaign.[35]

But campaign critics are increasingly pointing to ways in which the campaigns undermine popular support for the police. Some have argued that constant campaigns create great nervousness among average citizens, harming daily commerce and undermining economic growth. At the same time, when high-profile campaigns become routinized, citizens gradually lose faith in their effectiveness in controlling crime.[36] Looming behind this discussion of popular nervousness is a very carefully worded debate over the sensitive topic of false arrests and punishments. Many officials have stressed how the pressure to produce quick results leads to sloppy, overly anxious investigations. A municipal Public Security official in Hebei province has written disparagingly of the substandard investigations and evidence gathering that *yanda* campaigns have produced in his own city.[37] His carefully worded insistence that improper investigations have not *yet* produced any false cases in *his* bureau clearly suggests a belief that false cases were occurring in other jurisdictions. There is even some official statistical evidence indicating that pressure to crack cases may lead to an increased use of coercion and torture to extract false confessions. The Supreme People's Procuratorate's official published data on torture cases reported between 1990 and 1996 indicate that during the campaign year of 1996 these cases spiked to their highest levels during this period. While these statistics must be treated with the greatest caution, it is nevertheless noteworthy that such patterns would be evident even in officially controlled data. Reformist police officials and scholars have spoken strongly of the bad impact that this has on popular impressions of the police and the state.[38]

LONG-TERM INEFFECTIVENESS

But among public security analysts, probably the most powerful critique against campaign-style policing is that over the long term it simply does not work. Many reformers have attacked the "deterrence" justification for campaigns by arguing that these campaigns have no staying power. Within a little more than a year after the end of the 1983–1987 campaign, several senior security officials and scholars began noting that official crime statistics had quickly resumed their rapid upward trends almost immediately upon the cessation of the campaign.[39]

One of the boldest attacks on the long-term ineffectiveness of campaign-style policing has been levelled by two senior public security scholars, Liu Renwen and Tang Junqi, who write the "Social Order Trends" chapter in the Chinese Academy of Social Science's highly respected annual "Blue Book" on social trends in China. Writing in early 1996 at the very outset of the largest *yanda* campaign since 1983–87, the two government advisors drew upon past campaign results to flatly forecast its failure—predicting that any downturn in crime statistics resulting from the campaign would prove temporary and the upward trend in serious crimes would soon resume. One year later, when official crime statistics had proven their forecasts correct, the two authors wrote a refreshingly bold "I told you so."

> In the 1996 Social Blue Book, we forecast that "there is a rather great likelihood that after the 'yanda' concludes, amidst general stability, there will be an impetus for crime to return to its upward trend, especially a return to the upward trend in serious, major crimes." The facts have demonstrated that this has been the case.[40]

Liu and Tang illustrate their case rather dramatically by using rarely published month-on-month statistics on criminal cases nationwide, which make clear the overall similarity in crime patterns between the campaign year of 1996 and the post-campaign year of 1997. Their data also show that almost immediately after the 1996 *yanda* campaign concluded with the perennial pre-Lunar New Year's police crackdown in February 1997, criminal cases immediately began to resume through the remainder of the year. By September 1997, monthly crime rates were virtually the same as they had been at the high-point months of spring 1996 when the campaign was launched.[41]

Police analysts have put forward several explanations for the long-term ineffectiveness of campaign-style policing. A number of local officials have argued that campaigns draw police energy away from many of the activities that contribute to crime prevention. During campaigns, local police leaders are under terrific pressure from above to show statistical results, in particular an increase in the number of arrests and the percentage of all formally opened cases that are "cracked." Personnel and energy end up being focused almost exclusively on "investigation, attacks, and arrests." Preventative social order management activities—such as patrolling, household registration, strengthening neighborhood resident groups, and management of guns, explosives, and other dangerous materials—all slip by the wayside, with consequences for crime that are only likely to be felt after the campaign has ended.[42]

Other analysts have blamed what we might call cycles of political attention and the lack of "follow-up" for the unsustainability of campaign results. After the high tide of attack in a campaign, many local leaders quickly lose interest in social order management, leaving the fundamental sources of crime unaddressed. Moreover, despite universal support for the rhetoric of crime prevention and the long-standing policy slogan of "comprehensive management of social order," local Party committees are usually reluctant to put their money where their mouths are. Critics complain that budgets for prevention activities are rarely forthcoming, further underscoring the charge that *yanda* campaigns are an effort to get crime "on the cheap." One official has ridiculed this political cycle of attention and neglect as "seeing the doctor only when your head hurts." The ultimate effect, he argues, is that "the deterrent power of the campaign is slowly dissipated."[43]

In response, some officials have argued that the effectiveness of *yanda* campaigns can only be improved if the number of campaigns decreases and ordinary police work is strengthened, professionalized, and better managed. Liaoning PSB Chief Guo Dawei indicates that in 1993 his bureau put forward the proposal that, for the most part, "concentrated attack operations" in Liaoning be suspended while the police focus on strengthening regular police work. In particular, Guo contended that police departments needed to strengthen investigatory skills, interdepartmental cooperation to improve patrol work and hunt down mobile or fleeing criminals, police links to mass organs and social and economic units, control over computers, etc. In particular, Guo insisted that Party committees and governments at all levels had to greatly increase funding to recruit more and better-trained police officers, further confirming the interpretation that *yanda* campaigns have been used, in part, to compensate for inadequate local funding and staffing. Guo argues that stronger, more professional police forces can do a far more powerful and accurate job of attacking and punishing criminals, noting pithily that "wounding ten of their fingers is not nearly as good as breaking one of them."[44]

REOPENING THE DEBATE OVER DETERRENCE

The failure of *yanda* campaigns to staunch the long-term upward spiral in crime has driven reformist criminologists to question the very theories of deterrence upon which these campaigns are based. The focus of this criticism has been the assumption that criminals calculate their actions based mostly on the severity of punishment. Reformist criminologists such as Liu Renwen and Tang Junqi, by contrast, have drawn on both Chinese and foreign research to point to a different deterrent calculus in which the potential offender's *perceived probability* of being punished looms larger than the actual severity of punishment. They have criticized campaign advocates' "superficial" and even "superstitious" faith in "incessantly seeking to increase the severity of punishments." They argue that this ignores the fact that "the effectiveness of punishments is absolutely not a matter of whether or not the punishment is severe, but rather whether or not there are any loopholes in the net." So long as serious, career criminals believe they are able to escape execution or a long term of labor reform by laying low during a campaign, they will not be deterred.[45]

HISTORICAL-INSTITUTIONAL DEBATE AND THE FUTURE OF *YANDA* CAMPAIGNS

As this article has demonstrated, many senior police officials and scholars have put forward powerful arguments and evidence to chip away at the official "institutional lesson" that campaign-style policing is an appropriate and effective tool of social control during the reform era. Still, of course, the practice has no shortage of defenders, either among the upper levels of the public security system or among the broader political leadership. In the face of mounting evidence and criticism, staunch defenders have clung to the politically appealing—though analytically unfalsifiable—proposition that "stern blows" campaigns would still be an effective deterrent to crime if only the leadership would really be more "stern." The failure is not in the strategy of campaigning *per se* but rather that since 1983 the punishments have not been tough enough. Former Shandong provincial Public Security Bureau Chief Meng Qingfeng, for example, has decried the fact that in his province the percentage of convicts sentenced to labor reeducation between 1983 and 1992 declined by 20 percent.[46]

To be sure, given the strong institutional defences the Ministry of Public Security has made of past *yanda* campaigns—plus Deng Xiaoping's personal involvement in launching the 1983 campaign—an official declaration of their ineffectiveness is unlikely to be forthcoming. Since the 1996 campaign, however, there have been official signs of backing away from campaigns as a cornerstone of social control policy. This is evident in the changing official weight given to the other great social control policy slogan of the post-Mao era, the more prevention-oriented "comprehensive management of social order." Since the promulgation of this socially intrusive catchall policy in the early 1980s, a tension has existed between advocates of greatly strengthened crime prevention and social management measures and more hard-line advocates of stern punishments, deterrence, and campaigning. Throughout the 1990s, the latter group has insisted that "stern blows" was the "key link" in crime fighting, and that the punishment and deterrent functions were the only reliable premise for effective prevention measures. This view at times has won the endorsement of Party and state central leaders.[47] Advocates of a greater focus on prevention and "management" won a modest victory in 1997, when Jiang Zemin's Report to the Fifteenth Party Congress officially adopted the formulation that China should "combine [stern] blows with prevention, taking prevention as the key element" (dafang jiehe, yufang weizhu). In the wake of the congress, reformist security officials have used Jiang's formulation to turn the tables on campaigners, contending that without adequate prevention measures, "stern blows" are ineffective.

But a new policy slogan—even from Jiang's lips—is still a far cry from the policy commitments necessary to institutionalize an effective new form of policing adequate to the challenges of China's more mobile society. And prevention advocates are unlikely to dominate the institutional battle unless they can put forward a policy alternative that looks likely to be effective. But serious crime-prevention techniques will require the center to persuade local Party committees and governments to commit significant resources to expanding and professionalizing China's chronically underfunded and undertrained police forces. It is sobering in this context that more effectively policed Asian countries (e.g. Japan, Taiwan, South Korea) have police/citizen ratios as much as three times that of China. It must also find an effective system of public monitoring to replace the now largely ineffectual "work-unit" (danwei) system that provided such a critical invisible subsidy to policing in the Maoist era. It remains to be seen if the use of "contracting" and semiprivatizing security and guard work (highlighted in the recent research of Michael Dutton) will be effective. Finally, as any observer of law enforcement policy in the United States knows, the political appeal of an anti-crime policy of "stern punishments" rests not only on its effectiveness in deterring or preventing crime, but also on its visceral appeal to revenge and the desire of political leaders to outdo each other in showing that they are "doing something about crime." These last points mean that in the institutional debates over policing, critics of *yanda* campaigns are likely to operate at a political disadvantage for some time to come.

NOTES

1. These estimates come from Amnesty International's remarkably well-researched list of executions reported by the Chinese mass media. *China: Death Penalty Log, 1996 (Parts I and II)*, July 1997, ASA 17/35/97; see also the subsequent analytical report, *People's Republic of China: The Death Penalty in China: Breaking Records, Breaking Rules*, August 1997, ASA 17/38/97.

2. Deng's remarks are quoted in the memoir of his Public Security minister at that time, Liu Fuzhi. "Wei baohu gaige zuochu 'yanda' de juece," (Taking the decision for "stern blows" in order to protect reform), *Dang he Guojia Zhongda Juece de Licheng* (Accounts of important party and state decisions), vol. 5 (Beijing: Hongqi Chubanshe, 1997), 450–57 (hereafter Liu Fuzhi, "'Yanda' de juece").

3. Details of organizing the campaign, including the figure of three million, can be found in *Zhongguo Yanda de Lilun yu Shijian* (Theory and practice of stern blows in China), (Beijing, Zhongguo Renmin Gongan Daxue Chubanshe, 1998), chapter 1. The police personnel figure is for the year 1982, and it is from Ministry of Public Security Political Department, *Gongan Renshi Guanli* (Public security personnel management) (Beijing: Qunzhong Chubanshe, 1997), 67–68.

4. Murray Scot Tanner, "State Coercion and the Balance of Awe: The 1983–87 'Stern Blows' Anti-Crime Campaign," *The China Journal*, July 2000, 93–125.

5. Harold M. Tanner, *Strike Hard! Anti-Crime Campaigns and Chinese Criminal Justice, 1979–1985* (Ithaca, N.Y.: Cornell East Asian Series, 1999), especially the introduction, 1–4.

6. Michael Dutton, "Dreaming of Better Times: 'Repetition with a Difference' and Community Policing in China," *Positions* 3, no. 2 (fall 1995), 415–47.

7. Murray Scot Tanner, "State Coercion and the Balance of Awe," esp. 95–98.

8. For a defence of the campaign published as recently as 1997, see Liu Fuzhi, "'Yanda' de Juece."

9. See, for example, Hao Hongtao "Shenru Xuexi Deng Xiaoping Renmin Minzhu Zhuanzheng Sixiang" (Deeply study Deng Xiaoping's thought on the people's democratic dictatorship), *Gongan Yanjiu*, no. 4 (1997): 1–2, 13.

10. See, for example, the discussion of the campaign's successes in the very recent official MPS history, *Zhongguo Renmin Gongan Shigao* (A draft history of the Chinese people's public security), (Beijing: Jingguan Jiaoyu Chubanshe, 1997), esp. 380–81.

11. Børge Bakken's discussion of deterrence is in "Crime, Juvenile Deliquency and Deterrence Policy in China," *The Australian Journal of Chinese Affairs* (now *The China Journal*), no. 30 (July 1993): 29–58.

12. Such terminology is still in widespread use. As one police official has written, *yanda* campaigns such as in 1983 "can both serve the 'kill one to warn a hundred,' 'shake the mountain to frighten the tiger' function of terrifying criminal elements who are in the process of committing crimes or about to commit crimes, and can also stir up the courageous activism of the broad masses of people to see the righteous and do it." Su Yingjie, "Dui Danqian 'Yanda' Tongyi Xingdong Wenti de Jidian Sikao" (A few reflections on current problems of "stern blows" unified operations), *Gong'an Yanjiu*, no. 6 (1994): 22–24, 35. A classic analysis of the ancient origins of these notions of severe punishment, deterrence, long-term social learning, and "behavioralism" in legalist and pre-Confucian thought is chapter 8 in Benjamin I. Schwartz, *The World of Thought in Ancient China* (Belknap: Harvard University Press, 1985), especially 323–335; see also Geoffrey MacCormack, *The Spirit of Traditional Chinese Law* (Athens: University of Georgia Press, 1996), esp. 189–92.

13. Zhu Daren, "Guanyu 'yanda' douzheng de xianshi sixiang" (Some practical thoughts concerning 'yanda' struggles), *Gongan Yanjiu*, no. 4 (1996): 1–5.

14. Amnesty International, *Breaking Records, Breaking Rules*.

15. Amnesty International was among the only organizations which actually totalled up available official reports from "only a few places in China" and recorded the executions of over 600 individuals during the most intense period, from late August to about early November 1983. Western journalists estimated more than 1,000 had been executed by mid-October 1983, while foreign diplomats reported that central officials had assigned a nationwide target of 5,000 executions by the end of October 1983, broken down into provincial subquotas. Chinese jurists cited by the Hong Kong press and Amnesty International reported over 10,000 people had already been executed by January 1984. See Amnesty International, *China: Violations of Human Rights. Prisoners of Conscience and the Death Penalty in the People's Republic of China*, (London, Amnesty International Publications, 1984), 54–55; *Agence France Presse*, Hong Kong, October 21, 1983, in FBIS-CHI, October 25, 1983, pg. K 6; Victoria Graham, *Associated Press*, September 15, 1983. This last report claimed that Guangdong province had been assigned a quota of 500 executions, or 10 percent of the national total.

16. *The Chinese Communist Party's Forty Years in Power*, cited by Harold Tanner, "The Theoretical Bases of Labour Reform," *China Information* (Leiden), vol. 9, nos. 2/3 (Winter 1994/1995).

17. *Dangdai Zhongguo Shenpang gongzuo [shang]* (Contemporary China's adjudication work, Vol. I), (Beijing: Dangdai Zhongguo Chubanshe, 1993), 309.

18. Zhang Qingfu, ed., *Fazhi jianshe shinian, 1978–1988* (Ten years of legal system building, 1978–1988), (Beijing, Luyou Jiaoyu Chubanshe, 1988), 173–74, citing figures from Chief Justice Zheng Tianxiang's April 1988 Supreme People's Court Work Report.

19. There are two very strong indicators of this conclusion. First, as noted, of the total 2.048 million persons sentenced during the entire campaign, a full 42 percent were sentenced in those first five months. Second, the percentage of all sentencees who received the toughest sentences (five years imprisonment or worse) clearly declined over time (August 1983–December 1986, 39.7

percent; August 1983–December 1987, 38.18 percent; and therefore, from January to December 1987, 99,488 persons or 30.4 percent).

20. Zhang Qingfu, ed., *Fazhi jianshe shinian*, 173–74.

21. "China Says Death Sentences, Immediate Executions Reduced" Beijing *Xinhua* in English, February 11, 1998, and "China Formatting Regulations on Execution by Lethal Injection," Beijing *Xinhua* in English, February 28, 1998, translated by BBC Summary of World Broadcasts, on Lexis-Nexis. Other critical comments on the death penalty during the 1996 campaign by Chinese officials and scholars are cited in Amnesty International, "*Breaking Records, Breaking Rules.*"

22. Meng Qingfeng, "Dui xingshi fanzui dajibuli wenti jidai caiqu de jiben duice" (Several basic policies urgently awaiting adoption to deal with the problem of not striking forcefully enough against crime) *Gongan Yanjiu*, no. 6 (1994): 18–21, see especially 21.

23. Zhu Daren, "Guanyu 'yanda' douzheng de xianshi sixiang" *Gongan Yanjiu*, 1996, Number 4, 1–5.

24. Dai Wendian, "Shehui zhuyi chuji jieduan yu fanzui yanjiu" (Research on the initial stage of socialism and crime) *Gongan Yanjiu*, no. 2 (1988).

25. Li Maolin quoted in *Gongan Yanjiu*, no. 1 (1993): 3; see also Fu Hongjie, *Gongan Yanjiu*, no. 1 (1996): 32–33.

26. For widespread examples of this during the 1983–1987 campaign, see "Zuigao Renmin Fayuan guanyu Renmin Fayuan shenpan yanzhong xingshi fanzui anjian zhong juti yingyong falü de ruogan wenti de dafu [yi]" (The SPC's responses to several questions from people's courts on concretely using the law in adjudicating serious criminal cases [Part One]) September 20, 1983, in Ministry of Public Security, comp., *Zhifa shouce* 4 (1984), 45–52.

27. Dong Shenwen, "Guanyu 'yanda' douzheng xingshi de sikao" (Thoughts on the forms of "stern blows" struggles), *Gongan Yanjiu*, no. 1 (1996): 52–57, esp. 52.

28. Li Zhihui, "Yao zhongshi tigao 'yanda' de shehui xiaoguo"(We must pay attention to raising the social effectiveness of 'stern blows'), *Renmin Gongan*, no. 3 (1989): 11–12. At the time, Li was deputy secretary of the Hunan Provincial CCP Committee Political-Legal Committee. See also Dai Wendian, "Shehui zhuyi chuji jieduan yu fanzui yanjiu"; and Mou Xinsheng, "Shilun shehui zhuyi chuji jieduan renmin gongan jiguan de zhineng" (An initial discussion of the functions of the people's public security organs during the initial stage of socialism) *Gongan Yanjiu*, no. 1 (1988): 7–9.

29. Interview, Beijing, 1998.

30. Su Yingjie, "Dui dangqian 'yanda' tongyi xingdong wenti de jidian sikao" (Several reflections on current problems of 'stern blows' unified operations), *Gongan Yanjiu*, no. 6 (1994): 22–25, esp. 23.

31. Dong Shengwen, Guanyu yanda douzheng, 52.

32. Wang Mingxin, *Gongan Zhandouli Lun* (On public security fighting strength), (Beijing: Jingguan jiaoyu chubanshe, 1993), 183.

33. Dong Shengwen, Guanyu yanda douzheng, 52–53.

34. Su Yingjie, Dui dangqian yanda, 23–24.

35. This evidence and Deng's speech are discussed in Tanner, "State Coercion and the Balance of Awe," 98–108.

36. Dong Shengwen, Guanyu yanda douzheng, 52–53.

37. Su Yingjie, Dui dangqian yanda, 23; Wang Mingxin, Gong'an zhandouli lun, 183.

38. The torture data is in Wang Gangping, ed., *Xingxun bigong zui* (The crime of tortured confession), (Beijing: Supreme People's Procuratorate Press, 1997), 9. I have discussed this point in greater detail in Murray Scot Tanner, "Shackling the Coercive State: China's Ambivalent Struggle against Torture," *Problems of Post-Communism* (September–October 2000), 13–30)

39. Mou Xinsheng, Shilun shehui zhuyi, 7–9; Dai Wendian, Shehui zhuyi, 15; Li Zhihui, Yao Zhongshi tigao, 11–12;

40. Liu Renwen and Tang Junqi, "1996–1997 Nian Zhongguo shehui zhi'an xingshi de fenxi yu yuce" (1996–1997 Chinese social order trends: analysis and forecast) in Chinese Academy of Social Sciences *Shehui Lanpi Shu: 1996–1997 Nian Zhongguo shehui xingshi fenxi yu yuce* (Social Blue Book: 1996–1997 Chinese social trends: analysis and forecast), (Beijing, Zhongguo Shehui Kexue Chubanshe, 1997), 162–72, esp. 168–69; also Liu Renwen and Tang Junqi, "1997–1998 Nian Zhongguo shehui zhi'an xingshi de fenxi yu yuce" (1996–1997 Chinese social order trends: analysis and forecast) in Chinese Academy of Social Sciences *Shehui lanpi shu: 1998 Nian Zhongguo shehui xingshi fenxi yu yuce* (Social Blue Book: 1996–1997 Chinese social trends: analysis and forecast), (Beijing, Zhongguo shehui kexue chubanshe, 1998), 235–45, esp. 239.

41. Liu Renwen and Tang Junqi, Nian Zhongguo shehui, 239.

42. Su Yingjie, Dui dangqian yanda, 23.

43. Liu Renwen and Tan Junqi, Nian Zhongguo shehui, 166–67.

44. Guo Dawei, "Guanyu jianchi 'yanda' fangzhen qianghua jingchangxing gongzuo de jidian sikao," (Several reflections on strengthening the "stern blows" direction and strengthening regular work) *Gong'an Yanjiu*, no. 3 (1993): 1–4, esp. 2–3.

45. Liu Renwen and Tang Junqi, Nian Zhongguo shehui, 167.

46. Meng Qingfeng, Dui xingshi fanzui, 18–19.

47. An excellent example is Meng Qingfeng, Dui xingshi fanzui, 18.

Toward a Government of the Contract: Policing in the Era of Reform

MICHAEL DUTTON

ECONOMIC REFORM: FROM A COVENANT OF GRACE TO THE CONTRACT

The year 1978 was a turning point in China. It was the year that the secularized covenant of grace that had tied Mao to the people in an unmediated relation best described, in the language of Claude Lefort, as the people as one under the supreme Other[1] was abandoned and replaced by a new and very different set of conventions. Gone was the Maoist logic of politics in command, and in its place came economic reform. Deng Xiaoping, China's new paramount leader, issued a series of economic measures that foreshadowed a new form of governmental power. Unlike Mao, Deng's legitimacy rested largely upon a multifaceted modernization program. This, in turn, would lead to economic changes that brought forth the need for an endless series of petite contractual arrangements organized around the production of goods and services. These rather modest contracts would end up turning the logic of the economy into that of government.

Begun in 1978 with the announcement of the responsibility system in agriculture, this economic reform agenda would soon spread to other domains. Indeed, as the economy filled with responsibility systems, bonus systems, and contract systems of various sorts, other, more socially orientated areas of life were infected with the language and logic of economic reform. Where once everything operated under the aegis of Mao, now, it seems, everything was to be put under contract. Where once Mao's covenant of grace with the people operated under the sign of politics and "class struggle," under Deng's society of the contract, every new arrangement was signed with the word "economy." Law was essential to this process. Without a strong legal code there could be no system of individual contracts, and without these there was no way to offer material incentives to spur the masses to carry out more efficient production.[2]

The foundation of such modern contracts, as Sir Henry Sumner Maine had long ago argued, lay in the historic transition from family dependence to individual obligation,[3] and while the Chinese trajectory may be differently configured, it is similarly inspired.[4] The desire to replace the Maoist-induced collective dependence upon the state with a notion of rationally calculable individual obligation was central to Deng's reform program. It was the contractually based notion of individual obligation that was to fuel China's economic reform program and, as a result, the development of a substantive legal code would, by necessity, be an essential component of this process. It is, after all, through law that contracts are made legally enforceable.[5]

In the China of Chairman Mao, there was neither individual obligation nor a commitment to substantive law. Indeed, as the Chinese press in Mao's time made clear, any discussion of law presupposed the centrality of legal elasticity.[6] Without such legal flexibility everything from the mass dictatorship of the 1950s to the all-round dictatorship of the 1970s would have been impossible. Legal elasticity was the hallmark of both the Maoist-style continuous revolution as well as his campaign style of political life. Little wonder, then, that the much-vaunted criminal code that circulated within Party ranks from 1954 until the early months of 1957 was never ratified and fell victim to what later Chinese scholarship would describe as Mao's legal nihilism.[7] China under Mao was ruled by generalized, publicly promulgated regulations, specific and detailed internal Party edicts, and *People's Daily* editorials and commentaries. The land that produced a political covenant of grace that unified the people and their leader also promoted a form of governance that demarcated legitimate and illegitimate actions not on the basis of the law but on the basis of class struggle. This, almost by definition, buried any notion of formal legal equality. Indeed, by 1959, Chinese legal circles talked freely of the need for the rule of man to replace any lingering attachment to the rule of law.[8]

It was just this type of legal flexibility that was to become the target of a series of debates in China after economic reform resurrected the need for law. The rule of man would become the target of Chinese legal scholars' criticism. Chinese scholars, after all, had long and constantly pointed out that the market economy is a legal-system economy.[9] If law was essential to guarantee stability, then elasticity was the dragon that must be slain to ensure the success and stability of the economic reform program. The needs of the economic reform program not only brought on critiques of legal elasticity but also established the theoretical ground upon which the Party could promote legal construction work. Thirty years after the rule of man seemed to have been set in stone, the rule of law made a comeback.

In the debates that followed, legal reformers overturned the left view that law was a mere reflection of the will of one dominant ruling class. Instead reformers suggested that socialist law increasingly embodied the common good and all social needs.[10] As this form of "classless" law developed, it would increasingly serve a multiplicity of ends and reinforce a range of objective economic conditions.[11] It was, therefore, impossible to tie law back to class.[12] These types of arguments helped bolster the stability and legitimacy of the newly developing legal culture which, in turn, was said to contribute to the process of economic reform. As the Chinese legal scholar Zhang Shuyi makes clear, the basic point in establishing the legal system from 1979 onward was to promote the socialist commodity economy. He notes that the legal system was established in accordance with the needs of that commodity economy, and it was being developed in concert with the socialist commodity economy.[13]

As emphasis began to be placed upon the development of a legal-based culture, the legislative basis upon which policing was undertaken was also questioned. As law won the day, a vast array of legislation was devised and then enacted to ensure that policing, too, was placed on a legal footing. In the twelve-year period between 1979 and 1991 alone, over 50 percent of all the nation's laws and regulations governing public security were enacted. In the same period, a further six hundred regulations governing police actions were enacted by local governments and regional peoples' congresses.[14] With laws beginning to dictate and limit police actions and procedures, their traditional Party-based function as defenders of the dictatorship began to erode. This shift from a covenant of grace to a legally based society of the contract not only seemed to herald the arrival of policing as a form of law enforcement, but it also looked like the Western history of policing was about to be retold with Chinese characteristics.

EUROPE AS PRECURSOR?

Under very different conditions, the same sort of rearrangements to life and economy that are currently being witnessed in China began to unfold in Europe in the latter part of the seventeenth century. These European shifts not only led to the reification of the contract form, but more significantly, they marked the birth of the modern bourgeois state. In Europe, this modern bourgeois constitutional state developed secularized contractual relations that drew upon the religiously based covenant of grace that had proven central to the constitution of Christian faith.[15] The secularization of such compacts was central to these changes, for as Oestreich notes in his sociological synopsis of this European transition, it was the shift from the cleric to the lawyer that marked the opening moments of what we have come to call modernity. Oestreich plots this transition from the last decades of the seventeenth century onwards. It was at around this time, he argues, that "the business of writing gallant verses is taken over mainly by lawyers."[16]

These "new gallant verses" of the early modern era would be written as statutes and their poetry styled in the language of the contract. Tied to the market, this emerging form of constitutionalism would avow blindness to past forms of privilege and power. Economic transactions were legitimized under a code that claimed an autonomy and independence from all political arrangements. Yet this was, quite obviously, a fiction. The development of the market could not take place independently of politics for it was through the politically inspired law of the contract that market order was actually constituted.[17]

For market-orientated economic relations, the law of the contract lay at the intersection of market and state power and, as such, was (and arguably still is) central to the constitution of the modern bourgeois state.[18] It was under the influence of these types of politico-legal rearrangements that professional policing came into being. Only under this universalized code of law, operating as a secular and social contract, could the police begin to develop the character of a secular force for legal enforcement. This secularization of policing, witnessed in Europe in the early modern period, was accompanied by a process of professionalization brought on by other, more earthly, concerns.

Early definitions of police related to the maintenance of good government in relation to the interconnected concerns of the moral, political, and economic order.[19] This economy of policing began to break down from around the seventeenth century as the static, stable, rural communities of Europe began to break up. At this time, there was a huge movement of the population into urban areas. This not only increased urban density but produced social dislocation and new forms of urban life-styles. It also produced a social panic leading to increased demands being made upon government to more effectively and professionally deal with the growing list of social problems.[20] Community self-policing began to give way to professional policing and this, in turn, resulted in the reinvention of police as a force charged with the new, specialized task of crime prevention.[21]

Similar concerns fuelled a very different but no less professional model of policing in England after the War of Austrian Secession in 1748.[22] Rawlings chronicles the growing list of concerns that led in this direction. He argues that from around the latter part of the seventeenth century, a whole range of social problems emerged to fuel the fires of the later Fielding brothers' reforms. The unparalleled economic expansion of the time coupled with the beginnings of industrialization accentuated the already existing pull of the towns but added to this potent mix some radical new social problems.

The development of industries increased the degree of wealth disparity, leading to increased degrees of social envy and crime. Struggles over the introduction of new labor-saving technology resulted in Ludditism and other such social movements. New industries and technologies increased the need for labor in the city and this, in turn, upset the demographic stability of city populations, further exacerbating existing social divisions. Marx, of course, had pointed to just these problems when he spoke of the disenfranchising effect of the enclosure laws upon the peasants. But while Marx would examine this period to understand the formative moments of the working class, Rawlings examines it to understand the social conditions that led to the need for professional policing.

It was not just that there appeared to be more crime, it was also that this new crime appeared to be qualitatively different from the crimes of the past. More frightening, unpredictable, violent, gang-based, and indiscriminate than in the past,[23] crime came to occasion a moral panic and this, in turn, led to calls for radical action that would, eventually, lead to the formation of a professional police force. It was in this regard that the fathers of the Bow Street Runners, the Fielding brothers, made their greatest contribution. Rawlings argues that the Fieldings not only laid down the key ideologies of the modern professional police bureaucracy but also argued for recognition of the need for professional expertise in policing. This, in turn, largely reduced the role of the populace in policing. The implication of what the Fielding brothers were saying, writes Rawlings, was that "only experts could separate the criminals from the generality of the laboring poor."[24]

At a time when new levels of social mobility not only brought forth crime in the cities but also broke up the old self-policing rural communities, these were important arguments to make. Eventually they became more than arguments. In 1829 the British Home Secretary, Robert Peel, pushed through the Metropolitan Police Act and thus gave birth to the new, professional, and specialized police force.

MONEY TALKS

This now-familiar Western concept of the police only began to arrive at the scene of the crime in China after economic reform.[25] From this time onward, police increasingly claimed to be operating on the basis of the law, not Party dictates.

As the old command economy gave way to market socialism, the life-world of China was transformed. The agnatic, almost rural, nature of Chinese city life under Mao gave way to cities of a more familiar form. The all-encompassing work units of China were transformed into economic enterprises, and peasants who were once tethered to the land by a castelike system of household registration[26] were transformed into (formally) "free" workers and drawn into the city in ever increasing numbers. Greater wealth disparities coupled with greater degrees of social and demographic mobility spelt the beginnings of the now-familiar story of social dislocation that we call the history of modernity. It was under these conditions that the Party clerics were slowly replaced by the professional lawyer, and the Chinese police began to speak of the need to professionalize, specialize, and with their newfound respect for law, legitimize their work. It was with this latter goal in mind that the Chinese police would slowly and hesitantly begin to question their traditional role as a tool of the Communist Party.

The problem was that as the Party dictatorship faded, the new specialized and professional police sirens no longer stirred the masses to action. Increasingly, it seemed as though the only thing that would open their eyes was money. Nor was this attitude confined solely to the urban populace. As the old Maoist slogan about the forward march of socialism (*yiqie xiang qian kan*) was parodied and replaced by a new colloquial expression that spoke of the forward march of money, millions of peasants packed their bags and marched to the cities in search of work and wealth. Some found it but others lost their way. Those that lost their way became known as the floating blind (*mangliu*), and it was with regard to that group that an urban fear of a new, mobile, and dangerous criminal class emerged.[27] While this transient or mobile criminal group would remain one of the most intractable problems facing contemporary China, it was far from being the only one. Indeed, it was as though market reform had, quite literally, produced its nemesis: criminal reform.

New crimes began to emerge just as old ones, long considered vanquished, reappeared. Moreover, all crimes, new and old, appeared in unprecedented numbers. The market not only produced a new money-making ethos and new social mobility but also brought in its wake a dangerous and paradoxical situation: crime figures would rise just as the old social control structures fell. These social control structures would begin to crumble because they had been built upon the activism of local Maoist-inspired mass-line organs and kept in place by a tight system of demographic policing organized around the household register. This system had worked well in the era of the plan but would prove far less successful in the depoliticized and fluid conditions of the new marketized economy. From the pull of the cities with their need for labor to the tug of a newly monetarized economy with its fetishization of material things, reform produced a new demographic and social mobility that eroded the old Maoist social structures and ideological certainties.

No longer could China claim to be the land where no one picked up other's things from the road and no one needed to lock their door. Instead, it was the land of crime waves where each new high tide of crime seemed to exceed the last.[28] Little wonder, then, that this new and quite unprecedented wave of crime occasioned something of a social panic and led to calls by Party and government officials for a reform of policing.[29] Hence just as the Great Leap had called forth its own Great Leap in policing, so too economic reform now demanded its own version of police reform. These reforms would closely follow the contours of the main social agenda of economic reform. This meant that the politico-moral methods once used under Mao to improve police performance gave way to a series of money-based bonus systems, responsibility systems, and other contractual arrangements favored by Deng Xiaoping. In terms of content, reform would bring forth the rhetoric of professionalization, specialization, and adherence to the law. Unfortunately, the methods used to improve performance, namely the monetarized reward system, would end up driving the professionalization, specialization, and respect for the law agenda off course.

Publicly, of course, the Chinese police admitted no such conflict between monetary incentives and their professionalization agenda. Instead, all were thought of as modern and therefore part and parcel of the move to the rule of law. Much would be made of the new police academies and the new professional specialist courses. Much was also made of the fact that formally taboo disciplinary areas such as Western criminology, criminal psychology, and the rule of law were now being taught in police training institutions.[30] On the streets, reform led to a range of new policing techniques. From the institution of mobile police patrols to the adoption of the Japanese *koban* (pillbox) system, from the emphasis on forensics to the promotion and spread of the 110 emergency number system, the Chinese public security forces appeared to be following a reform program that drew heavily upon Western and Japanese policing practices. Taken together, such reforms implied that the open-door policy was leading toward the adoption of a scientific discipline of law enforcement.[31] The Western concept of the police, it seems, had arrived in China.

Yet there was another side to this police story that belied this image. It was a side that was no less inspired by economic reform, but it was one that would send policing practices spiraling off in an entirely different direction. Rattled by rising crime rates and the gradual erosion of their once-strict but static form of community control, the Chinese police opted for a partial revival of their past Maoist traditions. This revival included a return to a more visceral and populist response to crime. As this began to take shape, it was a policy that came to shadow and problematize the process of professionalization, specialization, and the rule of law that had been promised in the rhetoric of scientific law enforcement.[32] Foremost among these more visceral and populist responses to crime were the Maoist-inspired police campaigns and the so-called comprehensive management of social order.

While campaign-style policing emerged as a significant strategy in May 1981 after the five-city[33] security conference, it was not until 1983, with the announcement of the first of the severe strike campaigns against crime, that the full consequences of this strategy became apparent.[34] Leading to the arrest of over 1.5 million people overall, the severe strike campaign would follow the traditional Maoist three-stage approach to campaigning perfected in the 1950 campaign against counterrevolutionaries.[35] The difference was that while the campaigns of Mao were disciplinary and targeted political crimes, the campaigns of the Deng era were punitive and focused upon more orthodox forms of crime. Nevertheless, the severe strike campaign and all other subsequent police campaigns would adopt methods that appeared to be similar to those of the prereform period.

Nor was the campaign the only thing the police would resurrect from their past. While campaign-style policing focused upon the short, sharp shock, the other significant innovation revisiting the socialist past was called the comprehensive management of social order.[36] Where this differed from the campaign was that it was said to offer a more lasting and reintegrative crime-fighting model. Thus, while both campaigns and comprehensive management relied upon a wide range of local social forces coming together under the leadership of the Party and the police, the former focused on attacking crime while the latter emphasized the longer-term goal of crime prevention and social reintegration.[37]

This idea of comprehensive management emerged in June 1979 with a call from various organs for the Party to pay more attention to juvenile crime.[38] By the time of the 1981 five-city security conference, comprehensive management was being touted alongside campaign-style policing as a partial solution to the rising crime rates nationwide.[39] Given that both comprehensive management and the police campaign were reliant upon the participation of community activists, they required not only the reemphasis of Party committee leadership[40] but also the revival of the increasingly moribund mass-line security organs. It was with regard to the revival of the latter that the use of monetary incentives began to make its appearance within community policing. As this style of policing was revived, it almost inevitably bumped into the rhetoric of scientific law enforcement.

With a strategic need to coordinate all social forces to prosecute the anticrime campaigns and run the comprehensive management strategy that ran alongside it, local Party committee leaders were once again thrust to the fore. This ran counter to the rhetoric of specialist and professional police leadership and could potentially even lead to a challenge of the rule of law. Yet the rule of law would be challenged in a more fundamental, subtle, and paradoxical way by these innovations.

Mass-line organs, as products of the Mao era, had always and would always require a degree of legal elasticity in order to operate effectively and this, quite obviously, was in conflict with the new and highly publicized commitment to the rule of law. Nevertheless, and despite appearances to the contrary, this revival did not signal a return to Mao. Paradoxically, the revival of these once-Maoist organs and techniques flagged the return of something that was anathema to Mao's thinking. That was the use of monetary incentives.

Ironically, the revival of populist Maoist-inspired forms of organization in the reform years signaled the demise, not the rebirth, of left politics. It was this slow process of depoliticization and use of monetary incentives that would change the nature of mass mobilization in China forever. The new motor of mass-line policing was money, not political commitment, and this would lead to the diminution of politics and, for the police, to a politics of financial dependence. Police reliance upon monetary incentives was to have its own hidden costs. The more the police employed financial incentives to bring back the mass-line, the less they could rely upon their old political ways of mobilization. In the end, the police were left with no other options other than to allow the spread of monetary incentives throughout the entire policing system.

Police stations, police beats, even snouts were all put on contract. Mass-line organs would sell their household registration licenses to finance their own incentive schemes just as police increasingly invoked fines to finance theirs. Even private policing was introduced, in part, to offer police a profitable sideline. Effectively, economic reform reshaped the nature of policing in China and fundamentally altered the basis upon which it would recruit, mobilize, and operate. It is at this point that one notices another side to the economic reform process.

China had, in effect, become the land of the economic contract, and good social order had become the product that police were being contracted to supply.

It was Weber who once insisted that the spread of money and market mentalities requires not only law but also the law of the contract.[41] In terms of Chinese policing, the growth of the contract actually leads to the revival of organs that, in quite important but modest ways, challenge substantive law. In other words, the rule of law would be seriously compromised by the expansion of the economic contract when this contractual form was used to resurrect paralegal organs and promote paralegal policing tactics. Economic reform produced both the need for the rule of law but also the mechanisms that enabled its (partial) abnegation. It is this struggle between the desire for a rule of law and the necessity for legal elasticity to ensure social control that one finds being played out both on the streets and among police scholars.

RETHINKING POLICING

It was in 1988 that the preeminent Chinese police studies journal *Public Security Studies,* borrowing from the spirit of earlier reform-era legal debates about the status of law as a class tool, opened up a debate about the correct relationship that should be established between law and policing. Momentarily, it appeared as though police debates would closely follow the legal debates of the early and mid-1980s that had resulted in the resurrection of the rule of law. If that was the intention, it quickly went awry.

As the student protests of 1989 loomed ever closer, a new harder line began to emerge from within the Party and the police. Despite this impending disaster, the advocates of policing as law enforcement still had a day in the sun. It was the police scholar Liu Zaiping who offered the most cogent defence of the rule of law. Beginning with a critique of policing as a tool of the Party dictatorship, Liu suggested that this position obscured the inherently democratic function (*minzhu zhineng*) played by the force in the era of economic reform. For Liu, to regard the police as merely a tool would not only overstate the coercive role of the police but would also mask their changed function in the era of reform.[42] It would also lead to misunderstandings about the nature of the force and ignore the special nature of the dictatorship in the period of economic reform.

In contemporary China, Liu argued, the special quality of the dictatorship ensured that citizens were supreme, that there were guarantees about the equality of rights given, and that power was distributed evenly. Policing, under these circumstances, worked to uphold socialist principles, promote socialist law, and guarantee social order.[43] By promoting the rule of law, police helped establish a stable social order, and this was the precondition for the development of both democracy and the economy.[44] Moreover, with economic reform, Liu seems to suggest, democracy would develop both at the economic base as well as within the ideological superstructure.

The social base for democratic politics, he provocatively argues, rests upon a commodity economy. This, in turn, he adds, means that the role of the police in defending the socialist commodity economy against corruption, profiteering, and other acts of criminality not only benefits the people but also helps advance the democratic process.[45] But this was not the only way the Chinese police force advanced democracy, he contends. Of equal importance was their new primary role of law enforcement.

In Liu's view, economic reform resulted in significant changes in the nature of policing. Police were no longer a force designed simply to protect the Party but had become relatively autonomous of both Party and government. Their overarching guide to action in the period of economic reform, he insists, comes first and foremost in the role allocated to them under the constitution.[46] As police duties gained legal specificity and recognition, the security forces began to have an investment in the law, and this was also an investment in democracy as both the rule of law and democracy relied upon the principle of equality. While a defence of the law would always require coercive powers, Liu suggested that as democracy expands, the dictatorial function of the police would diminish.[47]

With the student struggles of 1989 just around the corner, however, the diminution of coercive police powers seemed far from the police agenda and this argument was to find little support. Particularly after 1989, this argument gave way to a chorus of calls for a return to a more class-based form of total policing. These arguments bemoaned the decline of the preventative Maoist policing model and the lack of class analysis that had accompanied the headlong rush to promote economic development.[48] They critiqued the tawdry state of politico-ideological education, which, they argued, had left Chinese youth unprepared for the seductions of capitalist ideology and the money economy. Tying these complaints together and employing language eerily similar to that which Mao had used against Yugoslavia and the Soviets in an earlier era, one senior police commentator, Tan Songqiu, wrote of the events of 1989 as part of a worldwide movement to bring about the peaceful evolution of socialist China.[49] If the sugar-coated bullets of the West were seducing Chinese youth, then action was needed. Only a renewal of mass-line policing along with a return to a class analysis of crime and a reliance upon campaign-style coercion and propaganda could start to set things right, it was suggested.[50] Through these methods the police could revive the structures that had given them stability in times gone by.

The Mao period, then, offered a set of methods and organizational forms that were conserved in the reform era as inherited structures and techniques the police could not do without. Thus long after most other domains of life had abandoned the mass-line ideology, it seemed to live on in relation to social control. Tan Songqiu's arguments point to the fact that while this mass line in policing gave the appearance that little had changed since the days of Mao, in truth, everything had, and it was Deng's all-round dictatorship of the economic relation that had seen to that.

Through the logic of economy, Deng has succeeded, quite literally, in putting Maoist-style police campaigns on a contractual basis and, in doing this, he has changed forever the nature of Maoist campaigns and the mass line without appearing to do so. It was in developing this contractual form of mass-line policing that a new era in public security in China opened up.

The spread of the contract into noneconomic domains such as policing was the result of its stunning success in increasing production in agriculture at the beginning of the eighties.[51] So successful was it in producing peasant enthusiasm for work and a calculable set of material outcomes that contract forms were thought worthy of emulation and adaptation in other domains.[52] In the end, the spread of the contract led to a virtual contractualization of Chinese life. This not only transformed the economic opacity produced by Mao's politics in command into something more calculable and productive, but in the process it revolutionized both urban and rural life-styles and mentalities.

In terms of economic relations, the employment of a "purposive contract,"[53] as Weber would no doubt have called it, broke down the established politico-moral bonds within traditional Maoist arrangements and reordered them into a discrete series of calculable domains and items. Under Deng, the Maoist homologization of all facets of life under the rubric of politics gave way to a dispersed set of economic calculations modeled upon the disaggregation of things. Thus, while Deng still had his Four Cardinal Principles[54] to protect and promote the Party's political belief system, most emphasis in the reform period would be placed upon the promotion of rapid economic development. It was as an extension of this logic that a new contractual model of social life emerged. While contracts had begun as a relatively simple means of developing the economy, their spread into social domains ate away at the political certainty and unity of the Party. And the more the moral core of the Party was eaten away, the more the Party required the economic contract to produce enthusiasm for the work of modernization upon which Party legitimacy rested. In the end, even their public security forces succumbed to the contractual temptation. The irony was that it was principally Maoist-style mass-line policing that was being brought back to life by these economic contracts.

Beginning in the early 1980s, increases in the overall crime rate, in the number of prison escapees, and in recidivists began to cause alarm. Worried that instability would offset economic gains, Party authorities began demanding that the public security forces improve their performance. They called upon the police to return China to the halcyon days of stability represented by the social order situation of the mid-1950s. Given the changed nature of social relations brought on by economic reform, however, many within the force knew that such demands were utterly unachievable.[55] Nevertheless, it was clear that Party orders must be followed and police reforms undertaken. What better way to demonstrate their determination to bring down crimes rates to the levels experienced in the 1950s than to revive 1950s-style policing techniques! Moreover, as transient criminals, drug addicts, and prostitutes were the new face of crime in the early reform years, the problem areas of 1980s policing in China looked eerily similar to those successfully overcome by the public security forces back in the 1950s.

From the early 1980s onwards, police began to revive earlier solutions to solve the problems. To revive past practices, however, involved trying to recreate similar social conditions to those that existed in the past, and here the police struggled. Nevertheless, central to their efforts in this regard were their ongoing attempts to moderate peasant migrant flows into the cities. By regulating this peasant flow, they hoped to restore the type of demographic stability that had underpinned good social order in both rural and urban regions in the prereform period. With the tight internal migration laws becoming something of a dead letter by the 1980s, however, this problem proved daunting. By the 1980s, huge numbers of peasants were entering Chinese cities in search of higher-paid work.[56] To deal with this growing problem the police would employ both external carrots as well as internal sticks.

The external carrot they offered came in 1984. Police augmented the household registration laws with a resident identity-card system designed to streamline procedures for those making legitimate travel arrangements. By this stage, the biggest of the external sticks was already in place. In 1982, police had tightened up on illegitimate travellers by reinvesting in the shelter and investigation centers (*shourong shencha*). These had proven useful in dealing with transients in the past, and in the face of the rising illegal migration that reform brought in its wake, it was thought that such centers might prove useful once again. Just how useful they would end up becoming was greatly influenced by the 1986 refocusing of the severe strike campaign.

From 1986 onwards, it was decided that the spotlight of the severe strike campaign should shine more directly upon transient criminal activity and criminals on the run. To facilitate this new stage in the campaign, shelter and investigation centers became the key detention facilities used to incarcerate suspected transient criminals. The problem was that these centers were run down and insufficiently funded. Indeed, by the mid-1980s even the Ministry of Security that ran these centers admitted internally that they were the worst form of detention in China.[57] Of even greater concern than living conditions, however, was the flexible nature of the regulations governing their employment.

If shelter and investigation centers led to the revival of certain draconian traditions, the attempts to resurrect the old static model of community policing in rural areas showed the way the police were willing to take up certain lessons learned in the process of economic reform. Apart from direct state investment in rural areas to boost the number of police stations,[58] the security forces also began to experiment with the use of financial incentives to revive their rural mass line. From the early 1980s police had begun to employ monetary inducements to reinvigorate their rural village-security pact system. Success in this arena led to further initiatives. In factories and mines all internal security arrangements were made subject to economic contracts. By June 1981, all police stations in China's five main cities were ordered to introduce a responsibility system that directly linked financial remuneration to the success of local security forces in maintaining law and order.[59] By the mid-1980s contractual arrangements were employed on a trial basis throughout China's remaining cities. By August 1982 financial remuneration was also said to be the key to the successful implementation of the comprehensive management of social order.[60] Other than being fanned by monetary reward, however, such policing innovations ran absolutely counter to the logic of economic reform.

Whereas Deng's economic innovations had principally involved a disaggregation of things, programs like comprehensive management and the mass line were an attempt to totalize and unify social forces in the fight against crime. Indeed, one might go so far as to suggest that things like comprehensive management were yet another example of the miniaturization and specialization of the basic attributes of the Maoist all-round dictatorship of the proletariat, for both comprehensive management and the all-round dictatorship turned on a desire for total control based upon mass-line organs.

Formal state police agencies were closely linked into the work of mass-line or-gans, educational institutions, and work-unit security sections, and together these organs would devise and build up a system of crime prevention.[61] From so-cial help and education to establishing jobs and training schemes for ex-crimi-nals,[62] the comprehensive management of social order craved the type of total control central to the Maoist strategy of an all-round dictatorship.[63] Yet this crime prevention model was driven not by socialist inspiration but by financial inducements. Without financial inducements such innovations were impossible because, as Xu Hanmin makes clear, reliance upon mass consciousness had left many areas with organizational names but little else.[64] To maintain social order, police clearly required more than names: it needed monetary inducements.[65]

From the mid-1980s onwards, even the Maoist-style police campaign would be brought to life not by revolutionary enthusiasm but by monetary incentive. In 1983, during the severe strike campaign, police began a trial implementation of the responsibility system in policing. The success of these experiments led to the sys-tem being adopted nationwide at the beginning of the second stage of this severe strike campaign in 1984. In authorizing contract-based policing, the Central Com-mittee pointed to experiments that had taken place in Guangzhou. Through the use of the contract, one area boasted that its overall crime rates had dropped by 18 percent and breaches of the public security regulations dropped by 20 percent.[66]

"This experience is worth drawing lessons from and extending to other places," claimed the Central Committee.[67] And draw lessons and extend this idea they did. By the beginning of 1985, the idea of financial remuneration was already clearly es-tablished. In January, Chen Pixian insisted that all neighborhood committees, vil-lage committees, and mediation workers be given remuneration packages that offered material rewards alongside the longstanding spiritual ones. Only this com-bination, he concluded, would enable these organs to once again become active.[68] In the following year, Qiao Shi announced the contractualization of base-level police work, and from that time onward, the purposive contract became one of the key de-vices used to ensure an active base-level policing system.[69] It was through contracts that local police and mass-line organ results were made predictable and, for local ac-tivists, profitable. Moreover, because mass-line organs could now renew their ranks using monetary incentives, the police could continue to rely upon and even strengthen the area-based system of policing inherited from the Mao era.

Not all the effects of such financial incentive schemes, however, led to "best practice" policing. Financial changes put pressure upon the *tiaotiao kuaikuai* or dual leadership system. This system came into being with the accession of Mao to the Party leadership in the Yan'an period. It was designed to ensure that Chinese security organs operated very differently to those in the Soviet Union. Whereas Soviet security organs had become a law unto themselves, the Chinese Party insisted upon local Party political control over all security organs. From that time onward, therefore, the security system operated under a dual leadership system. This meant that they would be led by local governments and local Party committees at their administrative level (that is, horizontal leadership, *kuai*), but when it came to professional leadership, they would look to higher-level public security organs (vertical leadership, *tiao*). While this *tiaokuai* system had worked well throughout the Mao era, it was significantly challenged by the forces unleashed by reform.

In theory, it should have been challenged by the demand for professionalization, specialization, and the rule of law for these pointed to the need to strengthen professional leadership over the leadership of the local Party and government organs. In practice, however, economic incentives seemed to have produced almost the opposite result.

On the ground, an ever-increasing portion of the financial burden for local policing was pushed back onto the shoulders of local governments. Strapped for cash and overworked, these local governments began demanding that their local police do their work. They ordered police to collect local taxes and grain allocations, police the one-child policy in their jurisdictions, and carry out a range of other non-policing tasks that were, essentially, the responsibility of local government and not the police.[70] In effect, the police were being employed as the administrative assistants of local governments just as they had formerly been used as the tools of the Party.

Even more worrying was the fact that many of these local governments were themselves in such financial difficulty that they no longer had the capacity to fully maintain local police station work. They, in turn, passed on the financial burden of maintaining the local police stations to the stations themselves. In effect, police stations were being told to (partially) self-fund their activities. The result was disastrous. In Gansu, for example, reports began to filter in of local governments refusing to fully fund police stations and demanding that the local police fill the budgetary gap. Local police stations reacted by extensively exercising their powers to levy fines and fees. They did this not as a means of deterrence, but simply to pay the wages of their officers![71] Increasingly, fines replaced punishment, and nowhere was this more in evidence than in those ambiguous administrative areas that lay on the edge of criminality.[72] Prostitution was one such area subject to administrative sanction that lent itself to this extended use of the fine.

As noted earlier, prostitution had become one of the problem crimes of the reform period. Nevertheless, police and Party officials continued to hold the view that prostitutes were victims, not criminals. Hence criminalization was thought inappropriate in most cases, and in place of that, a dual strategy of education and deterrence was put in place. The educative side of this strategy relied upon the revival of the once-successful 1950s strategy of detention and education. From 1982 onwards women's education and support-through-labor units began to appear, and these would operate in a very similar fashion to the earlier women's production education and fostering institutes (*Funü shengchan jiaoyangyuan*). These latter institutions had been established shortly after the revolution in 1950 to reform prostitutes through meaningful labor. While the role and responsibilities of these units were in many respects similar to the prison sector's reform-through-labor program, they differed in that they were not based on the criminal code. Indeed, initially they were developed without any legislative basis whatsoever![73] Women could therefore be sent for rehabilitation at the behest of city-level public security bureau chiefs alone.[74] Given the enormity of the problem, however, only a very small percentage of the prostitutes caught were actually sent. Instead police employed another, more lucrative method to deal with first-time or minor offenders. That, of course, was the employment of the fine.

Cash-strapped police forces began to employ the new financial logic of economic reform to try to remedy the ancient problem of prostitution. Increasingly, however, police began to look at prostitution not as an area in need of reform, but rather as a milk cow that would pay, through fines, for the vast array of financial incentive schemes that held the local public security system intact. A mechanism that had begun life as a deterrent had very quickly degenerated into a money-making business, as the police critic Song Haobo explains:

> Lots of people, including law enforcement agency staff, were enticed by money and this was to have a negative influence upon them and resulted in the commodification (*shangpinhua*) of administrative management. Hence there was an exponential growth in the use of fines and this malady became quite serious. It created situations in some places, where the law enforcement agencies took prostitutes and their clients in, not to detain, control or educate them, but simply to extract fines from them.[75]

With such an ethos coming to dominate, the situation deteriorated well beyond the use of fines to finance bonus packages. In one area, the local government even allowed the police to invest a percentage of the money they had earned. This amount proved to be so great that police began investing in a range of office buildings which the general public began calling gambling and prostitution buildings, for it was commonly known that these purchases had been financed through fines levied on these two particular industries. According to Song Haobo, this led inevitably to the commodification of legal implementation and ensured that criminals with money could avoid the detention, education, and other control measures.[76] By the time of the six evils campaign[77] in late 1989 which specifically targeted prostitution, the police were forced to introduce very strict and detailed guidelines to limit the use of fines for they feared justice was being seriously eroded.[78]Fines may have distorted justice, but the money it brought into the system was still needed to cover the cost of policing. While some of these costs would be covered by government expenditure, the spread of the police responsibility system meant that there would always be financial pressure upon the system. The problem was that it was only through contracts and re-sponsibility systems that local policing was able to keep the lid on crime. The sta-tistics alone told the story. Unfortunately, as these statistics were analyzed, they also began to tell another, more troubling, story.

The decreases in local crime rates that followed in the wake of the introduc-tion of the responsibility system, it was found, proved to be more a reduction on paper than on the streets. The responsibility system in policing, it seems, had produced a decrease in police reporting but not necessarily in the actual number of crimes committed.

This problem first came to the notice of senior police officers in 1987. In that year, the Fujian provincial police department undertook a study of fifty-seven po-lice station records across the country. What their study revealed was that huge gaps existed between the number of known or real crime cases and the number of cases reported. Indeed, reported cases constituted only 12.75 percent of the total number of all known cases. Even in relation to serious crime where stricter procedures op-erated, the investigators discovered a glaring discrepancy between known cases and those pursued. In this instance, only 58.33 percent of all serious cases were actually recorded.[79] The reasons for such a low rate of reporting, it was discovered, related in part to the performance criteria of the security responsibility system.[80]

Expectations upon local police were simply too great. Quotas set on clean-up rates in some places were as high as 85 percent of all cases and 95 percent of all serious criminal cases. This was much higher than existing clean-up rates that have long been estimated to be around 70 percent and above.[81] As a result of this discrepancy, police were seriously in danger of missing out on their bonuses and worse still, even incurring a penalty for failing to reach their allotted targets. In effect, underreporting was their way of coping. Not only did this tactic help police avoid the penalties associated with missing their targets, but it also had the added advantage of allowing police officers to avoid the mundane paperwork associated with opening cases. Best of all, it meant they would gain their financial bonus and receive praise because nonreporting, when translated into police statistics, equaled a high clean-up rate.[82]

While the Fujian police study acknowledged a lack of sufficient statistical evidence to make any definitive claims on this front, further studies have tended to support their findings.[83] Indeed, the most recent nationwide study of the problem undertaken in 1997 discovered that even then only 80 percent of known cases were being reported and of these only 30 percent were actually recorded. Moreover, of this 30 percent, only 37 percent were actually solved.[84] Other studies pointed to the way this problem of underreporting was not restricted to the formal police force. Responsibility systems, it seems, were distorting the crime profile right across the mass line.[85]

In 1989, the Yichang-area police undertook a study of the effects of the responsibility system on neighborhood security committee policing and the internal protection sections of work units.[86] Again, the study found a similar trend to that which was taking place within the formal public security force. Indeed, responsibility systems were proving such a disincentive to crime reporting at this level that even ordinary staff at enterprises failed to report crime. In one incident in a department store in Zhijiang county, Yichang, the fear of being financially penalized for not meeting the contractual obligations of the security responsibility system led staff to cover up the theft of four watches and pay for them out of their own pockets.[87] Despite such anomalies, neither the police force nor their mass line could survive without these sorts of financial incentive systems. They were the basis upon which police had been able to reinvigorate their work and revive the mass-line para-policing support base that was essential to their work. This could not have happened had it not been for the use of such incentive schemes.[88] The trouble was this slavish adaptation of the methodology of economic reform to para-policing organs had other hidden costs that only become visible when one closely scrutinizes the adoption of these systems within the mass-line organizations themselves.

THE MONETARIZATION OF MASS-LINE ORGANS

With a whiff of financial ammonia, it was thought that the basic-level Maoist mass-line security committees could be brought back to life and help solve the deteriorating crime situation much as they had done in the past. The first phase of this strategy to revive these organs involved raising the basic wage levels of participants. By the 1980s, reforms were being instituted to massively increase wages paid to mass-line activists. For too long, it was argued, local governments had used the October 1954 City Residency Committee Organizational Regulations that stipulated a monthly stipend not in excess of fifteen *yuan* per committee member. The inflation produced by economic reform made this wage rate completely untenable and, by the early 1980s, the committee structures were falling into disarray at an alarming rate. One study found that 20 percent of these organizations at a village level and 25 percent of them at a city level were either inactive or totally paralyzed. In 1989, the Ministry of Civil Affairs conducted a nationwide survey and found that in addition to the decline of these mass-line organs, 20 percent of all grassroots Party and government organizations at a village level were inactive, while a further 25 percent of them were completely paralyzed. Meanwhile, in the cities, street committees and security groups were found to be very weak because of a lack of funds and an inability to generate revenue while work-unit security units often existed in name only.[89] As a result a whole range of new policies were introduced. To deal with the decline of mass-line organs, a new regime was instituted that raised participant wage rates to over 100 *yuan* per month and, in some cases, to over 300 *yuan* per month.[90] In addition to this, a number of city-based security committees began offering monthly bonuses of over 100 *yuan* per month for heads and deputies who put in good performances.[91] Through these methods, the police were able to redevelop, albeit unevenly, the local-level security committees and small-group structures that constituted the backbone of all local-level community-based policing arrangements (see table 7.1). Despite this, the vagaries of financial opportunities were to leave their mark.

In cities, where other, more lucrative financial opportunities existed, security committees and groups still tended to be heavily reliant upon an ever-aging group of retirees (see table 7.2). In contrast, rural areas could still rely upon tradition and a lack of other opportunities to ensure a large number of youthful recruits to the mass-line organizations. This difference resulted in a major age disparity between rural and city committees and groups and, as a flow-on from that, a huge discrepancy in the value of these committees to police operations.

Table 7.1.   Public Security Committees and Small Groups

		Internal*	City and Town	Village Committees	Total Number
Public Security	1986	291,548	154,084	728,824	1,174,456
Committees	1989	309,366	170,525	695,619	1,175,510
(zhibao hui)	1990	319,382	163,560	711,668	1,194,610
	1991	317,867	216,087	717,074	1,251,028
Personnel	1986	1,580,426	858,943	2,866,078	5,305,447
	1989	1,574,887	951,519	2,656,167	5,182,573
	1990	1,664,592	884,810	2,728,069	5,277,471
	1991	1,564,331	857,719	3,464,249	5,886,299
Public Security	1986	407,763	394,300	2,247696	3,049,759
Small Groups	1989	394,199	474,849	1,617,866	2,486,914
(zhibai xiaozu)	1990	433,162	472,653	1,719,692	2,625,807
	1991	422,091	472,671	1,624,389	2,518,151
Personnel	1986	1,312,576	1,083,385	4,347,475	6,743,436
	1989	1,344,700	1,291,364	3,950,499	6,586,563
	1990	1,455,800	1,293,810	4,321,080	7,070,690
	1991	1,448,384	1,303,877	4,697,617	7,449,878

While less than 2 percent of all rural committee and group members are retirees, in the cities retirees make up around 25 percent of all members. In quite a number of cases, however, retirees make up 60 percent to 70 percent of committee and group members.[92] The large number of retirees in city committees and groups prompted one Chinese scholar to speculate that there may be no more cadres after this generation of neighborhood committee members.[93] Their only chance of survival, in fact, lay with a more extensive use of the incentive schemes. The only problem with such an extension, however, was who was going to pay?

Costs involved in running such incentive schemes devolved to the local communities themselves as the economic reform program promoted a "user-pays" model. Hence in neighborhoods it was resident-users that were the greatest source of financial support for these committees and groups.[94] The introduction of monetary incentives tended to be quite unpopular with local residents, and the public resentment that was building up forced police and the committees to experiment with other methods of recouping the costs for local neighborhood security work. One method involved trying to redevelop neighborhood solidarity and reinvent the voluntary basis of the neighborhood security system.[95] Yet another method involved charging visitors' fees for residency rights.[96] While the former method could never work adequately in the cities where money talked, the latter only further exacerbated the growing division in Chinese cities between the locals and the poor outsiders. It

Table 7.2.   Retired Workers and Cadres Involved in Security Work

	Internal*	City and Town	Village	Total Number
Retired Workers and Cadres Involved in Security Committee Work				
1986	44,298	248,967	34,737	328,022
Percent of participants	2.8%	29%	1.26%	6%
1989	69,112	301,109	46,136	416.438
Percent of participants	4.4%	31.7%	1.7%	8%
1990	89,143	304,231	52,802	445,176
Percent of participants	5.4%	34.4%	1.9%	8.4%
1991	84,835	304,674	57,644	447,153
Percent of participants	5.4%	35.5%	1.7%	7.6%

	Internal*	City and Town	Village	Total Number
Retired Workers and Cadres Involved in Small Group Work				
1986	45,195	359.985	39,799	444,979
Percent of participants	3.4%	33.2%	0.9%	6.6%
1989	1,574,887	951,519	2,656,167	5,182,573
Percent of participants	6.1%	34.9%	1.5%	9%
1990	1,664,592	884,810	2,728,069	5,277,471
Percent of participants	7.3%	37.1%	1.6%	9.3%
1991	1,564,331	857,719	3,464,249	5,886,299
Percent of participants	6.6%	37.1%	1.5%	8.7%

*Internal means internal to the enterprise or work unit
Source: All tables drawn from information given in Wang Zhongfang, 1989; Law Yearbook of China 1991, 1992, 1993. No information available after 1993.

effectively criminalized that class that couldn't afford to pay for registration, creating even more problems for the system by introducing a disincentive to register. Ongoing problems with the mass line such as these reinforced police determination to professionalize, but in the context of local policing this meant relying upon paid help rather than volunteers. Nowhere is this shift more in evidence than in the professionalization of the informant system. Once again, professionalization involved the "dumbing down" of politics.

FROM EYES AND EARS TO SNOUTS[97]

Informants have been an important source of police intelligence since the formation of the Yan'an city police squad back in May 1938. As with contemporary policing, the Yan'an city police were reliant upon mass-line organizations to carry out their grassroots work, but given the wartime setting, they were particularly reliant upon those within the mass line whom they described as backbone mass-line elements. These people became known as *Lianluoyuan* or liaison personnel. It was their job to give the police detailed information about the political reliability of neighborhoods and families in which they themselves lived.[98] After 1949, this activist-informant system was expanded and formalized. In 1950, the Ministry of Public Security issued an internal document outlining "The methodology for temporarily managing the focal population" (draft), and this placed special emphasis upon the role of these activists in assisting police to control those deemed politically suspect. The task of the liaison personnel was to carry out covert surveillance of these people and report anything untoward to the police. To put this into effect, the public security forces secretly selected and recruited local activists from within the ranks of mass-line organizations.

From 1956 onwards, information on those deemed politically suspect was held in a subcategory of the household register known as the focal or special population register. Because any information given to police would be added to the suspect's household registration details, those who kept covert surveillance on them became known as the "eyes and ears of the household register" (*hukou ermu*). Like many other things, the "eyes and ears" system dissolved during the Cultural Revolution but was revived with economic reform. By this time, however, their duties had expanded beyond covert surveillance of the special population. Increasingly they were now being directed to carry out covert activity monitoring common criminals. This too resulted in a name change. From this time onward they were known as the eyes and ears of public order (*zhian ermu*).[99] Far more significant, however, was the changing composition of those who would carry out the job.

Mass-line organizations no longer provided the activist base from which to recruit eyes and ears. Instead police were relying upon minor criminals and those with criminal records to do this work. It is estimated that in some cities, 60 percent to 70 percent of all eyes and ears are now ex-criminals. No doubt in part because they are ex-criminals, they have proven to be enormously useful to the police. On the basis of police statistics covering nineteen cities and provinces from October 1984 until February 1985, eyes and ears provided 60 percent of all evidential material enabling police to crack cases. A further 58 percent of clues that helped police crack criminal cases also came from them. In Zhejiang province alone, eyes and ears not only provided clues in over 5,129 cases, but their information was directly responsible for the clean-up of 2,059 criminal cases.

The shift away from recruiting activists to employing informants may have helped police maintain social order, but it came at the cost of a further monetarization and depoliticization of the Chinese policing system. While police documents insist that this system is nonprofessional in character, eyes and ears are now owned by particular police stations that recruit, register, and pay them for all information given. Indeed, the leadership of a police station must approve their nomination and their status, as their status as informants must be entered into their personnel file details along with anything else relating to their work. In effect, eyes and ears are now almost identical to registered police informants in the West.

If money can be said to have fundamentally altered the nature of the mass-line policing within the community at large, on the other side of the work-unit wall, it was having an even greater deleterious effect. Ironically, the financial incentive schemes that have been used to keep the appearance of the mass line alive in the wider society proved to be the very devices that have more or less begun to kill off the mass line within enterprises. Internal work-unit security units have all been put on contract, and as a result, they are increasingly concerned only with their own workplace. This is a far cry from their original mass-line role.

INTERNAL PROTECTION UNITS

Internal protection work began in Ruijin in September 1931, but it was only later, in Yan'an, that these protection units would develop into a permanent part of work-unit life. It wasn't until the takeover of the cities and the development of a stronger communist industrial base, however, that these protection units became a prominent and ubiquitous feature of Chinese city life. Only after 1948 did work-unit staff, rather than specialized protection cadres from the Party's social section, begin to take over this work, and while work-unit staff would come to completely replace the professional Party security agents, the political influence of this latter group left its mark. Thus when the system of internal protection was formalized and standarized across the country in 1949, the security units were made entirely enterprise based even though they were still clearly Party in nature.[100] Indeed, as Mao himself pointed out, "Protection work must especially stress the role of Party leadership and in real terms they must get direct leadership from the Party committees; otherwise things could become very dangerous."[101] Economic reform tended to sever this Party link, and as a result, the situation within work units has become very dangerous indeed, especially for the Party's cherished concept of comprehensive management! The beginning of the diminution of Party influence within work units began as a direct result of economic reform.

To raise production, enterprise autonomy was encouraged and the role of the Party committee restricted to overtly political matters. As a result of this administration-Party split, internal protection work was said to have drifted into the enterprise administrative sphere.[102] With managers administering their own workplaces and a reward system geared to production, security matters tended to drop from workplace agendas.[103] Hence despite the massive growth in the number of enterprises in China over the reform period, the number of protection workers has remained more or less at the level it was in the 1950s, that is, at around 100,000 cadres.[104] With the new administrative arrangements, however, not only were security organs short of staff but the nature of their work also changed.

Prior to reform, protection units would carry out both public and covert action to stop counterrevolutionary wreckers from disrupting production. This made the work units an integral part of a security system that flowed from work unit back into society. In post-reform China, the work focus remained on those things that adversely affected production, but this was no longer tied to a search for politically inspired wreckers and began to focus instead on safety matters and work practices within the enterprise that were deleterious to production. This new focus on the factory was further advanced when a contract responsibility system tying security workers' salaries to improvements in safety and production matters was brought into effect in the 1980s.[105] Where once the internal protection sections within work units had been made up of backbone elements in social and community policing and had been central to the formation of para-policing *lianfang* groups (the joint-protection defence groups), their agendas now focused almost exclusively upon enterprise production, industrial espionage, and internal work-unit affairs.[106] With this new agenda these organs had little to do with the formal police force, and they were no longer interested in or tied to police professional leadership.

With enterprise managers in charge and an agenda geared to increasing enterprise production, the right of public security units to determine internal protection appointments, stipulate security staff numbers, or set their work agendas was withdrawn.[107] This decline in police influence within the internal protection units would create significant problems for the police generally and for the concept of comprehensive management in particular. In the past, work-unit security organs had fed directly into police work by establishing dossiers on the dangerous,[108] undertaking surveillance, investigating and interrogating suspects, and opening criminal and administrative cases for the police. While all these powers have always lacked any legal basis, they nevertheless were accepted by a diminutive police force as essential for the maintenance of social order.

Indeed, without the local knowledge these units offered, police would find it hard to maintain their impressive clean-up rates. It is estimated that somewhere between 70 and 80 percent of all work-unit-based administrative and criminal cases rely upon the internal protection units in order to be cracked. Thus despite constant complaints from within the police force that these internal units are professionally weak, the police are utterly dependent upon them.[109] Today, however, their usefulness is severely limited by enterprise management that looks only at the bottom line (profit) and by a criminal code that limits their powers. Given these problems, the police have attempted to deal with this question in a different way.

In 1985, with enterprises increasingly taking control of their own internal security, larger enterprises began to request a more formal police presence within their workplaces. Their requests were met with support and, despite the lack of any legal basis allowing the scheme to proceed, by the early 1990s in Hunan alone, some 979 enterprises had established their own public security units employing some 7,596 cadres within their workplaces.[110] All that was needed for these police units to be established was the approval of the local government and a higher-level police unit. Despite the need for governmental and higher-level police approval, it was, once again, enterprises that would pay the wages, and as a result, these new structures very quickly began to run into familiar problems. Paid by enterprises rather than the government or the police, these units ended up following enterprise orders rather than those issued by public security units. The result could sometimes lead to unforeseen and quite deleterious consequences.[111]

While these enterprise police would often wear police uniforms and carry public security identification,[112] they were, in fact, not part of the police force. Neither the quality of recruits nor the training they were given was up to formal police standards. Indeed, in one survey undertaken into the quality of enterprise policing, it was revealed that in ten enterprise police stations with fifty-one officers, around 80 percent of the staff had received no training whatsoever, while a further 30 percent could not even do their work. This particular attempted reform of internal enterprise policing, therefore, merely replicated the problems that plagued the internal protection units. While all attempts to reform and revive mass-line-based enterprise policing have proven problematic, one new reform that relies upon the experience of Western policing has proven to be a great success and has actually increased the power of the formal public security forces within enterprises and work units. There is a double irony in this. First, this other reform comes about because of foreign investor pressure rather than because of any concerns about Party-mindedness. Second, it emerged not through any attempt to revamp mass-line structures, but by avoiding them. The development we are alluding to is the establishment of a private security industry.

PRIVATE SECURITY FIRMS (BAO'AN FUWU GONGSI)

The first private security firms in China came into existence at the behest of foreign investors and private enterprises. These investors wanted a type of security organization within their enterprises that was concerned with economic, not social, profit and would abide by the law of the land rather than Party "red banner" documents.[113] In these types of foreign-owned or partially owned enterprises (the so-called three types of capital enterprise or *sanzi qiye*), the Party organization would not participate in management and would not be involved in administrative, security, or specialized police work.[114] While these types of enterprises all recognized the union movement, they were nervous about having communist mass-line security forces within their ranks and requested another form of security that was more in keeping with international business practice. The result was the development of a private security company system.

Given this background, it is hardly surprising to discover that the first private security company appeared in 1985 in the Shenzhen special economic zone.[115] In 1986, a similar security company was set up in Beijing and within a few years most other major cities had them. The growth of these companies has been spectacular (see Table 7.3). By 1998 they collectively employed over 300,000 employees. In Shanghai, private security guards were said to number 27,000 officers, which makes private security operations about half the size of the Shanghai city police force. In Beijing the growth has been even more spectacular. There are over 34,000 security guards in the Beijing company which means, in terms of officers, it is about the same size as the city Public Security Bureau.[116]

Chinese private security companies differ from those in the West, however, in that they are all wholly owned subsidiaries of the local branches of the Ministry of Public Security, and it is their bureaus that directly own and operate these businesses. Not only do the public security forces have a monopoly over this industry, but they also have complete control over staffing. Hence the police force has allocated all senior staff positions within these companies to formerly high-ranking officials from within either the provincial Public Security Bureau or from the

Table 7.3.   Private Security

Year	No. of Companies	No. of Personnel
1985	1 (Shenzhen)[a]	over 50[b]
1988	99	over 10,000[c]
1991	1,000	over 100,000[d]
1995	2,200	over 200,000[e]
1998	n.a.	over 300,000[a]

[a]Interview with head of the Beijing Private Security Company (August, 1998).
[b]Ye Huaming (1989), "An Exploration of the Socialisation Model", 24–27.
[c]Public Security Studies, no. 3 (1988): 39.
[d]An Outline of the Public Security History, 384.
[e]Law Yearbook of China, 1996, 168.

Ministry of Public Security itself.[117] It is estimated that these companies now cover about one-third of all police work in the cities, and it is in guarding banks, restaurants, and other such establishments that they derive most of their profits. Ironically, then, police control over enterprise security is strongest where it appears least "communist." More importantly, perhaps, the emergence of private security takes the ongoing commodification of security matters, which the police-reform agenda has promoted, to an even higher level.[118] With the emergence of these firms, the point being made here is visible. Security has become commodified, and like any other commodity it can now be bought and sold.

This commodification of security was, I would argue, the inevitable end point of the ongoing process of contractualization. This is because the contract does not just make things calculable or economically viable or visible, it also produces new mentalities and value systems that lead to a reification of money and commodity exchange.

The contractualization of most parts of the Chinese life-world, therefore, offers the crucial means by which to train Chinese out of the politically imposed egalitarianism of Maoism and into the "equality of opportunity" logic proffered by market relation. The police have also played their part in this process. Ironically, the sections most favored by Mao and the Maoist revolution, and most feared by Western entrepreneurs as they entered China, has now become the principal vehicle for the promotion and training of capitalist values. The mass line in security has become one vast network of tiny little workshops that train cadres to think in terms of the market, the contractual relation, and monetary reward. It is, in effect, marketization with a Maoist face. This marketization is a gift delivered via the contract from economic reform and, like any gift, the only thing really given has been time.[119] Time for the police to reform their structure in line with the new demands of a modernizing China; time for them to shift tack and move from a preventative to a more responsive form of policing; time too for them to plug the structural holes in the system and change things so that a code of professionalization can replace a system that required revolutionary zeal. One might, however, suggest that this gift of time was essential.

The police scholar Zhang Min, while not suggesting this, offers evidence in support of this conclusion nonetheless. He argues that policing in the reform period can be divided into three overlapping stages. In the first, which lasted from the beginning of the reform period until the early 1990s, a revival of the traditional socialist policing system took place. This revival relied upon police stations to operate as the leadership backbone of a vast network of security committees and groups that operated under their purview. The second stage of reform was said to have run from the early to the mid-1990s. In this period, argues Zhang Min, a new set of policing strategies was devised to augment the revived mass-line system. In particular, Zhang Min notes the development of the police patrol system in cities.

While economic reform may have reinvented the concept of the main shopping street, the mass-line residency and work-unit policing strategies were area-based and did not offer these new areas adequate protection. By the end of 1995, however, the situation had been rectified. By that stage, 2,217 large-and medium-sized cities had established police patrols and, nationwide, the patrol force boasted some 110,000 officers. From the mid-1990s onward, while still relying on the revived mass line to maintain order, police themselves became more mobile. They developed command centers in their city police stations, and these would monitor and react to calls placed on the emergency police number 110. By 1996 over 200 stations had set up this particular type of system,[120] and for Zhang Min, the story of growing police comprehensiveness is more or less complete.

While one may doubt the smoothness of the transition described or the evenness of the trajectory plotted, it is clear that the first brick in this new edifice of police reform was the revival of the mass-line policing structures. Its revival, however, was not a return to the past but a contract into which participants entered. In effect, this contract bought the police time, and in the time they had, they set about establishing a more mobile, reactive police structure. It is this force that is now coming to dominate city life. Whether one turns to the more traditional police system operating in rural China or looks to the new professionalism encouraged in the cities, all reforms are utterly dependent upon monetary incentive. This is the road down which the public security forces are now travelling and which flags the end of a long Maoist tradition of socialist policing.

CONCLUSION

In 1988, when the police began to formally question their status as a tool of the People's Democratic Dictatorship, the script line for their new life as law enforcement agencies seemed clear enough. For economic reform to succeed, stability must prevail. That, in turn, was dependent upon overcoming any remnants of the rule of man in favor of the rule of law. Under these circumstances, police would become law enforcement agencies. Economic reform produced a sea change in attitudes and new policing practices reflected that. The growth of police academies, the teaching of legal studies within them, coupled with a new professional attitude and desire for specialization, all suggested that police were in step with these changing times. As the role of the dictatorship in legitimating police actions diminished, law came to replace it, and as it did, it more and more framed police actions. Law was central to economic reform because it was through law that stability could be achieved and calculable outcomes forecast.

At the same time, however, while economic reform required stability, it did not produce it. On the contrary, it created the conditions for social dislocation. In some respects, economic reform was to be a trip down memory lane. The redevelopment and rustification of cities that took place from 1948 onwards and resulted in a system of urban and industrial villages known as work units is in the process of unravelling and returning the Chinese city to a form it knew before the arrival of the communists. The stilling of the population upon which planning and socialist policing were predicated has given way to a new social mobility. Mobility is, of course, a requirement of market economies hungry for labor to fuel the development of city construction and the service industries. Yet in relying upon the market, in promoting a money economy, and in freeing the population to move in a manner that the economy dictates, the old social ills of capitalism have been revisited upon the new China. Drug addiction, prostitution, economic crimes, and an endless sea of troublesome transients have been but a few of the negative side effects of this reform program. At first these social ills would prove embarrassing. After all, the curing of such things was one of the great boasts of the Chinese revolution. If nothing else, the relapse into crime, vice, and other social ills that accompanied the development of the economic reform program suggested that there were lessons to be learned from the history books of an earlier socialist policing era. Perhaps also, the Party demands to return China to the crime-free days of yesteryear suggested that the solutions of yesteryear might still have some purchase. Whatever the reasons, and there were many, the mass line was still very much in vogue in the early reform years. This is despite the very real and growing emphasis within the police force upon professionalization, specialization, and a respect for the rule of law. It is also in spite of the fact that in order to operate, mass-line organs would always require a degree of legal elasticity. Pragmatically, there was little else the Chinese police could do other than to rely upon the mass-line structure. More to the point, it was a model the police had real difficulties in thinking beyond. This situation resulted in a contradiction between the rhetoric of legal reform and the concrete need to maintain stability by relying upon the remnants of the mass line. It thus ensured that there would always be attempts to square this circle by putting the mass line in policing on a legal footing. And while such rules and regulations were to prove important, it was another type of law, the law of the contract, that became the crucial catalyst of change. This is not to disparage claims by Chinese commentators that the Chinese police are increasingly a law enforcement agency. Rather, it is to broaden this issue and ask a more profound question about the type of society they are being called upon to police.

Past mass-line communist solutions to combat crime had succeeded precisely because they were holistic (comprehensive) and involved turning their backs on the money economy. Instead of capital, communist cadres offered participants in the system a form of symbolic capital. The mass line was a vision of a communist future, and enthusiastic participation in it was the cost of the entry ticket. With economic reform, this historical materialist vision came crashing to earth, and it was from the rubble that a new type of materialism emerged. It offered a new means by which the Chinese police could mobilize and enthuse the masses in a world where comprehensiveness was no longer possible. That new means was, of course, money. Moreover, because money was always tied to performance, local communist cadres would be retrained and disciplined into the work habits of the market economy. By slowly commodifying mass-line policing through contracts, responsibility systems, and bonus programs, the authorities, in effect, would unwittingly transform the mass line into one long conveyor belt of capitalist values. Ironically, then, it was these most communist of organizational forms, the mass-line organs, that became the schoolhouses of these new value systems. In this light, the rhetoric about the need for the rule of law takes on a very different hue.

"Only in commodity production does the abstract legal form see the light," wrote the one-time doyen of Soviet jurisprudence, Evgeny Pashukanis.[121] His argument was simple enough. All legal relations, he insisted, were relations between formally equal subjects,[122] and this legal equality mimicked the myth of equivalence that was central to market economics. The dominance of a money-based contract system, therefore, signaled the dominance of an ideology of equivalence, and it was through this myth that markets and commodities came to appear both normal and even natural despite the fact that they were so alien to the planned economy of the past.

Economic reform, in this light, is one vast program of reform through labor inculcating participants with the values of the money economy. The contract responsibility system it has relied upon reinforces a type of equivalence that is central to the new Chinese value system. Moreover, the police, in devising their own money-based version of this strategy in order to reinvigorate the mass line, have become one more agent of change despite the fact that they are all too often regarded as a conservative (read leftist) force in the West. Chinese police have indeed become law enforcement agencies and are themselves increasingly subject to the law. But the main law they are subject to and their main task of enforcement is with regard to the law of the contract. It is this law that has transformed the mass line into a mass-production line for the maintenance and extension of values that the revolution once fought against. This perhaps is the final irony and lasting legacy of the mass line in policing and quite possibly the end of socialist policing in China. If nothing else, however, it is the end of this version of their story.

NOTES

This paper is based on parts of my forthcoming book, *Policing Chinese Politics* (Duke University Press). The research was undertaken with the aid of an Australia Research Council grant. Thanks to Shaorong Baggio for help reformatting and researching this paper.

1. Claude Lefort, *The Political Economy of Modern Society: Bureaucracy, Democracy, Totalitarianism,* ed. John B. Thompson (Cambridge: Polity Press, 1986).

2. Kong Lin and Zhang Weiguo, "Qiyue zhidu: fazhan shangpin jingji de falu xuanze," (The contract system: selected laws for the development of a commodity economy) *Faxun* 73 (Law Science Monthly), no. 12 (December 1987): 5–7.

3. Henry Sumner Maine, *Ancient Law: Its Connection with the Early History of Society and Its Relation to Modern Ideas,* ed. Raymond Firth (New York: E. P. Dutton, 1971), 168.

4. Interestingly, this point is not lost on Chinese legal scholars. They now celebrate Maine's thesis and argue that the story of the contract is the tale of modernization, freedom, autonomy, and equality. See Albert H. Y. Chen, "The Developing Theory of Law and Market Economy in Contemporary China," in *Legal Developments in China: Market Economy and Law,* ed. Wang Guiguo and Wei Zhenying (Hong Kong: Sweet and Maxwell Asia, 1986), 9–10.

5. Max Weber, *Economy and Society,* vol. 2, ed. Guenther Roth and Claus Wittich (Berkeley: University of California Press, 1978), 669.

6. Indeed, as Hazard notes, Communist China began by following the Soviet idea of stability very closely, but by 1957 it had veered toward the necessity of elasticity to ensure that the revolution did

not die out. The Soviets were scathing in their criticism of this and, according to Hazard who is quoting the Chinese press, demanded that law "possesses definite elasticity, and may be called an elastic measure" See John N. Hazard, *Communists and Their Law: A Search for the Common Core of the Legal Systems of the Marxian Socialist State* (Chicago: University of Chicago Press, 1969), 99.

7. He Qinghua, ed., *Dangdai zhongguo faxue xinsichao* (New trends in law studies) (Shanghai: Shanghai shehui kexun chubanshe, 1991), 3.

8. He, *Dangdai zhongguo*, 3.

9. Chen, "The Developing Theory," 4.

10. He, *Dangdai zhongguo*, 17, 36.

11. For example, Zhou Fengju, "Fa danchun shi jieji douzheng de gongju ma?" (Is law purely an instrument in class struggle) *Faxun yanjiu* (Studies in Law), no. 1 (1980): 39; Wu Buyun, 'shilun shehuizhuyi falu de jiejixing he keguanxing," (A tentative analysis of the class character and objective nature of the socialist law) *Faxun yanjiu* (Studies in Law), no. 5 (1980): 11.

12. While there was an array of voices that rejected this position, e.g., Tang Congyao, "Zaitan shehuizhiyi fa de jiejixing," (Once again on the question of the class nature of socialist law) *Faxun yanjiu* (Studies in Law), no. 5 (1980): 7–9, it was this view that tended to predominate. For a recent summary of these new debates in law, including this and the rule of law/man debate, see He, *Dangdai zhongguo*, 16–6.

13. Quoted in He, *Dangdai zhongguo*, 51.

14. *Zhongguo renmin gong'an shigao* (An outline of public security history) (Beijing: Jingguan jiaoyu chubanshe, 1997), 404.

15. Oestreich details the prehistory of modern contractualism by tracing the development within the Church of the covenant of grace and from there to the secularized forms of contract. His argument is that, since Weber, this covenant of grace within Protestantism has largely been ignored as all eyes turned instead to predestination. Yet for Oestreich the recovery of this part of theology is crucial for any understanding of more modern forms of contractual obligation in the process of secular state building. See Gerhard Oestreich, *Neostoicism and the Early Modern State*, eds. Brigitta Oestreich and H. G. Koenigsberger, trans. David McLintock (Cambridge: Cambridge University Press, 1982), 135–54.

16. Oestreich, *Neostoicism*, 165.

17. Hugh Collins, *The Law of Contract*. (London: Weidenfeld and Nicolson, 1986), 4, 6.

18. Collins, *The Law,* 11.

19. Michel Foucault, "On Governmentality," *I and C*, no. 6 (Autumn 1979): 11.

20. Oeconomy means the "correct manner of managing individuals, goods and wealth within the family . . . and making it thrive" See Foucault, "On Governmentality," 11.

21. Oestreich, *Neostoicism,* 156.

22. Here we are not trying to suggest that continental models and the English model of policing are the same. Rather we are merely alluding to the fact that the process of professionalization was occasioned by similar sorts of pressures.

23. Philip Rawlings, "The Idea of Policing: A History," *Policing and Society* 5 (1995): 136.

24. Rawlings, "The Idea of Policing," 139.

25. Even if we adopt the very broad definition of police as used by Clifford Shearing, that is, as a force for the "preservation of the peace," there would still be difficulties describing the prereform Chinese public security forces as a police force. This is because they were designed to protect and promote the revolution, *not* the peace. Indeed, the prereform pubic security forces were quite often a central force in the prosecution of the Maoist-style political campaigns, making them, if anything, disruptions to the peace. See Clifford D. Shearing, "The Relation between Public and Private Policing," in *Modern Policing,* ed. M. Tony and N. Morris (Chicago: University of Chicago Press, 1992), 399–434.

26. Gong Xikui, "Household Registration and the Caste-Like Quality of Peasant life," in *Streetlife China,* ed. Michael Dutton (Melbourne: Cambridge University Press, 1998), 81–84.

27. Police figures tell us why this would be the case. The growth of "transient crime" has become one of the major issues in contemporary policing in China. The problem first appeared in the 1980s when police discovered that crime committed by itinerants was coming to constitute a rising percentage of all crime. In one study led by the former Deputy Minister of Public Security, Yu Lei, the rising trend of itinerant crime throughout the 1980s was examined. Cases that involved the floating population constituted only about 15 percent of the total in 1985, but rose to 17 percent in 1987, and then 18 percent in 1988. See Yu Lei, ed., *Zhongguo xian jieduan fanzui wenti yanjiu zongjuan* (Studies on current Chinese crime problems) (Bzzeijing: Zhongguo renmin gong'an daxun chubanshe, 1993), 172. While Yu Lei's study offers a general picture, it tends to disguise the nature of the problem, which is demographically concentrated in the cities. As the police scholar Gu Xinhua has noted, the problem of "floating crime" becomes much more significant when one concentrates on market areas and large population concentrations. See Gu Xinhua, "suzhou jingji fazhang fangshi yu nongcun fanzui bianhua," (The mode of economic development in Suzhou and economic development and the changes in rural crime) in *Gong'an yanjiu* 13 (Public Security Studies), no. 5 (1990): 47–50. Hence if one closely examines key market areas and population concentrations, one discovers that the percentage of crime committed by itinerants rises dramatically. In the Shenzhen economic zone, for example, it was discovered that over 90 percent of all serious crime was perpetrated by the so-called "three have-not" people from the countryside. These three have-nots (*san wu*), are those who have no long-term employment, no legal identification, and no long-term residency. While one may claim Shenzhen is a special case, Guangzhou is not. Yet in 1996 a study found that 85 percent of all arrests were of itinerants, and while this is unusually high, the general trend it suggests is evident in just about every city. See He Qinglian *Xiandaihua de xianjing* (The traps of the modernization.) (Beijing: Jinri zhongguo chubanshe, 1982), 65. In 1996 a study in Shanghai found that itinerant crime had increased fifteenfold in just thirteen years. Some 55.86 percent of cases were about itinerants. See Shanghai

jingcha xuehui ketizu (Policing studies group), "teda chengshi nongmin fanzui wenti de yanjiu," (Studies on peasant crimes in large cities) in *Gong'an yanjiu* 61 (Public Security Studies), no. 5 (1998): 17–20. In Beijing in 1994 police found that 46 percent of all arrests were of itinerants. Given that stability is needed in order to promote economic reform, transient and itinerant crime has becomes one of the key concerns of the police (He, *Xiandaihua de xianjing*, 254, 255, 265).

28. There have been five high tides of crime in China since 1949. The first of these occurred shortly after the establishment of the PRC. In 1950 this tide reached its peak with 513,461 crime cases being prosecuted. This meant that the crime rate was about 93 per 100,000 people. Serious cases numbered around 47,000, which meant they constituted 9.22 percent of all criminal cases. These crimes mainly involved counterrevolutionary sabotage and so-called remnant crimes such as drugs, prostitution, and the trading of human beings. The second high tide peaked in 1961. In that year, crime cases reached 420,000. These cases involved new types of crimes by new types of criminals. In the main, these were committed by young people and juveniles and were said to be a new type of criminal raised in the new society. The key characteristic of these two high tides was that they dropped off sharply after they reached their peak and countermeasures were undertaken. The third tide rose during the Cultural Revolution (May 1966–October 1976). It reached its peak in 1973. The next two high tides came during the reform period. The fourth emerged around the late 1970s and early 1980s and peaked in 1981. In that year over 890,000 criminal cases were logged and the crime rate was estimated to be running at about 1,989 per 100,000 people. The fifth wave began in the late 1980s but continued into the 1990s. By 1991, the number of crime cases had reached 2,360,000 and the crime rate was said to be around 200 per 100,000 people. Unlike previous periods, the reform era was to witness only minor fluctuations in what, by Chinese standards, is an inordinately high crime rate. In terms of the fifth wave, it is still too early to predicate when it will peak. For more information on these five waves, see Yu, *Zhongguo xianjiedaun*, 37–47. For an alternative view that only registers four waves (that is, it does not include the Cultural Revolution), see Wang Zhimin and Huang Jingping, *Jingji fazhan yu fanzui bianhua*, (Economic development and changes in crime) (Beijing: Zhongguo renmin daxun chubanshe, 1992), 48–49.

29. Evidence of the degree of this social panic can be found in the text, *Ni ganjue anquan ma*? (Do you feel safe?). This text summarizes the results of a survey undertaken by the PSM between 1988–1989. Questioning some 15,000 people across fifteen provinces and cities, seventy-five areas, 150 city districts, seventy-five counties and 750 neighborhoods, this survey was the most comprehensive of its type ever undertaken. The results for the police were not good. While judgements about social order and personal security suggest that they were barely satisfactory (77.5 percent of people said social order was either just satisfactory or below par, while 58 percent of people said the same about their own personal security), the popular judgements about sentencing was that it was too lenient (nearly 60 percent of people answered that it was too lenient). See Ministry of Public Security Public Safety Group, Ministry of Public Security, Public Security Research Unit, *Ni ganjue anquan ma*? (Do you feel safe?) (Beijing: Qunzhong chubanshe, 1991), 40, 46, 150–59, 250–59. It should be added, however, that despite no significant improvement in the law and order situation in the 1990s, more recent surveying witnessed something of a reduction in popular anxiety about crime. A follow-up survey in May /June 1991 discovered that while only 7.3 percent of the population felt safe, 43.7 percent felt "relatively safe," and a further 17.9 percent felt

the situation was "average." Average and below for personal security therefore account for 48.4 percent, which is a decrease of just under 10 percent. In terms of social order the situation was perceived to be even better, with only 58.7 percent of the population feeling that the situation was average or below. See Ministry of Public Security Public Safety Group, Ministry of Public Security, Public Security Research Unit, *Ni ganjue anquan ma?* 58–64. There is little space to develop these points, but for those interested in a more detailed articulation and analysis of these figures, see Michael Dutton and Lee Tianfu, "Missing the Target? Policing Strategies in the Period of Economic Reform," in *Crime and Delinquency* 39, no. 3 (July 1993): 319–22.

30. From 1978 onwards, the Ministry of Public Security began opening professional police schools (that is, specialized secondary schools). These schools offered training programs for recruits who had graduated from high school. From 1978 to 1987, there were eighty-three of these police schools built and approximately 80,000 graduates were sent from these schools into the police force. See Yu Lei, ed., *Dangdai zhongguo de gong'an gongzuo* (Contemporary Chinese public security work) (Beijing: Dangdai zhongguo chubanshe. 1992), 440–48. By November 1984, the Ministry of Public Security was closely attending to the issue of police training. At that time it convened the national public security educational work meeting that suggested a coordinated and national approach to the question was needed. This resulted in a call for central, provincial, and regional level governments to work toward creating a multi-leveled and diverse public security educational system offering intensive educational and training programs for police. At the same time, this meeting also drew up a six-year training program for police. As a result of these initiatives, it is said that police educational and training programs have undergone rapid development. From the early 1980s police academies began to reappear, and by 1986 they were joined by five police cadre management academies. The academies offered two- to three-year courses, and these included a variety of legal, political, cultural, and professional subjects as well as specialized police subjects such as public security, public order management, and crime investigation. See *Zhongguo renmin gong'an shigao*, 410. Higher education institutions run by the police have also developed in this period. From 1978 to 1987, three police universities (with four-year degree programs) and eleven institutions (with three-year degree programs) were established. These fourteen institutions had 10,979 students in 1987. See Yu, *Dangdai zhongguo*, 448. The subjects offered in these degree programs included public security management, detective work, preliminary trial preparation, public order management, security guard work, public security political work, document examination, forensic medicine, crime photography, traffic management, household registration management, radio communication, television techniques, graphic communication, computer application, as well as other specialization. See Yu, *Dangdai zhongguo*, 450. Some police universities have also established law programs. See Yu, *Dangdai zhongguo*, 453. On the creation of police patrols and the emergency 110 telephone number system, see Zhang Min, "Qianxi zhiding zhi'an jingwu fazhan zhanlu yingdang zhuyi de jige wenti," (A brief analysis of a number of issues to be considered when formulating a police development strategy) in *Gong'an yanjiu* 69 (Public Security Studies), no. 1 (2000): 31.

31. On the development of the *koban* pillbox system, see Hao Hongkui, "Fanzui huodong de shidaixing bianhua yu fanzuizongti duice detiaozheng," (The regulation of comprehensive counter measures to be taken against crime and the changing nature of criminal activity) in *Gong'an*

yanjiu 8 (Public Security Studies), no. 4 (1989): 16, 37. On forensics see Yu, *Dangdai zhongguo*, 450, 453. On the creation of police patrols and the emergency 110 telephone number system, see Zhang "Qianxi zhiding zhi'an," 31–33.

32. One Western observer goes so far as to suggest that the 1983 "severe strike" campaign was an attempt on the part of the police to reassert their power in the "balance of awe" between police and offenders. See Murray Scot Tanner, "State Coercion and the 'Balance of Awe': The 1983–1987 Stern Blows Anti-Crime Campaign," *China Journal*, no. 44 (July 2000): 93–125.

33. Beijing, Tianjin, Shanghai, Guangzhou and Wuhan.

34. Harold Tanner, *Strike Hard! Anti-Crime Campaigns and Chinese Criminal Justice, 1979–1985* (Ithaca: Cornell East Asia Series no. 104, 1999), 72.

35. See Tanner, *Strike Hard!*, 83–104. Also see tables at end of text.

36. Tanner, *Strike Hard!*, 66–72.

37. There are a number of accounts that claim to offer a "behind-the-scenes" look at why campaigning returned to policing. Most of these have been summarized in Tanner, who concludes that Deng Xiaoping gave the order to the newly installed Minister of Public Security, Liu Fuzhi (See Tanner, *Strike Hard!*, 85–86). One well-placed informant I consulted offered yet another variant on this tale, suggesting that campaigns came up as a strategy during a discussion Liu Fuzhi was having with Deng about the social order situation in a number of areas in Guangdong province (Interview, February 1996).

38. Wang Zhongfang, ed. *Zhongguo Shehui zhi'an zonghe zhili de lilun he shijian* (Theory and practice of comprehensive managment of public order in China) (Beijing: Qunzhong Chubanshe, 1989), 8.

39. The diversity of the various organs that called for this policy and were later included in it is indicative of the type of "comprehensiveness" being called for. The eight organs that petitioned the Party were the Ministry of Propaganda, the Ministry of Education, the Ministry of Culture, the Ministry of Public Security, the National Labor Bureau, the National Workers' Union, the Communist Party Youth League, and the National Women's Federation. Wang, *Zhongguo shehui zhi'an*, 7.

40. Dai Wendian, ed., *Gong'anxue jichu lilun yanjiu* (Basic theoretical research on the Chinese public security) (Beijing: Gong'an daxue chubanshe, 1991), 253.

41. Weber, *Economy and Society*, 671–72.

42. Liu Zaiping, "Shilun gong'an jiguan de minzhu zhineng – jianlun renmin minzhu zhuanzheng de duixiang," (Examination of the democratic function of public security units) in *Gong'an yanjiu* 7 (Public Security Studies), no. 3 (1989): 8.

43. Liu, "Shilun gong'an," 9.

44. Liu, "Shilun gong'an," 11.

45. Liu, "Shilun gong'an," 11.

46. Liu, "Shilun gong'an," 11.

47. Liu, "Shilun gong'an," 12.

48. See Liu Wenqi, "Renmin minzhu zhuanzheng lilunshang de hunlun bixu chengqing," (It is necessary to clear up confusion about the theory of the people's democratic dictatorship) *Gong'an yanjiu* 10 (Public Security Studies), no. 2 (1990): 21 and Yang Zhaoming and Wang Gongfan, "Cong donglun he baolun toushi dangqian de jieji douzheng wenti," (Viewing the current state of class struggle through the period of turmoil and chaos) *Gong'an yanjiu* 9 (Public Security Studies), no. 1 (1990), 8.

49. Tan Songqiu, "Dui woguo xianjieduan de jieji douzheng he renmin minzhu zhuanzheng weiti de jidian renshi," (The class struggle in the present period in our country and a number of points to know about the people's democratic dictatoriship) in *Gon'an yanjiu* 10 (Public Security Studies), no. 2 (1990): 3.

50. Liu Wenqi summed up this conservative position and offered criticism of the Party in the process. He spoke for many within police ranks when he bemoaned the lack of class analysis and class focus in police work. In relation to class struggle he said that "in any particular period, because we have refrained from using these types of concepts and methods to proceed in examining international and national questions, when we are faced with the development of an internal rebellion and chaos, we are not in a position to provide answers to the troubles that come about" (Liu, "Renmin minzhu zhuanzheng," 21). For their part, Yang Zhaomin and Wang Gongfan would write that "in recent years we haven't paid enough attention to class struggle" (Yang and Wang, "Cong donglun," 8). What these left complaints do not say is that it was the police themselves who were no longer employing categories like counterrevolutionary crime that would flow from a class-based analysis of crime. In clear contrast to the prereform years, counter-revolutionary crime had become a marginal category in contemporary China. Only about 0.1 percent of all cases were treated under this banner in the reform years. Moreover, even this small number of counterrevolutionary crimes was declining. In 1979, around 1,000 criminal cases involved the charge of "counterrevolutionary crime" while in the prisons about 7 percent of all inmates were so labeled. In 1990, after the arrests that followed the events of 4 June, there were even less "counterrevolutionaries" in prison and far fewer up on these charges. In that year, only about 400 cases came before the courts and only 4 percent of the prison population were regarded as "counterrevolutionaries." The reason why this category has become dispensable, then, was because police were no longer employing it. In fact, what they appear to have been doing was criminalizing political dissent. In the months that followed 4 June 1989, *Public Security Studies* offered a breakdown of the motivations of those arrested and discovered that nearly 30 percent of them were unreformed recidivists who were said to harbor resentment against the authorities, and a further 50 percent were defined as social dregs that the police already knew about but whom they had neither arrested nor prosecuted. In addition to these, a further 3 percent were said to be profiteers and corrupt officials while a "small but active number" were labeled spies and secret agents of foreign powers (Yang and Wang, "Cong donglun," 10). So little used was the category of

counterrevolutionary criminal that it disappeared altogether from the amended criminal code of 1997. In place of this category was the charge of "endangering national security".

51. David Zweig, K. Feinerman Hartford, and Dang Jianxu, "Law, Contracts, and Economic Modernization: Lessons from the Recent Chinese Rural Reforms," *Stanford Journal of International Law* 23 (1987): 320. Xu Hanmin, *Renmin zhi'an 40 nian* (Forty years of people's policing) (Beijing: Jingguan jiaoyu chubanshe, 1992), 149.

52. Zweig et al. dates the introduction of the contract from 1982, but contracts were beginning to be introduced from around 1981. By 1982, as we shall go on to show, they would not only spread into other domains but also go deeper into the society. Indeed, as Zweig et al. show, by April 1985 the unified purchasing of grain that had been operative since the central plan came into being in 1953 was replaced by a system of voluntary contracts between producers and the state. As Zweig et al. conclude, "The success of the current rural economic reforms depends upon whether contractual relations will facilitate rural China's transformation from a command economy to one based on an amalgam of indicative planning and market mechanisms." See Zweig, Hartford, and Dang, "Law," 319–64.

53. The purposive contract in Weber is juxtaposed to the status contract in that the former is programmatically applied and temporally limited. For more details see Weber, *Economy and Society*, 668–81; Michel Rosenfeld, "Contract and Justice: The Relation between Classical Contract Law and Social Contract Theory," *Iowa Law Review* 70 (1985): 810–14.

54. Articulated in 1979, these were the socialist road, the dictatorship of the proletariat, the leadership of the Communist Party and Marxism-Leninism, and Mao Zedong Thought.

55. Note, for example, the position taken by Wang Zhimin, Li Tianfu, and Huang Jingping in the pages of the key police journal *Public Security Studies*: "How is it possible to compare the situation today when modernization is in full swing and when the scale, speed and scope of change in society, politics, economics and cultural systems is so great with that of yesteryear? Given that the situation with regard to law and order is the result of objective environmental factors, it seems hard to imagine the likelihood of a return to the 1950s. Under the influence of such evaluation criteria, public security organs undoubtedly neglected the actual conditions and were eager to achieve success by resorting to any short-term measures, even those which ran contrary to their own interests." Huang Jingping, Li Tianfu, and Wang Zhimin, "Gong'an guanli xianzhuang," (The situation with regard public security management) in *Gong'an yanjiu* 4 (Public Security Studies), no. 4 (1988): 6.

56. Zhang Qingwu pointed out in an interview in 1994 that since the end of the 1980s, population flows had "stabilized" at around fifty to sixty million people per day on the road in China. He added, however, that this would double if one were to include intraprovincial movement. Professor Zhang was then the director of the Population Research Institute, China's Public Security University, Beijing.

57. *Yushen kanshou gongzuo shouce di 2 juan* (Handbook on preparatory investigations and watch-house work, vol. 2) (Beijing: Qunzhong chubanshe, 1985), 188–89.

58. In 1979 there were 12,719 police stations throughout China. This increased to 16,112 by 1980, and a large part of that rise was with the development of a more extensive rural police station network. Something like 4,000 new police stations were established in rural areas in that year. Indeed, the growth of rural stations has been highly significant. At the beginning of reform in 1978, there were 5,276 rural police stations, 3,515 urban ones, and a total nationwide of 11, 480. By 1983, after substantial investment in the police station system, there were 25,434 rural stations, 4,357 urban ones, and 30,441 overall. Clearly there had been some significant investments, but what is interesting was the way they were directed at the countryside, no doubt in part to prop up the ailing household registration system and the burgeoning rural crime rate. These figures are drawn from interviews from scholars who asked not to be named.

59. As far as I can tell, the first document to put this system forward came in June 1981. A copy of this document can be found in *Shehui zhi'an zonghezhili zhengce fagui huibian* (A collection of rules, regulations and policies on the comprehensive handling of social order) (Beijing: Qunzhong Chubanshe, 1992), 1–4.

60. Comprehensive management was a system devised to tie mass-line organs and formal policing agencies more closely together by building up a total security network that could prevent crime before it actually occurred. See Wang, *Zhongguo Shehui zhi'an*, 8–14; Tanner, *Strike Hard!*, 297–99. Running counter to many of the reforms which disaggregated things, comprehensive management wed formal police agencies to mass-line organs, educational institutions, work-unit security sections, and so on to build up a system of total control. Indeed, one could view the campaign as a miniaturization of the Maoist all-round dictatorship and the application of that logic to crime prevention work.

61. Wang, *Zhongguo Shehui zhi'an*, 8–15; Tanner, *Strike Hard!*, 297–99.

62. Liu Chenggen, "Promote Community Developments, Control Serious Cases of Repeat Offence" (Unpublished paper presented at the International Conference on Education, Training, and Rehabilitation of Prisoners in Correctional Institutions (Chengdu: October 1995).

63. Social help and education, according to Shao Daosheng is "a means to mobilize sectors of society to educate youth who have committed minor offences in order to help them correct their mistakes and to encourage them to embark on a path of healthy development. It is neither an administrative sanction nor criminal punishment, but is a form of political and ideological education of youth. It is a necessary measure to maintain social order and bring about an improvement of the social environment. It is a new form of and a new invention in mass participation in the comprehensive treatment of youth crime." As he goes on to note, it is also used as a means to police newly released prisoners who are still on parole. Those charged with the task of helping and educating are the "people living and working with the young people who have committed minor offences" as well as locals with a high political consciousness such as cadres, model personalities, advanced workers, or colleagues, teachers, neighbors, schoolmates, relatives, or parents of the recipients. Shao concludes, "Because there are emotional ties between these people and the juvenile offenders, they are in the best position to understand what those young people think, what they do and what they need. This contingent of educators is thus highly motivated and consists of progressive, honest and upright people who are at the same time

committed to youth education and are capable of undertaking this task." See Shao Daosheng, *Zhongguo Qingshaonian fazui de shehuixue sikao* (Considerations on the sociology of youth crime in China) (Beijing: Shehui kexue wenxian chubanshe, 1987), 196–209.

64. Xu, *Renmin zhi'an 40 nian*, 149.

65. For an example of one very well-developed set of regulations from Shanghai indicating the nature of the inducements and they way the system worked, see Bai Yihua and Ma Xueli, eds., *Jumin weiyuanhiui gongzuo shouce* (A handbook on neighborhood committee work) (Beijing: Zhongguo shehui chubanshe 1990), 207–8.

66. Xu, *Renmin zhi'an 40 nian*, 149.

67. *Shehui zhi'an zonghezhili zhengce fagui huibian*, 113.

68. Quoted in Bai and Ma, *Jumin weiyuanhiui*, 194.

69. Qiao Shi gives a good summary of the way in which policing work at base levels would be reinvigorated by a system of contracts in his speech to the National Politics and Law Work Meeting. In this speech he begins by outlining the third stage of the severe strike campaign in 1986. Redirecting this campaign onto the streets and toward transient crime, he highlights the way in which base-level work can be strengthened. He said,

> Strengthening base-level organs and raising the fighting power of these organs is germane to the program. Only by doing this can the various measures implemented in these places truly be put into effect and the comprehensive management of social order ensured. This work involves building up all base-level party and government powers, bringing them into play so that they are of use in organizing the comprehensive management of social order. To do this we need to advance and put into effect the security contract responsibility system and the safety security responsibility system and this will give each security committee of the neighborhood committees and each mediation unit new life. We have already successfully put in place the security contract responsibility system in rural areas, and these have, on the whole, resolved the problem of financial remuneration for people involved in the (village) security committee and mediation work. This, in turn, resolved the problem of inadequate recognition of their skills, inadequate linking of their work to rewards and penalties which was all a part of the philosophy of eating from the big pot. Through this, the activism of these people can be brought into play and this will speed up the process that is changing the face of public security. So this system has received a warm welcome from the broad body of the masses. . . . We have already implemented the safety security responsibility system within factories, mines and enterprises. On the whole this has meant that as the economic contract responsibility system has already strengthened the responsibilities of the entire cadre and worker body, this has meant that in relation to security departments these people are now much more active in relation to both production matters and grasping safety practices. On the basis of these sorts of experiences we now need to contentiously summarize this basic experience and from this generalize and extend to other areas.

See Qiao Shi's speech in *Shehui zhi'an zonghezhili zhengce fagui huibian*, 52–55.

70. Li Wennan, Jin Lu, "Guanyu gong'an guanli tizhi gaige de sikao," (Some thoughts on the reform of the public security management system) in *Gong'an yanjiu* 59 (Public Security Studies), no. 6 (1998): 25.

71. Wan Shengzi et al. 2000: 1, V69, 23.

72. Indeed, the use of fines to replace punishment had become such a widespread phenomenon by the end of the 1980s that the phrase describing it, *yifa daixing*, had become a common colloquial expression.

73. Legislation did come to cover these institutions in 1985, but even then it was in the form of an internal notice from the Supreme Court and seven other relevant departments. For an example of this legislation see Dutton, *Streetlife China*, 125–29.

74. The information on prostitution centers comes from interviews conducted in 1990, but this was not the only zone of revival. The 1950s revivals to deal with renewed outbreaks of old crimes or misdemeanors is a constant feature of the Chinese justice system. Note, for example, that the reemergence of a Chinese drug problem has occasioned the revival of clinics modeled on the early 1950s *Jieyansuo* or anti-smoking clinics, while the reappearance of large-scale transient crime led to the revival of the shelter and investigation centers (*shourong shencha*) until their abolition due to international pressure in 1996.

75. Song Haobo, "Xian jieduan maiyin piaochang xianxiang toushi," (A perspective on the current situation with regard to clients of prostitutes) *Qingshaonian fanzui yanjiu* 144 (Juvenile Crime Studies), no. 6 (1994): 3.

76. Song, "Xian jieduan," 3.

77. The six evils are 1) prostitution; 2) manufacturing, selling, and spreading indecent materials; 3) kidnapping and trading women and children; 4) planting, smoking, and dealing in drugs; 5) gambling; 6) using superstitions to trick people. See *Shehui zhi'an zonghezhili zhengce fagui huibian*, 150.

78. Similarly strict guidelines also came to dominate the treatment of gamblers. In terms of prostitution the internal regulations promulgated during the "six evils" campaign of 1989 state that custodial sentences, not fines, should be used in the following situations:1) Where the prostitute has already been dealt with in the past by the police (i.e., had prior convictions); 2) Where the crime was particularly severe (like where the entire family had moved into a city or town to live off the proceeds); 3) Where it involved sex with foreigners; 4) Where the case involved multiple counts of sex; 5) Where the prostitute is actively soliciting customers. See *Shehui zhi'an zonghezhili zhengce fagui huibian*, 146–49. Similar sorts of guidelines were also issued on gambling.

79. Fujian Public Security Department, "Dui li'anbushi wenti de diaocha yu sikao," (Some thoughts on an investigation into the underrecording of the criminal cases) in *Zhongguo xianjieduan fanzui wenti de yanjiu lunwenji diyijuan* (Ministry of public security studies on current Chinese crime problems, vol. 1), ed. Yu Lei (Beijing: Zhongguo renmin gong'an daxue chubanshe, 1989), 332–40.

80. The other main reason given was also financial. High legal costs were said to be responsible for people avoiding legal remedies and dealing with matters privately. Wu Zhongfei and Chen Yuanxiao, "Jiaqiang chengben kongzhi, cujin lianxing fazhan, tigao jiguan jiayu shehui zhi'an de nengli," (Enhancing cost control, promoting virtuous development, and improving the public security organs' capacity to control social order) in *Gong'an yanjiiu* 69 (Public Security Studies), no. 1 (2000): 27.

81. Fujian Public Security Department, "Diaocha yu sikao," 337; Yu, *lunwenji diyijuan*, 491.

82. Fujian Public Security Department, "Diaocha yu sikao," 337.

83. Yu, *Lunwenji diyijuan*, 47, 562.

84. Wu and Chen, "Jiaqiang chengben kongzhi," 271.

85. Yichang Administrative Area Public Security Section Research Group, "Guanyu xingshi an'jian li'an bushi wenti de taitao," (Studies on the problem of underrecording criminal cases) in Yu, *Lunwenji diyijuan*, 344.

86. Yichang Administrative, "Guanyu xingshi an'jian li'an," 345–46.

87. Yichang Administrative, "Guanyu xingshi an'jian li'an," 346.

88. Yu Haibing, "Bao'an fuwu mianlin de wenti ji duice," (The problems faced by security companies and some countermeasures) in *Gong'an yanjiu* 7 (Public Security Studies), no. 3 (1989): 28.

89. Yu, *lunwenji diyijuan*, 234.

90. Bai and Ma, *Jumin weiyuanhiui*, 184.

91. Bai and Ma, *Jumin weiyuanhiui*, 162. For more detailed regulations stipulating wages, subsidies, and bonuses in Shanghai, see Bai and Ma, *Jumin weiyuanhiui*, 207–8.

92. *Zhi'an jichu gailun* (A basic outline of grassroots level security) (Beijing: Zhongguo renmin gong'an daxue chubanshe, 1987), 247.

93. Bai and Ma, *Jumin weiyuanhiui*, 184.

94. *Baowei gongzuo shiyong jiaocheng* (A course in the uses of protection work) (Beijing: Jingguan jiaoyu chubanshe, 1990), 247.

95. It was for this reason that the spirit of Fengqiao was revived and revisited. Once a Maoist model of mass dictatorship, this model was suitably adjusted for the new political climate. In the era of reform it became known as Fengqiao community crime control. This time around, the work principle that "small matters are dealt with locally without passing on to the village, big matters are dealt with at the village level without being sent on to the town and contradictions are not sent to higher authorities" was no longer a sign of mass democracy but of voluntary self-help. See Zhou Zhangkang, "Lun Fengqiao shequ fanzui kongzhi moshi," (Theorizing crime control in the Fengqiao community) *Qingshaonian fanzui yanjiu*, 141–142 (Research into Juvenile Crime), no. 3–4 (1994): 142.

96. In 1987 the police reported favorably on voluntary schemes operative in both Wuhan and Chongqing which organized residents into groups of fifteen and rotated the responsibility between them. For details of this see *Zhi'an jichu gailun*, 247. For a dramatic example of the user-pays household registration experiments, see Dutton, *Streetlife China*, 99–102.

97. The following information on informants is drawn from *Zhi'an jichu gailun*, 261–88, unless otherwise indicated.

98. *Zhi'an jichu gailun*, 262.

99. This was made "official" in October 1984 when the Ministry of Public Security issued an internal document entitled "Temporary regulations concerning the establishment of public security eyes and ears." For further details see *Zhi'an jichu gailun.*

100. *Neibao gongzuo shouce* (Internal protection work handbook) (Beijing: Gong'an daxue chubanshe, 1991), 19–21.

101. Quoted in *Neibao gongzuo shouce*, 25.

102. *Neibao gongzuo shouce*, 25.

103. Hu Yongming, "Xinshiqi jingbao gongzuo yeyao shixing zhengqi fenkai," (Economic protection work in the new era also needs to be separated from administrative and enterprise responsibilities) in *Gong'an yanjiu* 28 (Public Security Studies), no. 2 (1993): 58.

104. Hu, "Xinshiqi jingbao gongzuo," 60; Gao Feng, "Neibao gongzuo gaige quyi," (A brief discussion of the reforms in internal protection work) in *Gong'an yanjiu* 2 (Public Security Studies), no. 2 (1988): 17–21.

105. *Neibao gongzuo shouce*, 29.

106. Zheng Yuhua and Cen Shengting, ed., *Zhi'an lianfang shouce* (Joint security force handbook) (Beijing: Jingguan jiaoyu chubanshe, 1992), 7; Gao, "Neibao gongzuo," 19. The importance of the joint-protection defence force or *lianfang* cannot be underestimated. It began to be formed in the early 1960s and was formed by the security committees of the neighborhood committees (the zhibaohui), led by local governments and local public security forces, and was populated with civil and military personnel as well as local cadres and was designed as a local neighborhood security force. Currently boasting a cadre force of 2,500,000, it is estimated to have assisted police by discovering and cracking around 20 percent of crime cases. This, it is said, "helps reduce the problem of the shortage of police". It is the importance in this regard that has led to this group also beginning to experiment with responsibility systems and the replacement of unpaid retirees with salaried younger members. For more details see Zheng and Cen, *Zhi'an lianfang shouce*, 1–8.

107. Previously police would check and approve all appointments and ensure that these units were well staffed. Indeed, a quota of not less than 0.3 percent of total staff and workers was to be employed in these units in the prereform years. See Hu, "Xinshiqi jingbao gongzuo," 58.

108. Internal protection units organized dossiers on 1) Special cases; 2) Common criminal cases; 3) Cases requiring supervision; 4) Those under investigation; 5) Serious incidents; 6) Key projects; 7) Criminal detention; 8) Secret forces; and 9) Any other general documents deemed worthy of attention. See *Internal Protection*, 44, for further details.

109. Gao, "Neibao gongzuo," 18–19; Hu, "Xinshiqi jingbao gongzuo," 60.

110. Zhou Rongzhao and Yang Ming, "Qishiye gong'an jigou de libi ji duice chuyi," (A brief discussion of profits, losses, and countermeasures employed in the enterprise policing structure) in *Gong'an yanjiu* 1 (Public Security Studies), no. 1 (1991): 49.

111. In one well-publicized dispute between one enterprise and peasants over land in 1988, the enterprise chief sent the enterprise police out to arrest a number of peasants, and as a result, other peasants descended upon the factory and caused considerable trouble at the factory gates (Zhou and Yang, "Qishiye gong'an," 49).

112. The use of police uniforms and identification badges by nonauthorized personnel is yet another problem produced by economic reform. See Zheng and Cen, *Zhi'an lianfang shouce*, 58 and Zhou and Yang, "Qishiye gong'an," 48.

113. So-called Red Banner documents are those produced by the Party center for local high-ranking cadres. They are usually "top secret" and offer detailed arguments and evidence about specific items on the political and social agenda. Widely used in China prior to reform, they have a more problematic status today.

114. Chen Du and Gu Xinhua, "Yanhai weixiangxing jingji fazhan yu gong'an fazhang zhanlu," (The stratagies of developing public security work in coastal areas) in *Gong'an yanjiu* 3 (Public Security Studies), no. 3 (1988): 31.

115. Ye Huaming, "Shehui zhi'an guanli shehuihua muoshi de tansuo," (An Exploration of the socialization model of society's public order management)" in *Gong'an yanjiu* 7 (Public Security Studies), no. 3 (1989): 25.

116. The number of police in Beijing varies between 30,000 and 40,000 according to the head of the Bureau (Interview with head of Beijing PSB, August 1998). All other information from Ni Minle and Fang Lei, "Lun bo'an fuwuye de falu diwei ji weilai fazhan," (A discussion about the legal position and future development of private security companies) in *Gong'an yanjiu* 57 (Public Security Studies), no. 1 (1998): 64.

117. So derivative of the Ministry of Public Security are these forces that even the officer ranks within the security firms are based upon the organization of the police. All profits go back to the ministry but, in the case of Beijing companies, they are said at this stage to remain within the companies to allow further expansion. Taxes are high with a rate of 55 percent leveled on any profits earned (Interview with head of Beijing Public Security Bureau, August 1998).

118. Steven Spitzer, "Security and Control in Capitalist Societies: The Fetishism of Security and the Secret Thereof" in *Transcarceration: Essays in the Sociology of Social Control*, eds. John Lowman, Robert J. Menzies, and T. S. Pays (Aldershot: Gower, 1987), 50.

119. Jacques Derrida, *Given Time 1. Counterfeit Money*, trans. Peggy Kamuf (Chicago: University of Chicago Press, 1992), 41.

120. Ye Ming, "Qiantan xin xingshi xia paichusuo jichu gongzuo de xin fazhan," (A brief discussion of new developments in basic work within the station in the new situation) in *Gong'an yanjiu* 59 (Public Security Studies), no. 3 (1998): 65.

121. Evgeny B. Pashukanis, *Law and Marxism: A General Theory*, ed. Chris Arthur, trans. Barbara Einthorn (London: Ink Books, 1978), 118.

122. Pashukanis, *Law and Marxism*, 41.

Index

Page numbers in italics refer to figures and tables.

About the Editor

Børge Bakken is a Fellow in the Division of Pacific and Asian History at the Research School of Pacific and Asian Studies at the Australian National University. His main research interests include the modern history and sociology of crime and control as well as norms and deviance in China, particularly the development of crime and criminology in the People's Republic and the period of reform and modernization in the perspective of the *longue durée.*

Lightning Source UK Ltd.
Milton Keynes UK
UKHW010034180320
360487UK00008B/127